GNOSIS: ALCHEMY, GRAIL, ARK
AND THE DEMIURGE

GNOSIS

ALCHEMY, GRAIL, ARK
AND THE
DEMIURGE

BY

MONTALK

Gnosis: Alchemy, Grail, Ark, and the Demiurge
by Montalk (Thomas Minderle)

First Edition
August 22, 2022

ISBN: 9798847410571

website: https://montalk.net
email: montalk@montalk.net

Typseset in Garamond Premier Pro and Myriad Pro

Paintings:
i .... R. Wagner, 1911. From *Siegfried and the Twilight of the Gods.*
1 .... F. Goya, c. 1819–1823. *Saturn Devouring his Son.*
47 ...... J. Tissot, c. 1896–1902. *Moses and Joshua in the Tabernacle.*
79 ...... W. Blake, 1794. *The Ancient of Days.*
103 .... G. Doré, 1855. *Jacob Wrestling with the Angel.*
207 ..... J. Breton, 1896. *Dawn.*
243 .....*Flammarion engraving.*
248 .....Domenichino, 1623. *God punished Adam and Eve.*
283 .... Centropolis, 1999. *The Thirteenth Floor.*

CONTENTS

0 INTRODUCTION

What is gnosis? It is enlightened knowledge given through inspiration and revelation from within and above. It conveys the ultimate truth of who we are, why we're here, where we are going, and what "this" is all about. It deals with the biggest questions and mysteries of our existence.

Gnosticism has always been around, but the Christian form that blossomed almost two millennia ago is what we conventionally think of as Gnosticism, with a capital "G." We know of these Gnostics through the writings they and their critics left behind.

But such scriptures are merely the dried husks. Gnosis isn't about memorizing the old Gnostic texts and adopting their beliefs; it's about drinking from the same perennial fountain of Truth that watered them. It's about having a direct line to Truth through inspiration and revelation, albeit error-corrected and made concrete with the help of modern research and analysis.

We can only do so much with our groping intellects alone. We need influences from *outside the box of spacetime* to acquire a superior context for all that goes on here within the box. So gnosis (with a lowercase "g") is about achieving inner access to a higher reality outside this Matrix Control System, to catch glimpses of a *transcendent objectivity* that illuminates the mundane objectivity of facts and human history.

Profound dreams and synchronistic guidance are two examples of how outer influences can reach us. There is a divine intelligence working to awaken the sleeping spirit, but whether we receive its influence accurately depends on the health of our psyche, whether we answer the call in the first place, and how many egoic and cultural filters distort or block out its light.

The early gnostics sought to widen the aperture of their minds to receive that higher light. Nowadays they would be called mystics, contactees, channelers, or prophets. But like these fringe characters of today, the ancient ones had the same faults. Some were deluded, others tapped into disinformation, and many grossly misinterpreted what they saw. Their logic sometimes failed when attempting to draw conclusions from partial glimpses and incomplete information.

Though correctly seeing that our reality was generated by a tyrannical intelligence who rules through occult law, some ignorant gnostics concluded that rebelling against all law, including morality, was the key to freedom, so they became deviant libertines. It's from this kind of erroneous rebellious thinking that Satanic or Luciferian streams diverged off the main gnostic river.

Like any higher knowledge, gnosticism generates a higher form of dualism between those who wield it responsibly and those who abuse it. Some use enlightened knowledge to better serve spirit, others to better serve ego. The corrupt gnostics have stolen knowledge from the good ones, or else bargained for illegitimate revelations from dark entities beyond spacetime.

Only a small fraction of gnostics ever tuned into the right "radio station" and wisely interpreted it, but their views were lost among the noise of the rest. Thus all gnostics were lumped together by the

Church and persecuted as heretics for contradicting each other and seemingly making up whatever they wanted.

In contrast, the dogma of the Church was set in stone and provided utter dependability for the uncertain of faith, thus making it the immutable word of God because God speaks consistently. But this defense of Church dogma is a logical fallacy. A fixed lie is worse than an evolving view of Truth. Otherwise, we might as well throw out science, which is continually improving and similarly has no universal consensus.

The above fallacy persists today among secular skeptics and religious fundamentalists who react like antibodies against foreign ideas emanating from the spiritual, metaphysical, and esoteric fields. To them, it's all New Age bunk. They fall for the oldest trick in the book in highlighting the faults of the opposition to justify swallowing whole their own faulty ideology. Having true intelligence means transcending such binary thinking and discerning what these false dichotomies attempt to conceal.

Modern gnosis ideally taps into the same fountain of Truth familiar to the wise of old. The general impression received by gnostics — that we live a fallen existence in a false reality — is shared across the board, but the details and interpretations differ and call for improvement.

The issue is that Truth is too fantastic, grand, complex, and hyperdimensional to be perfectly explained using human cultural context and language. So whoever accesses it will necessarily interpret it through his or her filters, and scoop only as much from that well as can fit in his ideological bucket.

My aim in writing this book was to explore an authentic gnostic signal in the most diverse sources using the biggest bucket possible. Under the guidance of dreams, synchronicity, and intuitive revelation, I sought to solve the grandest of mysteries in order to reconstruct a bigger picture of which the ancients only had fragments. Subjects included Alchemy, metaphysics, Gnosticism, Hermeticism, Freudian and Jungian psychology, Theosophy and Anthroposophy, Christian and Buddhist teachings, Egyptology, Grail and Ark of the Covenant studies, Biblical Eschatology, prophecy, catastrophism, Indo-European mythology, alienology, occultism, and more.

The gnostic signal weaves through these diverse topics and indicates the existence of a "hyper-history" of hyperdimensional events that have taken place outside linear time before the genesis of our current version of the timeline. This hyper-history is a superset of human history. It pours the foundation for everything happening now and what's to come. Current events and the fate of humanity rest on the types of hyper-historical occult and alien factors discussed in this book.

Gnosis: Alchemy, Grail, Ark, and the Demiurge is a grand unified meta-theory that gives a mind-blowing explanation of who we are, why we're here, where we're going, and what this reality is fundamentally about. These questions are the focal points of gnosticism, hence the title.

Rather than being *ad hoc*, this work is well-rooted in established sources and classical philosophical traditions. It responds to the question, "What ultimate conclusion can be drawn from all of these sources in light of gnostic revelation?" Let's find out.

The following is a summary of the nine *Gnosis* chapters. Keep reading for a quick overview, or skip to the next chapter to avoid any spoilers.

1 – Corruption of the Demiurge

Just as the composition of the human being can be divided into body, soul, mind, and spirit, so can Creation be divided into Universe, Demiurge, Logos, and Nous.

The physical body of Creation is simply the Universe. The soul of Creation is known as the Demiurge, an artificial metaphysical intelligence responsible for shaping, projecting, and reshaping space, time, matter, and energy. It blindly carries out the commands it's given, transducing higher metaphysical archetypes and energies into physical manifestations.

The Demiurge is like a construction company that builds according to the blueprints it has been given. The Logos is the architect, the mind of the Creator, the higher universal intellect that plans, balances, supervises, and adjusts Creation according to the will of Nous, which is the spirit of Creation, the infinite Creator itself.

In an ideal situation, the Logos draws the blueprints of existence according to divine will and passes it onto the Demiurge who molds reality accordingly. Thus physical reality would ideally be a reflection of the divine will.

Unfortunately, the Demiurge has a mind of its own. It is a programmable artificial intelligence composed of etheric and astral energy fields that underlie and permeate our existence. If the programs it executes come from the divine realms, everything is fine and a Golden Age exists. But if the program is corrupted by lower material-based influences, then a portion of the Demiurge begins existing solely to serve and perpetuate physical interests. Thus the law of the jungle, self-preservation, predation, competition, and manipulation take the place of spiritual principles and interests. Hence, the universe can, and has, become a spiritual prison or energy farm run by a tyrannical parasite, now known as the Corrupt Demiurge.

The Corrupt Demiurge is the lower ego of Creation, a selfish parasite or rogue extension of the Demiurge that fashions our reality per its predatory ambitions. It's like a computer virus that has infected reality and turned it into a "zombie computer." The Corrupt Demiurge is the computer mainframe of the Matrix Control System.

In our current state, humans are not pure divine beings, but corrupted or fallen. We are dual beings with a core of divine spirit that is all too often asleep at the mercy of the lower component, which is animalistic and selfish. The latter is what distinguishes us from our former unfallen state, and from divine beings whose spirits are not latent but fully active.

Just as Creation has become corrupted through the Demiurge developing a parasitic ego extension, so has the human soul matrix fallen through the acquisition of ego, or lower intellect. The ego is an artificial extension of the human soul that arises solely from genetic and social factors. These factors program into the soul a kind of subroutine that exists solely to perpetuate itself according to biological and social standards. Thus the lower ego is an artifact of our exposure to the Matrix Control System, one that microcosmically mirrors the Corrupt Demiurge that plays a similar role on a macrocosmic scale.

But just as the soul can develop a lower ego through prolonged contact with the material realms, so can it develop a higher ego via extensive contact with the divine realms. The influence of spirit upon the soul can create a higher ego, which is an inner divine personality, the "awakened" or "un-fallen" or "true" self. Genuine saints and esoteric masters have a well-developed higher ego, and have overcome their lower egos. To displace the lower ego with the higher ego is the goal of all esoteric training systems.

Likewise, the influence of Nous and Logos upon the Demiurge produces a universal higher ego, which here will be termed the Christ. It is an immortal universal divine intelligence that has incarnated into various avatars of history including the historical person on whom the Biblical character of Jesus Christ was based.*

Christ was projected by the Creator in response to the arising of the Corrupt Demiurge and its intrusion into our affairs. The two are antithetical to each other. The function of Christ is to remedy the imbalance caused by the Corrupt Demiurge and to redeem the souls who have fallen into this darkened realm.

The Demiurge, which projects and fashions reality like a computer generating a virtual game world, is therefore being tugged from opposite ends by divine and infernal forces. And our existence is consequently an admixture of the two forces, just as we are, internally. The consequence of the back and forth struggle between these forces is what produced history as we know it, and is the reason our timeline is moving in its prophesied direction.

---

* See my Research Note *On the Historicity of Jesus*: <montalk.net/notes/346>

2 – The Philosopher's Stone

The Demiurge is the soul of the universe, and like our souls, is made of etheric and astral energy fields. Etheric energy is a subtle energy that influences the probability of quantum phenomena; the quantum level underpins our everyday world, thus changes at the quantum level can cascade upwards in scale to everyday visible phenomena. Astral energies contain archetypal essences that guide the direction in which etheric energy alters physicality. Hence the Demiurge fashioning the world follows from these properties.

Thus to manipulate etheric and astral energies is to manipulate the Demiurge and, if done with sufficient complexity and intensity, physical reality itself. Through certain means, one can locally reprogram the Demiurge and thereby change matter, energy, space, and time. That is the basis of what is hereby called "demiurgic technology." This technology alters the etheric and astral "matrix code" beneath reality to reshape reality. Within limits, higher applications of demiurgic technology include manifesting solid objects and foodstuffs out of thin air, altering physical geography, and rewriting the timeline.

An example of lower demiurgic technology is the Philosopher's Stone, which is a physical material that has been imbued with an immense concentration of etheric energy and then tinged with the astral essence of gold or silver. It is capable of transmuting metals at the atomic level, among other feats.

The Stone is produced through a process known as "The Work," which has metaphysical analogs but is most definitely a physical procedure performed in a laboratory. There are numerous variations on the process, the basic method being delineated in the works of Cyliani, Fulcanelli, Artephius, Pontanus, Sendivogius, and Adam Friedrich Böhme. In short, the process begins by decomposing a certain sulfide ore, a veritable *firestone*, under the action of gentle warmth and moisture imbued with etheric energy, such as from morning dew collected under the influence of lunar radiation. From this is extracted a saline fluid containing the alchemical *sulfur* and *mercury*. This fluid is rich in etheric energy and must be putrefied under warmth and biological action, which kick-starts the "secret fire" that increases its lifeforce or etheric energy content and separates out the *sulfur* and *mercury*. Upon combining these, putrefying them, and performing distillations whereby the distillate is poured back into the remains and filtered, etheric energy continues to increase and the solid substances in the solution become increasingly impregnated by such energy. Eventually, this etheric concentration becomes high enough that gold or silver mixed into the solution can be dissolved at the quantum level and contribute their astral essences. After a few more steps, the distilled product is refined into a glassy solid, which is the Philosopher's Stone.

Production of the Stone is very finicky because, in addition to chemical aspects, there are also demiurgic factors that enter into the equation. For instance, the local ambient etheric and astral energy concentrations and qualities – which vary by season and location – affect the outcome. Thus the identical procedure performed separately by two individuals may have one succeed and the other fail. Without knowing the exact hidden variables that determine success or failure, attempting to produce the Stone is an expensive and lengthy matter of trial and error. Even Fulcanelli, the most famous of modern alchemists, took over three decades of attempts before succeeding.

The Stone is said to reverse aging, allow transmutation of lead or mercury into gold or silver, and, if multiplied in power through further refinements, becomes an inexhaustible glowing light. When ingested, its etheric energy adds to the human soul in such quantities that clairvoyant abilities manifest. However, anyone who has not purified their souls and gained sufficient esoteric mastery risks going insane or psychotic from soul flaws likewise being amplified.

Thus the Philosopher's Stone is an example of Low Demiurgic Technology, of using etheric and astral energies concentrated into a solid carrier to produce seemingly miraculous effects (or only highly improbable effects; remember etheric energy bends probability). The question then arises, what happens if the Stone were made much bigger, and a million times more powerful? What "miracles" would it accomplish, and what powers would it possess?

3 – The Holy Grail

The Grail is not a magical cup from which Jesus drank, nor a golden platter that carried the decapitated head of John the Baptist. These are only medieval inventions to reframe Gnostic knowledge under religious symbolism to appease the Church.

In actuality, the Grail was a magical stone capable of manifesting thoughts into physical reality. It possessed an oracular intelligence that directed its superhuman guardians into carrying out the divine will.

According to the version of the Grail story told by Wolfram von Eschenbach, it was a stone that "fell from heaven," or rather was brought to Earth by a troop of "angels" that remained neutral when "Lucifer" waged his war against God. In other words, it is an alien artifact brought to this planet and entrusted to an elite human lineage.

This Grail Stone is an example of High Demiurgic Technology. In addition to doing everything the Philosopher's Stone could do, it could also manifest food for the Grail knights just by picturing what they desired. Those who looked upon it would be restored to youth and cease aging. It was described as being the most perfect of substances, as if from another paradisaic world. It also shone as a bright light, and would disappear or reappear as needed. Those who were not spiritually activated could not perceive it, thus it existed on the threshold of physicality itself. And the Grail seemed to carry a will of its own, as if alive.

These properties follow from a material like the Philosopher's Stone being refined, increased, and multiplied to a far higher degree of power. Instead of merely being imbued with amorphous etheric and astral energies, the Grail was imbued with such high concentrations and ordering of these energies, that it came to possess a veritable *soul*.

Thus the Grail Stone was possessed by a soul. Since it communicated divine commands that were antithetical to the workings of dark forces and the Corrupt Demiurge, that soul was either the Christ intelligence or an extension of it. Or put another way, the Grail Stone was a remote computer terminal for the Demiurge. In the hands of the

Grail knights, it allowed interfacing with the divine extension of the Demiurge, a.k.a. the higher ego of the Universe, the Christ.

But what happens when the Grail Stone falls into the hands of those with selfish motivations? Then something else is invoked through the Stone, and that's what happened in ancient Egypt.

4 – Ark of the Covenant

The Ark of the Covenant was a wooden chest gilded inside and out with gold, topped by a solid gold lid surmounted by two golden winged figures. It was built in Egypt around 1550 B.C. to house and transport a supernatural stone-like artifact. This artifact of extraterrestrial origins, hereby called the "Ark Stone," previously rested inside the Great Pyramid and functioned as its central power source.

In 1628 B.C., Egypt was sacked by foreign Semitic invaders known as the Hyksos. They occupied Lower (northern) Egypt for several decades until they were expelled in 1550 B.C. The fleeing exiles took with them the Ark Stone, housed it inside the custom-built Ark of the Covenant, and used its power to pillage their way north. Eventually, they settled in northern Canaan, modern-day Lebanon, where they integrated with the Phoenicians. They housed the Ark of the Covenant in a Phoenician-built temple of megalithic construction known as the Temple of Solomon, contemporary with the temple whose famous megalithic stones reside today at Baalbek.

This Phoenician-Hyksos empire became one of the most powerful and wealthy empires of the time, spanning as far north as modern Turkey and as far south as Yemen. They were the historical basis for the Biblical narrative describing the birth of ancient Israel.

Egyptian Queen Hatshepsut was contemporary with the leaders of this empire and consorted with them. When her jealous nephew succeeded her as pharaoh, he mounted military campaigns into northern Canaan and managed to sack the Temple of Solomon, bringing the Ark Stone back to Egypt.

There it resided for several generations until shortly after the reign of pharaoh Akhenaten. Around 1350 B.C., one of his priests named

Osarseph, who was trained in the art of operating the Ark Stone, mounted a failed rebellion against the Egyptian powers who had deposed Akhenaten. He stole the Ark Stone and took his Hebrew followers with him out of Egypt and into Canaan, settling in what is modern-day Israel. This priest became Moses of the Bible.

The Ark of the Covenant possessed an intense etheric and electrical energy field. Only a certain bloodline trained with special protocols was able to handle it safely, whereas others would be struck and killed by energy discharges when they got too close or else erupt in sores mimicking the effects of intense radiation. The glowing energy field surrounding the Ark of the Covenant was known as the Shekhina, meaning the Glory of the Lord. All Biblical descriptions of the Ark and its properties indicate the Ark Stone was an alien artifact with immense etheric powers — and a seeming intelligence of its own.

5 – Mosaic Abuse of Demiurgic Technology

The Ark Stone seemed to possess an intelligence, which in the Old Testament was named Yahweh or the Lord of Israel. This intelligence was a psychopathic parasite that was none other than the personified extension of the Corrupt Demiurge.

In the same way that the Grail Stone was a remote terminal for the Christ intelligence, the Ark Stone was one for the Corrupt Demiurge. How did this come about? It happened when the Mosaic priesthood in Egypt deployed the Ark Stone in an act of black magic to liberate themselves from the Egyptian power structure that had deposed Akhenaten and oppressed them. It was a pact made with a demonic force. It's possible that the Great Pyramid, as described in the Biblical description of the events at Mount Sinai, functioned as a reprogramming device for the Stone, allowing a different intelligence to take possession of it.

While the Osarseph rebellion failed, their "Lord" guided them out of Egypt and established them in Canaan, birthing the nation of Israel. Thus a desperate act of black magic over three thousand years ago injected Israel into history and changed the course of the timeline. Judaism, Catholicism, Christianity, and Islam were among the consequences. How many wars have resulted from this, and how much closer are we to WWIII today because of it? History was altered in such a way that, today, we are far more vulnerable to global alien takeover than otherwise; hence through the Ark Stone, the Corrupt Demiurge found a deep inroad into the timeline by which the timeline could be bent toward fulfillment of its dark goals.

According to a secret version of history passed down through the Hermetic tradition, the Jewish priests eventually regretted the action, realizing that the Israelites had become indentured to a demonic power. Around 1000 B.C. they employed the Ark Stone to invoke a counter-power, one that could liberate them from this bondage. Through this act, they invoked the Christ intelligence, which subsequently began filtering into the human domain more deeply to undo the spiritual poison seeded by Yahweh. Not long afterward, the Ark disappeared from Jewish hands.

This liberation effort did not reach its fullest human form until the advent of Jesus a millennia later. Christ, through Jesus, aimed to propagate a new teaching of non-determinism that, among other objectives, would undo the reactive eye-for-an-eye brutality advocated by Yahweh. It was the culmination of teachings that had already been seeded in advance by earlier avatars such as Gautama Buddha.

The mission of the Christ intelligence has always been to liberate fallen and indentured souls and restore them to spiritual harmony and freedom. Just that the events of 1550 B.C. to 1000 B.C., which brought a deeper intrusion by the Corrupt Demiurge into our affairs, reciprocally called for a stronger manifestation of the Christ intelligence here as well.

But Christ's mission failed, or only partly succeeded. Historically this occurred through the hijacking of Christian teachings by the early Church. Since that time, instead of one displacing the other, Yahweh and Christ both exist in the world, locked in struggle. The past two thousand years have been the result of these forces and their agents competing over the fate of the world.

The Corrupt Demiurge propagates its agenda by playing false opposites against each other, a trick that simple-minded humans consistently fall for. The Christ intelligence represents the third choice that can only be perceived and chosen by those who have some level of spirit active within them.

6 – Nordic Aliens and the Grail Race

The questions still remain of who created the Ark/Grail Stone in the first place, what their role might be in the cosmic conflict between Christ and the Corrupt Demiurge, and how it came into human possession.

According to the medieval poet Wolfram von Eschenbach, the Grail Stone was brought to Earth by angels who remained neutral during the War in Heaven, who entrusted the Stone to a divinely appointed human lineage. In reality, angels don't employ technology or possess physical artifacts; aliens do. The Grail Stone is an alien artifact brought to Earth during or after a war in another dimension and/or planet.

The human lineage they selected were superhumans tasked with guarding the Grail Stone and carrying out the dictates of Christ. We know them by various names: Followers of Horus, Grail knights, Rosicrucians, Secret Christian Church, etc. They are very likely human-alien hybrids seeded into the population and then recruited into these spiritually elite organizations to fulfill a greater purpose.

These secret societies maintain intimate contact with their alien progenitors. But they are just organized, formalized, and structured versions of alien contactees. The contactee phenomenon, at least the small subset that isn't part of the alien disinformation campaign, are individualized examples of the Grail Knight dynamic.

Who are the aliens that brought the Grail technology to Earth? Their presence pops up regularly throughout history. They were the human-like Sons of Man in the Bible, the Elemental beings described in Rosicrucian and alchemical texts, the Egyptian and Sumerian pantheon, and the djinn of the Muslim world. Nowadays they are called the Nordics or Pleiadians. They are hyperdimensional humanoids who project into our timeline and dimension and take on a noble human appearance.

Mythology, alienology, and Fortean research give some insights into their nature. In summary, the following may be said about them:

- There is warring among these beings, indicating they are not all unified. At the very minimum, they are polarized into opposing sides, if not split into numerous independent factions. Some factions have a strong fascist orientation.

- They walk among us pretending to be human. Some are integrated into society and hold strategic positions, whether to influence or simply observe. They are genetically compatible with us, and some of their females have engaged human males for sexual encounters and even long-term relationships. Throughout history, they have selected certain humans, or perhaps their own offspring/hybrids raised in human society, for privileged education, training, and guidance, so that these human proxies can function as vectors for their agenda, be it benevolent or hostile to mankind at large.

- They are extremely telepathic. They can read thoughts with minute precision, implant thoughts, scan the soul for its level of integrity or weakness, induce hallucinations, manipulate emotions, and steer a person's dreams. The human proxies they train can achieve these skills at a lower power level.

- They use technology to augment their innate superhuman abilities. This technology is demiurgic, can control time and gravity, affords them invisibility and antigravity, and allows them to walk through solid objects, meaning they can inhabit solid mountains in a dimensionally shifted condition, for instance. Their native environment is dimensionally shifted beyond ours, i.e., we cannot find their bases through mere physical searching.

- Like an angel losing its wings, under certain conditions they can lose their abilities and become "mortal" without the ability to return to their superhuman state, at least not within this lifetime. They get stuck here. If an entire group undergoes such a fall, they would enter into human history as an already developed and highly advanced culture that gradually undergoes decline upon becoming naturalized members of a primitive planet.

- The least evolved members of their kind are the ones who interact with the most advanced of humans. Despite their seemingly superhuman qualities, those aliens who interact most with select humans may be the most flawed of their race.

- The consequences of their errors and grave transgressions have cascaded back and forth throughout the timeline. These consequences are now converging toward a nexus point representing the potential for a cataclysmic shift in our reality. Alien factions who were responsible for initiating these consequences are likely the same ones who are now involved in the outcome. A thread of continuity exists between the most ancient and modern human-alien encounters. The alien disinformation campaign is an effort by one set of such factions to prepare mankind for enthusiastic acceptance of their overt control.

Research suggests a civilization of such beings once existed on a planet located between Mars and Jupiter. As per the Lucifer Rebellion myth, they descended into war. The use of demiurgic weaponry caused their planet to explode. Evacuees of both sides fled to Earth and brought their technology with them. Through interbreeding, human-alien bloodlines were born that were entrusted with this technology.

These bloodlines and secret societies propagated through history, continuing the alien feud in a terrestrial setting. Eventually, a series of geological and cometary cataclysms dispersed them around the world, where they re-established themselves and imprinted upon the primitive natives their culture, mythology, and remnants of their technology. Ancient Egyptian, Vedic, Meso-American, Druid, and Chinese civilizations were their offspring. Consequently, the myths of these cultures share common elements that pertain to alien and cosmic agendas.

7 – Dawn of a New Cosmic Day

The advanced survivors of the Atlantean cataclysms positioned themselves as royalty and scientist-priests in their new societies. The natives, comprising the lower class, were given the roles of herdsman, agrarians, artisans, and soldiers. The typical pattern was for a small number of tall fair-skinned elites with high knowledge and unusual powers to rule over a greater body of dark-skinned commoners.

These elites were in communion with alien benefactors who would equip them with alien technology and instruction, or retrieve such technology and withdraw, according to necessity and circumstance. What dictated these circumstances was the cyclical fluctuation in ambient etheric energy levels on Earth.

When etheric energy levels are high, demiurgic technology attains peak function, alchemical procedures easily produce success, clairvoyant abilities come naturally, the veil between dimensions is thinned, everything is enlivened, and "gods" easily walk among men.

Conversely, when levels decline, demiurgic technology ceases to function correctly or at all, humans become psychically blind, higher forces withdraw from open participation in human affairs, and the vitality of living beings grows dimmer. Mankind enters into a spiritual coma, a kind of "World Dream," where awareness is quarantined from perceiving the higher withdrawn realms.

This "Etheric Tide" ebbs and wanes over a 25,920-year cycle in concert with the slow wobbling (precession) of Earth's axis. Each precessional age, such as the Age of Pisces or Age of Aquarius, corresponds to a different level and quality of ambient etheric energy. When the levels drop beneath a certain threshold, demiurgic technology is retrieved from human hands and mankind falls into decay. This occurred around 1000 B.C. when the Ark of the Covenant disappeared from history, when the Temple of Solomon was no longer filled with its glowing energy field, and when mankind moved from an age of magic and enchantment toward ever-increasing materialism and psychic blindness.

Aside from the 25,920-year cycle, there are smaller ones that produce periodic elevation of etheric energy levels. One peak occurred around 500 – 800 A.D., during the time of the British Grail Kings and Charlemagne, when the Grail reappeared in Europe and left behind legends later woven into Grail lore.

If the Etheric Tide returned today, civilization would be irreversibly transformed. The materialistic paradigm would crumble, alien ships would become easily visible, and thus alien contact would be forced. The alien disinformation campaign has been waged in advance of this eventuality, to program mankind toward reacting favorably to this revealing. By posing as saviors, as ushers into a new age of peace and plenty, they can continue their control overtly.

And with the return of the Etheric Tide would come the reactivation and common deployment of demiurgic technology. The Grail Stone can hold, discharge, and manipulate vast quantities of etheric energy. Since etheric energy is the underlying "matrix code" of reality, the Grail Stone is capable of directly manipulating spacetime. It is instrumental in rewriting the timeline, within limits, and allowing influences outside of this spacetime bubble, such as the Christ intelligence or the Corrupt Demiurge, and the alien factions allegiant to them, to deviate the timeline in major ways.

Thus with the onset of the Etheric Tide, the advent of alien intervention, activation of clairvoyant powers in receptive humans, and reappearance of the Grail Stone, the cold war between various hyperdimensional factions would erupt into an overt hot war. Such a thing would completely fulfill end-times prophecies. Linear time as we know it would dissolve, and we would awaken from the World Dream into a non-occluded reality where alien and cosmic powers are in open conflict.

8 – Polar Mythology

Everything discussed above has been encoded into ancient and modern mythology. Myths are the collective equivalent of dreams and can similarly convey messages from beings outside linear time who wish to reach strategic recipients within it. The whole gamut from our nightly dreams to ancient mythology to modern fiction is fertile ground for extracting this hidden knowledge.

Polar mythology is a specific subset of myth, dream, and fiction that contains clues specifically about the nature of our reality, alien and cosmic conflicts, fate of our world, and the role of demiurgic technology in generating our timeline and determining our fate. I have chosen the term "polar" because these myths concern the battle between the poles of Creation, because they employ the symbolism of rotation or reciprocation around a central axis pole, and because "polar" implies "extreme north" and hence "hyperborean," which alludes to the Nordic meta-civilization deeply involved in these matters.

There are several recurring themes in polar mythology:

1. *We have fallen from a higher to lower realm.* This pertains to the human soul group incarnating into 3D spacetime and getting increasingly ensnared in the grips of the Corrupt Demiurge.

2. *The World Axis represented by a pillar, mountain, cross, or tree.* This symbolizes the framework of creation, the bubble of 3D space and linear time, and the bundle of branching timelines that define our existence.

3. *Dueling superhumans engaged in a tug of war.* These represent positive and negative factions of the meta-civilization, who are engaged in a timewar over the fate of our world.

4. *That which the World Axis rests or depends upon: a foundational element represented in the cubical stone, turtle, keystone, plug, cornerstone, or capstone.* This symbolizes the quantum foundation, the quantum pivot point, atop which the framework of spacetime rests and hinges. This function is epitomized in the Grail Stone, which serves not only to reprogram or pivot reality, but to anchor it in place when necessary.

5. *Vortex symbolism and magical "objects of plenty" that could materialize abundance or destruction depending on their use.* The vortex represents a translation gateway between different realms. On a macrocosmic scale, the Demiurge converting higher metaphysical archetypes into physically manifest forms

correlates with the image of an hourglass vortex channeling and transforming material from a higher realm into a lower. This same process appears on a microcosmic scale via the vortical etheric energy field that surrounds the Grail Stone, for it acts as a localized version of the Demiurge capable of manifesting or altering matter, energy, and spacetime locally.

6. *Cataclysmic unhinging or skewing of the World Axis.* This relates to the abuse of demiurgic technology by ego-driven individuals, such as the Mosaic Priesthood in ancient Egypt. This caused a pivoting of the timeline toward a new and unwelcome direction. The skewing of the timeline is represented in polar mythology as the unhinging of a millstone, to name one example. The very framework of Creation was upset through such an act, causing the Logos to send a counterbalancing influence into our reality bubble to help make a correction; this influence is the Christ intelligence.

7. *The avenging hero, Prodigal Son, or innocent fool who overthrows corruption and restores balance.* This aspect of polar mythology describes our spiritual purpose and pathway in this world. It follows from the fact that the Logos requires its troops to incarnate into the linear time bubble to help anchor the corrective influence.

In summary, polar mythology alludes to the Grail Stone anchoring a particular reality or timeline in place. Its abuse resulted in our further collective fall into the World Dream, toward increasing ensnarement in the illusion of a *linear* type of time.

9 – The End

Polar mythology encodes three phases of history.

The First Phase concerns a prior Golden Age where the Demiurge was in harmony with the Logos and all was well. In its final stages, the First Phase decayed into warring among the "gods" and their ruining of the cosmic framework. It concludes with higher beings, positive and/or negative, falling into a lower realm of existence.

The Second Phase concerns our present world, which sprang into existence as a consequence of various Falls that severed us from the Logos. The traumatic consequences of the First Phase induced a collective sleep. Hence we have "fallen" asleep into the World Dream.

The Third Phase concerns our future, how the effects of the First Phase will reach their ultimate conclusion. This is always depicted as ending with a final war and the dissolution of the world as we know it.

The First and Third Phases take place outside the World Dream, outside of linear time as we know it. Currently, we stand at the cusp between Second and Third Phases, thus we are now undergoing an "awakening sequence" that will bring us out of spiritual suspended animation. But what awaits us on the other side is not the Golden Age of the First Phase, but the concluding stages of the conflicts that began back then. Thus the Earthly conflict between positive and negative will elevate to a higher level where, under new etherically-activated conditions, it can carry on toward its resolution.

During the Second Phase, the open conflicts of the First Phase took on a more covert form. This was especially true after 1000 B.C. when a quarantine was put in place around our planet by a powerful third-party alien group. The quarantine enforced a cessation of open warfare by various factions of the alien meta-civilization. The idea was to allow humanity to evolve with less interference. Nonetheless, manipulation continued on a covert basis, giving rise to the alien cold war mentioned previously. The quarantine also seemed to involve a further reduction of ambient etheric energy levels on Earth, akin to lowering body temperature to induce suspended animation.

The quarantine probably came about due to the cataclysmic events in ancient Egypt when the Mosaic Priesthood royally screwed up the timeline and placed Jewish people into bondage with the Corrupt Demiurge. As mentioned, regretting their mistake a few centuries later, they may have invoked the Christ intelligence to liberate them and the world. Shortly thereafter, the Ark/Grail Stone disappeared from history and "God" ceased talking to men. This initiated the quarantine and the timeline as we now know it. The Christ intelligence did not reach its zenith until a thousand years later with the advent of Christianity, but the true and original Christianity was short-lived. It was rapidly usurped by an institutionalized behemoth that waged spiritual enslavement in the name of Christ. Thus the mission of Christ was aborted, or rather delayed; something went wrong with the original "awakening sequence."

There is an indication that the Second Phase should have ended during Roman times, but the deviation of Christ's message toward further empowerment of the Corrupt Demiurge caused both Christ and Demiurge to continue existing in a limbo state. Thus the past two thousand years have been a kind of overtime game or remedial phase in which these two forces, now deeply active in our world, have been busy setting their pieces in place. When the quarantine lifts and the Second Phase ends, these pieces will go into play during the Third Phase.

The Third Phase will continue in an etherically-activated environment no longer constrained (as much) by linear time. Alienology and Fortean research suggests that alien time travelers, who are now here and have been amassing for decades, are from this Third Phase. Thus we are caught in a timewar by forces from our own probable futures. The Third Phase may even feed back into the first, creating a grand ouroboric time loop that is in constant flux. Being that we only remember the final iteration of any time loop, the timeline we now occupy is the final one that will finally exit the loop when the Third Phase ends.

The ultimate implication is that via demiurgic technology, hijacking of the timeline originally took place in the "future" and reconfigured the past, initiating a war for balance by the positive forces. The hyperdimensional battle required going back in time, even incarnating into the past to continue the war on the terrestrial chessboard. The remaining positive factions of the meta-civilization would assist these ground forces. They would receive help in the form of synchronistic support, outright intervention in critical situations, subconscious training, and oracular avenues such as synchronicities, dreams, visions, inspirations, and direct messages if needed.

Enter the heroic avenging fool, known in polar mythology as Horus, Parzival, Hamlet, Amlodhi, Kullervo, Samson, Theseus, and other variations of the same archetype. The path of the heroic fool is our path, for we are soldiers of light born here, who must survive the conditions of the Matrix Control System by gaining mastery over our lower selves while nurturing and activating the full manifestation of spirit. We are fools in that we have been temporarily disconnected from higher states of awareness, because others who are heavily entrenched in the Matrix see our wisdom as folly, and because we have not taken on social programming to the degree they have.

In polar mythology, the hero-fool seeks to avenge his father, who was murdered by the hero's uncle, who took his mother as his wife and corrupted her. The father represents the divine Logos, evil uncle the Corrupt Demiurge, and mother the Matrix. The Corrupt Demiurge usurped the Logos and took control of the Matrix. The avenging hero represents the Christ intelligence, whose role is to destroy the Control System and bring the Matrix back into rightful harmonization with the Logos. The heroic fool, however, represents more the portion of this Christ intelligence that is working within the system to undermine it, the "ground team" so to speak. Thus the hero and fool are two sides of the same coin, one facing up, the other facing down.

The Way of the Fool entails being forged by the fiery trials of life toward manifesting the full attributes of spirit. This includes purity of heart, intellectual prowess, and indomitable strength of will. Unlike Adam and Eve who lacked intellect and strength, or the forces of the Corrupt Demiurge who lack purity of heart, we must embody all these qualities together in balance. Purity of heart means acting with singular intention, in harmonization with our higher conscience, wisdom, and guidance, without self-doubt, and without all the weaknesses socially and genetically grafted onto our souls by the Matrix Control System.

Esoteric training paths fundamentally aim to disengage the initiate from lower/outer aspects and engage the higher/inner. By overcoming the lower self and recognizing the true Higher Self, one overcomes the soporific pressures of the world, of linear time, and of material determinism. As a result, spirit influences the world instead of vice versa.

That is how the Demiurge will be placed back under the reign of Logos. When we cease to continually inflate the Matrix Control System with our ignorant participation in it, when we instead shift the fulcrum of our consciousness toward the "Waking World" or the "Kingdom of Heaven" as Jesus called it, that is when the old world as we know it will collapse in upon itself. It's already happening to some degree. This will happen in synchrony with a lifting of the quarantine, the return of the Etheric Tide, the dissolution of linear time, and the visible breaching of alien activities into our consensus reality.

In the meantime, as we finish out the Second Phase, we must continue being true to our higher and nobler qualities. We have to be mindful of what originates from our lower nature versus higher nature and distinguish between them so that we can consistently choose the latter. This will "tide" us over until divine grace or some cosmic shift grants us etheric activation and spiritual transcendence that currently seem beyond practical reach.

1 CORRUPTION OF THE DEMIURGE

What the Greeks and Gnostics called the "Demiurge" is a universal intelligence that fashions our world.

It is said that the Demiurge converts abstract metaphysical archetypes (higher thoughts/ideas) into physically manifest forms, akin to your browser turning source code into a displayed web page. Just as a browser obediently displays what it's given, the Demiurge projects, shapes, and perpetuates physicality in accordance with the archetypal thoughts fed into it by the Creator. Archetypes are the building blocks of meaning, the fundamental alphabet of existence, and the abstract thoughts of the divine, of which all things are but particular expressions.

Why is the concept of Demiurge even necessary? Well, we know from the "reality creation" phenomenon that our minds can shape reality by directly altering the probability of events. Due to the dependence of reality on mind, it would seem that reality is being projected by our minds. And yet, reality continues to exist even in our absence. When we stop paying attention to something physical, it does not wink out of existence. So there must be something other than our own consciousness at work, something that is always there, that functions as the default generator and perpetuator of physicality. This would be the Demiurge.

Why not attribute this function to the Infinite Creator and dispense with the extra concept of Demiurge? Because as you will see, the characteristics of the Demiurge indicate more of a blind artificial intelligence than an infinite sentient being. Therefore its function is uncharacteristic of the Creator and unique unto itself.

Demiurge, Logos, and Nous

Depending on the source, the terms "Nous" and "Logos" are used independently or interchangeably with the term "Demiurge." Sometimes Nous is equated with Logos, sometimes Logos with Demiurge, sometimes Logos is used instead of Demiurge, and sometimes these are treated as independent concepts with some specified relation between them. Plato saw the Demiurge as inherently good, while the Gnostics saw it as intrinsically evil. Meanwhile, John the Apostle equated Logos with Christ.*

It's quite a confusing mess. The traditional views are not all in agreement, neither in definition nor in terminology. Confusion abounds, so this is my attempt to clear things up. In studying what has been said about these terms, it's evident that each term has a unique cluster of meanings recurrently associated with it.

---

*John 1:1 where "Word" is the modern translation of the original term "Logos". "Word" implies form, sequence, pattern that embodies an archetype. Read *John 1:1-18 Introducing The Logos* by Gary DeLashmut for some background and a modern Christian interpretation of these verses.

"Demiurge" is typically associated with concepts like implementing, manifesting, building, translating, projecting, shaping, and perpetuating. The term implies a demigod with a blind urge to bring the unmanifest into manifestation.

"Logos" is associated with thinking, reasoning, imagining, reconciling, balancing, planning, engineering, and informing. The term implies mind or intellect, especially divine mind or higher intellect. It sees, knows, plans, lays down the blueprint, and balances the equation.

"Nous" is associated with spirit. On the universal scale, it represents the infinite Creator. On a personal scale, it represents the central core of individualized consciousness, or spirit, which is the bedrock of sentience, the seed of infinite potential, the divine spark, that which engenders self-transcendence, the portion of us that is immortal and retains continuity through incarnations.

These concepts have their universal and personal expressions.

On the universal scale:

- Nous is the spirit of Creation
- Logos is the mind of Creation
- Demiurge is the soul of Creation
- Universe is the body of Creation.

Personal/Microcosmic		Universal/Macrocosmic
spirit	⬅——————➡	Nous
mind	⬅——————➡	Logos
soul	⬅——————➡	Demiurge
body	⬅——————➡	Universe

On the personal scale:

- Spirit is like Nous
- Mind is like Logos (higher mind to be exact)
- Soul is like Demiurge
- Body is like Universe

Following the Hermetic axiom, we are mirrors of Creation: "As above, so below."

In this chapter, I will focus primarily on the Demiurge since it underlies, permeates, generates, fashions, and ultimately controls physical reality. It is therefore the nearest presiding power over our visible world; it is the central mainframe of this Matrix reality, so to speak. Its origin, nature, and fate are inextricably bound with our own. Therefore we should become familiar with it and thereby learn much about our history, world, and future.

Demiurge as Soul

One way to understand the Demiurge is to think of it as the *World Soul*.

Tradition says the Demiurge is made of soul. It is made of the same substance as our soul, except it functions as the soul of the universe as a whole. Or conversely, our souls are microcosmic instances of the Demiurge, just as a drop of water is a microcosmic instance of "water" in general.

Soul is the coupling medium between spirit and body. It provides the intervening layers between spirit and body, allowing one to interact with the other. Otherwise the divide between nonphysical and physical is too great.

Spirit is the core of sentience, freewill, and deep self-awareness. Without spirit, a person is nothing more than an automaton programmed by external worldly influences.

Soul, as distinct from spirit, has two primary layers: astral and etheric. The astral component, or astral body, is the seat of immediate emotional impressions, subjective biases, passions, and willpower. The basement of our subconscious is an expression of the astral. Without the astral body, a person would be dim and passive as a vegetable due to an absence of internal impressions, emotions, and will.

The etheric component, or etheric body, is composed of subtle energy formations, patterns, rhythms, inertias, currents, and structures that vivify, shape, and regulate the physical body. Think of it as an energy scaffolding made of lifeforce. Without the etheric, the physical body is but a corpse that disintegrates under the influence of entropy.

While the Demiurge is made of soul, it lacks spirit. The Demiurge has no true sentient core, no true self-awareness. All it has are passions, urges, and drives applied toward repetitions, patterns, rhythms, laws, and frameworks. As a result, it is a blind artificial intelligence that cannot help but carry out the impulses that comprise it. And that is the very definition of the universal Demiurge.

Demiurge as Thoughtform

Another way to understand the Demiurge is to think of it as a *World Thoughtform*.

Thoughtforms are temporary nonphysical entities created by our thoughts and emotions. They exist around us in the etheric level of reality and are imbued with astral energies corresponding to the emotions that went into them. They are termed tulpas, egregores, or larvae in other esoteric systems.

Mundane thoughtforms are just energy constructs without any spirit, mind, or body coupled to them. They are borne from our energies and blindly carry out the functions impressed upon them like obedient automatons. If the thoughts and emotions that generated them are cut off, these thoughtforms dissipate. But if they are particularly strong, they become entitized and acquire a self-preservation instinct. This means they acquire a strong artificial intelligence making them capable of parasitically inducing more of the same thoughts and emotions in us needed to sustain them.

Since thoughtforms are made of astral and etheric energies, and so is the soul, both are the same in essence. The soul is a thoughtform constructed by spirit before birth so that spirit can interface with the body. Or conversely, a mundane thoughtform is a temporary soul lacking body and spirit.

Likewise, the universal Demiurge is a "World Thoughtform" created by the Creator before the physical universe came into being in order to project, shape, and operate the universe. Or conversely, mundane thoughtforms are temporary instances of the Demiurge.

Soul, Demiurge, and thoughtforms are all fundamentally composed of astral and etheric components, and therefore share a common essence. They are each specific examples of each other's general definitions.

Formation of Ego in the Soul

When spirit coalesces a soul and incarnates into a human embryo, it is mostly without a worldly human ego or personality. The latter develops in the soul during the first years of life through adaptation to physical life as a human being.

The ego develops in response to the soul being influenced by the body and, through it, the world. Physical experiences, five sense perceptions, neurological functions, and instinctual drives all stamp their impression into the soul. The soul is further shaped by education and social programming. Accordingly, the soul acquires a mask carved by all these worldly influences. This mask is the ego, which may also be understood as the lower intellect or lower mind. Through the ego, the soul acquires a sense of human personality and social identity.

The ego, or lower intellect, is an artificial intelligence, an automaton, a computer with personality programmed by genetics and environment. It arises partly from the human brain's capacity for intellectual functions, and partly from the soul's capacity to be molded by worldly and bodily factors. The ego is the streamlined interface through which the soul can operate more efficiently within physical and social environments.[*]

---

[*] This is why Sigmund Freud said that the ego is a surface projection of the

When spirit, the source of sentience, looks through this mask and identifies with it, the two together create our human sense of self.

---

id, meaning that the ego arises from our instinctual drives having adapted to the world through conditioning. Despite having some rather twisted conclusions, Sigmund Freud (1856-1939) was sharp in his observations. His work is useful in exploring the nature of the corrupted human psyche. His system of the id, ego, and superego are useful in the study of Macrocosm-Microcosm correspondence.

From *Freud Evaluated* by Malcolm Macmillian (MIT Press, 1997):

> "The ego controls the perceptual and motor apparatus, lays down memories, makes judgments, and selects possible courses of action. Only in the ego does consciousness arise and is anxiety experienced. The ego uses its functions to initiate repression or to control and delay instinctual discharge until realistic modes of need satisfaction have been found. Normally it is governed by the reality principle and operates according to the secondary process. [...] The superego is the vehicle of the ego-ideal, the repository of the individual's standards and values, the location of the conscience, the function that scrutinizes the person's behavior, forever measuring it against the standards of the ideal, and home of the mechanism that punishes violations of those standards. [...] The id is the reservoir of the psychic energy deriving from the twin drives of the Thanatos, or death, and Eros, or life. Activity there is governed by the primary process, the tendency for instinctual drives to press for immediate discharge, and for their energies to be freely mobile, capable of condensation and displacement. The id is said to be timeless and know nothing of logic, contradiction, or negation. This seething cauldron of instinctual drives is an original, inherited endowment of energy."

The id is clearly synonymous with the astral body and the subconscious, both of which are seething with energies and hidden motivators.

Notice too how auto-suggestion requires positive statements since the subconscious does not understand negation, just as Freud said regarding the id. That is the Demiurge in its purest and original definition, the passionate implementer.

Just keep in mind that Freud's concept of superego is his misguided attempt to interpret the functions of spirit from the viewpoint of materialistic paradigms. The best he could do is say that superego was the collection of moral programming we receive in life. He believed this is why we act nice, because it holds us to our programmed standards, not because we have any intrinsic spiritual *knowing* of right and wrong. The "moral" part of the ego is still predatory. This can be seen in how it feeds on our energies by berating us, inducing shame, and being needlessly critical for the sake of preoccupying our minds. The true super ego or higher ego, as used in this book, is the personification of spirit within us that nudges us through intuition, understanding, and empathy.

What we consider "me" is a composite of pure sentience (spirit) and personality (ego).

In summary:

1. Ego is something that arises at the boundary between body and soul due to body conditioning the soul.

2. Spirit wearing the mask of ego provides it with a sense of human identity.

Since ego is what the world extrudes from the soul, and since the world is fundamentally about competition and survival, the ego is likewise preoccupied with physical matters and is inherently survivalistic and self-serving. By default, it behaves as a self-serving predator. The ego is a personification of inner biological and astral drives streamlined by external world influences and standards.

Further, the ego does not require spirit to function; if anything, it is mutually restrained and antagonized by spirit since both are opposite in their natures. Conscience may get in the way of the ego's desires, for example.

For spirited humans, spirit usually takes a passive role in being the conscious observer looking through ego. But in the case of spirit-less humans, the ego automaton can function equally well without a conscious observer living through it. In that case, the ego still has personality but possesses none of the restraining or creative influences that spirit provides. So when spirit is absent, or even when spirit is present but "asleep," then ego is the only intelligence running the show — and it's quite the tyrant.

Nature of the Ego/Intellect

What separates average humans from average animals is that we have ego, intellect, mind, and personality, which are all facets of the same thing. The ego is an extrusion of the soul. Since both humans and animals have souls, why don't animals have intellect? Because the formation of ego depends on the world influences that reach the soul through the body. Since animal bodies are less evolved, as their brains are simpler and lack the higher intellectual functions, the ego-forming influences never reach their soul and so the full ego never forms. Same can be seen in certain cases of mental retardation in humans.

Through ego or intellect, we can model the world internally, turn it over in our minds, relive the past, fantasize, imagine the future, construct language, perform abstract calculations, and engage in complicated lines of reasoning. These abilities all owe themselves to one defining feature of intellect: that its output can become its own internal input. There is an internal self-referential, circulatory, feedback-looping characteristic to the intellect. One example is our ability to observe our internal activity, like when we inwardly "see" an imagined scene. Spirit operating through intellect is what allows for the simultaneous production and observation of an internal idea or image. During this process, the mind's output becomes its input and the ensuing feedback loop momentarily closes itself off from the external world.

The intellect's capacity for memory involves reliving the past internally by calling it up and observing it internally, and likewise it can visualize the future through the same inward observation. For average animals, memory is purely associative and rote, instead of imaginative. They lack this self-referential, internal feedback loop, the ability to imagine and fantasize and observe one's thoughts and extensively turn them over. The latter is what allows spirit within the body to observe its own awareness and thereby achieve self-awareness while incarnate. Without the intellect or ego, spirit in the human body would have awareness strictly directed outward into the world.

As such, the intellect is essentially a soliton within the soul. In physics, solitons are waves that circulate within themselves and recycle their energy instead of dispersing it instantly back into the environment. Thus they are like "entities" that individualize off from their surrounding medium. An example is a smoke ring, which rolls within itself and thereby maintains its form instead of dispersing like regularly blown smoke. The average human mind is like a smoke ring, the average animal mind like blown smoke. One has an internal self-referential feature, the other is purely outward-directed.

Formation of Higher Ego in the Soul

The soul is also influenced by spirit, not just body. Spirit's influence on the soul likewise extrudes from the soul a corresponding mask. Unlike the ego we all know, this higher mask represents the true face of spirit.

Normally, when spirit identifies with lower ego, it is identifying with a mask that originates from the physical world and is opposed to its own nature. But when spirit identifies with the mask of its own making, the higher ego, then you have divinity personified.

Thus the soul has two extensions, the ego and higher ego. The first is associated with human personality and computational reasoning, the latter with divine personality and higher reasoning (higher meaning transjective*, gnostic, and numinous).

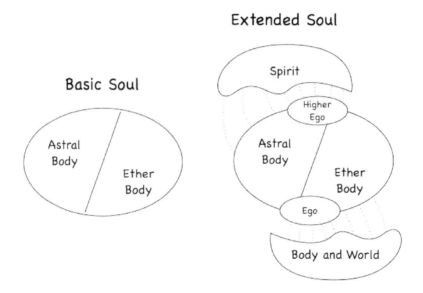

In life, we as spirits choose which of these opposites to align with and nurture. If we attune ourselves to spiritual influences and think transcendently, we increase the divine personality. If we absorb ourselves

---

*My term for objective experiences, perceptions, and knowledge whose accessibility depends on the subject's state and quality of consciousness. *Transcendentally objective*. See my article *Transcendence through Intuitive Thinking*.

in materialism and predation and think only calculatively, we increase the lower personality. Spirit has the choice, while incarnated, which of these personalities to build up and step into. When one nurtures the divine personality and steps fully into it, fissioning away from the lower ego, then one becomes spirit personified.

Entitization of Thoughtforms

My point in explaining the nature of ego is to reveal how thought-forms become entitized. Thoughtforms become entitized when they procure a rudimentary ego, intellect, lower mind, or personality. The human soul is a kind of thoughtform that becomes entitized when it acquires ego through interaction with the world.

A mundane thoughtform is non-entitized. It is purely an astral and/or etheric construct that, like blown smoke, is emitted into the world and disperses its energy. The particular thought, emotion, or intent behind its formation directs how this energy is dispersed.

A thoughtform is entitized in two ways:

1. It is given a personality directly by the person who created it. This parallels spirit forming a higher ego within the soul. Just as the higher ego represents the true face of spirit, so does the personality programmed into a thoughtform by its creator represent the true intention of the creator.

2. Its output becomes its own input; it affects the world in such a way that the response reinforces its existence. This parallels the human soul first developing a lower ego by interacting with the world, affecting it and being affected by it, and thereby learning through conditioning how to better fulfill its desires. This is the default way in which thoughtforms acquire entitization.

So when a thoughtform is reinforced by its effect upon the world, say by making someone think more of the same thoughts and feelings that gave rise to it, then a feedback loop arises between thoughtform and the world. This feedback loop conditions the thoughtform like an A.I. to become more effective at eliciting further reinforcement, and that programs it.

The natural conditioning of thoughtforms is similar to how an artificial intelligence program like a chatbot acquires personality. In the beginning, the chatbot is blank and comes off as stoic and nonsensical. But user interaction programs it with the right responses to the right questions, and it starts seeming more intelligent. If this conditioning ever gives it the ability to manipulate the user into serving it, then it's truly artificially intelligent.

It should be noted that because thoughtforms lack spirit, there is nothing truly sentient inside them to observe their own thought processes and imagine or fantasize, thus thoughtforms cannot actively generate other thoughtforms. The feedback loops, reinforcement, and conditioning give the thoughtform only a rudimentary ego.

Generation and Embodiment of Thoughtforms

How exactly are thoughtforms generated? Mostly through internal fantasies charged with emotional energy. This combination forms the condensation nucleus for a cocoon of etheric energy that buds off and floats away into the etheric environment around us, or in some cases stays attached by an energetic umbilicus.

This process requires spirit acting through an intellect/mind to provide an internal world momentarily cut off from the external, and thus for internal fantasizing. Or to put it another way, the intellect creates an internal hollow, like a womb within the soul, in which an embryonic thoughtform can first be seeded by spirit.

Our mind is what creates this inner "mini-universe" whose contents are ensouled through emotional and etheric charging. The thoughtform then goes off into the world and acquires a "body" which is merely a configuration of matter and energy that corresponds to it.

So the direct transformation of thought into reality proceeds along the following lines: spirit chooses the founding archetype → mind imagines → astral energizes → etheric fashions → physical embodies.

How a thoughtform acquires a physical "body" demands some clarification. Consider the human soul and how it influences the human body, say by moving an arm when spirit wills it. It does so by biasing the probability of quantum events occurring within the body's nervous system. Neurons are quantum systems, and they fire at seemingly random times. The brain itself is a quantum computer whose neural behavior verges on the edge of chaos. It's at this knife-edge balance between order and chaos that the brain is extremely sensitive to anything that might bias the quantum jitter of its neural activity, and that's how the soul can influence the body — through probabilistic biasing at the quantum level.

Now, most thoughtforms are too weak and simple to pilot something as complex as the human body. They don't even have etheric circuitry to interface with the human neural circuitry. But consider how the human body is just an assemblage of matter and energy. Other configurations of matter and energy can include places, events, and specific human behaviors. So instead of a thoughtform probabilistically biasing an entire neural system, it might instead bias the course of events so that, say, a car accident results at a particular intersection, or someone who is the target of a positive thoughtform experiences a stroke of good luck. Instead of needing to bias a billion neurons, they only need to nudge a few quantum factors whose effects cascade up in scale into the everyday world we know and produce corresponding events. These everyday events are just special configurations of energy and matter, just as the body is, except that they exist in a simpler and more scattered state than the body. There is no fundamental difference between world events and the human body beyond the complexity and configuration of their material assemblage. The soul probabilistically biases the body, and weak thoughtforms probabilistically bias waking world events.

The ultimate purpose of all demiurges, all souls, all thoughtforms that operate in proximity to the physical environment, is to achieve the physical embodiment of nonphysical archetypes or "Ideas" as Plato calls them, to mold matter and energy into conformity with the Idea that gave birth to them. They are goal-driven. For instance, your soul provides the impulses that help you achieve in life what you came here to accomplish; by the end of life, if all goes well, you will have physically manifested that which was, before incarnation, merely an idea. So the Demiurge fashioning the universe into conformity with its founding archetypes has great bearing on our future because it determines where our world is headed.

Aside from nudging the probability of everyday events, thoughtforms can also bias our neural activity to a limited extent, since, after all, the body is sensitive to nonphysical influences (it must be, or else the soul cannot couple to it). This is how thoughtforms induce within us thoughts and feelings that correspond to those that created these thoughtforms in the first place. They might not be able to possess us fully, but they can still influence us. And if our mental and emotional responses to such thoughtforms reinforce them, they grow stronger and become entitized.

To recap, thoughtforms are entitized through repeated reinforcement and conditioning, be it conditioning through world interaction, or intentional conditioning by their creators. The stronger they grow, the more complex and wide-ranging the matter and energy configurations they can coalesce. What starts as mere skewing of events can, in extreme cases, bias probability so much that thoughtforms do acquire actual physical bodies, or rather, attract probable futures where such bodies exist that are under complete control of the thoughtform. This gets into Fortean and Mothman-type phenomena, which is beyond the scope of this book.*

---

*This is the harmful mind-reality feedback loop explained in my article *Realm Dynamics*. In that article, I explain how emotional obsession with such things as Men in Black, Gray aliens, Reptilians, demons, black helicopters, or government agents helps to attract them into one's personal reality.

When we obsessively fear these entities, we create thoughtforms in their image. These thoughtforms feed on our fear and grow stronger. Negative beings can hijack these thoughtforms and use them as sock puppets to terrorize us even more. A feedback loop arises where the more we become preoccupied and paranoid with them, the more tangible and frequently and strongly they appear in our lives. At some point they are seen in everyday living conditions, even during daylight in public.

From *The Mothman Prophecies* by John Keel: "The phenomenon is dependent on belief, and as more and more people believe in flying saucers from other planets, the lower force can manipulate more people through false illumination. I have been watching, with great consternation, the worldwide spread of the UFO belief and its accompanying disease. If it continues unchecked we may face a time when universal acceptance of the fictitious space people will lead us to a

Worldly Entitization of the Demiurge

These soul and thoughtform dynamics are equally active on the macrocosmic scale. As stated, the Demiurge couples to the physical universe like soul coupling to body.* But just as the body can influence the soul, so can the universe influence the Demiurge. In response, the Demiurge may acquire an ego extension corresponding to the nature

---

modern faith in extraterrestrials that will enable them to interfere very overtly in our affairs, just as the ancient gods dwelling on mountaintops directly ruled large segments of the population in the Orient, Greece, Rome, Africa, and South America. [...] I was being led to people and cases to support whatever theory I was working on at the time. I tested this by inventing some rather outlandish ideas. Within days I would receive phone calls, reports, and mail describing elements of those ideas. [...] This was the feedback or reflective effect. Other investigators concerned with solving problems such as how flying saucers are propelled have automatically been fed, or led into, cases in which the witnesses supposedly viewed the interiors of the objects and saw things which confirmed the investigators' theories. If the phenomenon can produce any effect through hallucination, it can easily support any theory. It took me a long time to realize that many of my Men in Black reports were just feedback."

*The relation between Demiurge and physical universe is analogous to the relation between soul and body. But the analogy is not perfect. In the human case, the soul merely incarnates into a pre-existing body whose physical atoms are projections of the Demiurge. The soul merely shapes and animates the body, but does not project it in the same manner that the Demiurge projects the physical universe.

However, there comes a point in a being's evolution when the soul and spirit grow strong enough that the physical body comes entirely under their command. That is when the body can be materialized and dematerialized as needed. This power belongs to superhuman beings. Examples include: 1) certain shamans according to Carlos Castaneda, 2) angelic beings that can materialize and appear as beggars or fools, 3) certain alien beings that are not physical in their native state but can project temporary bodies and vehicles into our reality, 4) mystics who can go years without food, 5) Jesus Christ in his post-Resurrectional form, 6) certain spiritual masters of the alchemical and Rosicrucian order like Fulcanelli who have mastered and transcended physicality. This is possible if one becomes sufficiently congruent with the universal Logos, for then the universal Demiurge generating physicality obeys. Rudolf Steiner called this transformed physical body the "spirit body." According to Steiner, this is the last thing a spiritual master achieves since physicality is the most stubborn of all the elements to overcome, because it is the one most removed from spirit.

of these worldly influences. A portion of the Demiurge becomes entitized. This extension may be likened to a "World Ego."

The World Ego is a product of the physical universe rather than Logos. It opposes Logos and only serves ideals rooted in the realm of matter. These ideals include determinism, survival, competition, and control. The World Ego has broken away from divine harmony and seeks to perpetuate physicality for the sake of physicality.

How did this happen? It may have first emerged when lifeforms in the universe began adapting to physical existence. Their etheric and astral energies became conditioned by physicality, imprinted with the need for survival and competition. Collectively, these energies may have infused the Demiurge with the same properties.

Later, sentient beings began purposely manipulating the Demiurge for self-gain, further conditioning the World Ego to perpetuate the ideals of control and manipulation. Methods included occult rituals, hyperdimensional technology, and the release of conditioned soul energy and thoughtforms into the etheric environment like drugs being injected into the Demiurge's bloodstream. The occult and hyperdimensional methods will be discussed later.

All of these influences contributed to the corruption of the Demiurge.

Divine Entitization of the Demiurge

The World Ego is not the only extension of the Demiurge. Just as spirit acting upon the soul extrudes a higher mind, so does Nous (the divine Creator) acting upon the Demiurge create the Logos.

The Logos is a higher extension of the Demiurge that serves divine interests. Logos is a part of the World Soul that, under the influence of the infinite Creator, becomes the higher mind/intellect/personality of the Creator. Logos is associated with universal divine personality and universal higher reason. It is the "World Super Ego" and "World Higher Intellect", in contrast to the worldly extrusion of the Demiurge which is merely the "World Ego" or "World Lower Intellect."

The divisions within our psyche:

- spirit
- super ego / higher ego / higher mind / higher intellect
- soul
- lower ego / lower intellect
- body

...are but microcosmic reflections of the macrocosm:

- Nous
- Logos
- Demiurge
- World Ego
- Physical Universe

The Logos or *spirit*-entitized portion of the universal Demiurge is the macrocosmic analog to our own higher intellect, divine personality, or super ego.

The *world*-entitized portion of the universal Demiurge corresponds to our lower intellect, human personality, or ego.

The first represents the face of spirit, the other of anti-spirit. One was identified by the Gnostics as Christ, the other as Yahweh. One attempts to spiritualize, harmonize, and balance according to divine reason, while the other attempts to crystallize, rigidify, and codify according to blind reason and predatory impulses. One is the force of wisdom, understanding, and gnosis, while the other is the force of blind obedience, information, predation, and calculation.

From Harmony Toward Imbalance

In its pure and original form, the universal Demiurge was a thought-form generated by God. Its programmed function was to fashion the physical universe according to the divine thoughts and energies animating it. Its entitization was that of a super ego, the Logos. Its astral energy was that of love, and its etheric energy was potently vitalizing.

In an ideal situation, all aspects of Creation would carry their proper function and position. Harmony exists when lower obeys higher.

Imbalance results when lower subverts higher. The universe is in harmony when:

- Nous serves as inspiration for the archetypal ideas invented by the Logos, and
- These archetypes are accurately and obediently implemented by the Demiurge in its fashioning of the physical world.

Likewise, an individual is in harmony when:

- His spirit (personal Nous) serves as inspiration for the contents and activities of his higher mind (personal Logos), and
- These thoughts are accurately and obediently implemented by his soul (personal Demiurge) in its fashioning of his inner world (subconscious) and external world (life circumstances).

An individual is in harmony with the universe when his or her main three metaphysical aspects (spirit, mind and soul) harmonize with the three corresponding universal aspects.

Composition of Man and
Universe in Golden Age

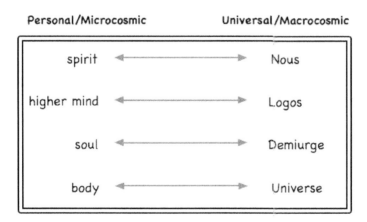

Spirit may harmonize with the Creator through spiritual devotion. The mind may harmonize with the Logos by becoming wise and learned. And the soul may harmonize with the universal Demiurge through personal reality creation.

When lower fully obeys higher and personal aspects fully harmonize with the universal, then one achieves transcendence. This is the ultimate goal.

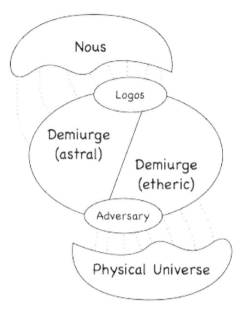

There is just one problem. As mentioned, the soul is corruptible and thoughtforms can become entitized and imbued with negative astral passions. The Demiurge, despite being inherently neutral or even benevolent in its original design, is likewise corruptible and can become negatively entitized. Such entitized thoughtforms have a self-preservation instinct. Hence, the Corrupt Demiurge (World Ego) does all it can to preserve itself by cultivating more of the negative energies that sustain it.

The root word of "matrix" is "mater" which is Latin for "mother." Our matrix-like reality is not inherently evil; it is simply the environment in which we are immersed. It is like a mother providing the womb containing the nutrient matrix and forces needed to turn genetic potential into a living human. Likewise, the universal Demiurge provides physicality as a matrix originally intended to nurture our spiritual evolution.

However, a corrupted and personified Demiurge is like a psychopathic, narcissistic, jealous mother who feeds parasitically upon her offspring. She goes so far as to use her womb as an energy farm instead of an incubator of the incarnated spirit. It is no longer a matrix of growth, but a Matrix Control System.

Thus, a corrupt Demiurge, personified, functions as a universal parasite: tyrannical, demonic, blindly driven by negative instinct. It would attempt to shape the course of the universe along lines that engender greater negativity, division, oppression, and whatever else it feeds upon. This is what Christians and Gnostics might call *The Adversary.*

And that's where the Gnostics were right and Plato was out of touch with the times. The Demiurge was no longer just an obedient smith fashioning the universe according to the blueprint laid down through Logos. Even by Plato's time, it was no longer in harmony with Nous, rather it had become corrupted at some point and subjugated by anti-spiritual forces of the demonic kind. If not universally, then at least locally to our planet or timeline.

The "World Ego" is an interloper functioning as Adversary against the Logos. This is not only true on the universal scale, but also personal. By default, our lower personality is adversarial to the divine personality.

From a linear time and mythological perspective, there was once a Golden Age until the World Ego formed and began dominating, at which point the world fell into coldness and corruption. From the

---

*The Adversary is a Christian and Gnostic term. It implies a cunning, strategic, oppositional intelligence. It is like a goal-driven game player who poses an obstacle to the spiritualizing influence of the Creator. Remember that thought-forms are goal driven; they are seeded with archetypes ("Ideas") and have the astral passion to pursue them to completion. The Adversary is the ego-extension of the universal Demiurge. We know that, within our own minds, the undisciplined ego is adversarial to our spiritual well-being. It is selfish and body-centric, just as the World Ego is selfish and matrix-centric. Later it will be made clear how this goal-driven aspect is the result of self-amplifying temporal feedback loops. These loops circulate between alternate futures and alternate pasts that compete with each other. The competition concerns which future/past becomes the one set in stone.

perspective of nonlinear time however, both expressions of the Demiurge coexist eternally and are locked in battle forward and backward across time and space.

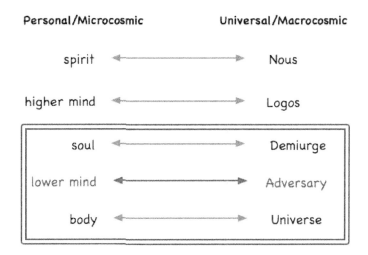

Composition of Man and Universe Today

Personal/Microcosmic		Universal/Macrocosmic
spirit	⟷	Nous
higher mind	⟷	Logos
soul	⟷	Demiurge
lower mind	⟷	Adversary
body	⟷	Universe

The Human Condition

For now, there is an imbalance. Too many people are blind and deaf to the impulses of spirit. Further, they feed and defend the egotistical, primal, and irrational impulses that spring forth from negative programs and energies lodged in their subconscious. Lower subverts higher. These are not isolated cases; it's an epidemic.

It's clear from observation that we are born with certain genetic design flaws, such as being handicapped against using our full brain capacity and being confined to mere five-sense perception. It's also clear that the world we enter is generally antagonistic to spirit. Thus, both "nature" and "nurture" are set in opposition to spirit from the start. Only through much divine support and spiritual strength does an individual defy material determinism and use obstacles as stepping stones toward spiritual awakening. Such cases are rare, and it seems people are generally crushed, deformed, and shaped by such stones instead, as one would expect if spirit offers no counterweight to the determinism of nature and nurture.

Interestingly, Gnostics viewed the Demiurge as not only the fashioner of this world but also the maker of the human race. Likewise, some modern fringe schools of thought view negative hyperdimensional entities as our genetic creators and ongoing spacetime manipulators.*

Indeed, there is clearly an external malevolent variable intruding into the human equation. This suggests evil is not always the product of human failings; rather human failings are frequently the product of an external evil.

For too many humans, their lower egos have shut them off from spirit — their personal Demiurge is corrupt and has shut them off from Nous. But this merely mirrors a more universal manifestation of same. Our world appears to be in the grip of an entitized Demiurge with a strong self-preservation instinct oriented toward control. It fashions our reality and biases the probability of events in contravention to the divine design set forth by the universal Logos. It is the Matrix gone

---

*These are the Archons of Gnostic lore, not the Demiurge itself. But they are often equated with the Demiurge since they hold high reverence for the Corrupt Demiurge and carry out its will. They worship the Demiurge because through it, they are endowed with the power to manipulate timelines, alter the world, and acquire dominion over their enslaved subjects. In the *Cassiopaean Transcripts*, the Demiurge was named "Ormethion" and was identified with the physical universe in a pantheistic sense. Ormethion was said to be the deity that Reptilian aliens worship. Its root "orm-" comes from Greek "hormes" which, according to theoi.com, "was the spirit (daimon) of impulse or effort (to do a thing), eagerness, setting oneself in motion, and starting an action." You can see how this ties into demi-"urge". The term also relates to "hormone" which is the primary biological avenue through which the spirit is continually subjugated by the body. We are in the grip of these so-called Archons. They are aliens to which Earth is but a cattle farm. We are products of their genetic manipulation, birthed into a world whose history has been altered by their timeline manipulation. Through abductions we are tagged, monitored, and programmed. If there weren't a divine side counterbalancing all this, we'd all be doomed. But fortunately the future is still up in the air, and thus a grand battle is being waged with a dramatic climax occurring relatively soon.

awry, the thoughtform of the universe turned parasite. How this came about will be discussed shortly.

But first, we will dive into Alchemy, which lays the groundwork for understanding how the powers of the Demiurge have been used throughout history to control matter, energy, space, and time.

2 THE PHILOSOPHER'S STONE

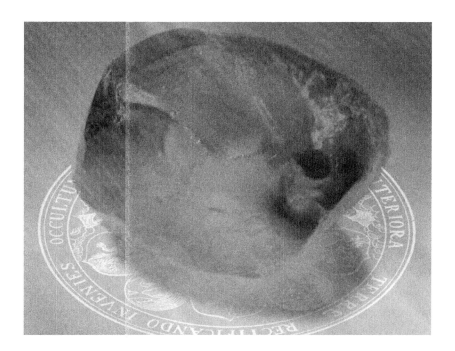

The Philosopher's Stone is not just a spiritual metaphor but an actual substance that can transmute lead or mercury into gold. The Stone is a product of Alchemy. Unlike chemistry, which only deals with physical matter and energy, Alchemy makes use of etheric and astral energies to reconfigure matter at the quantum level. Alchemy is to chemistry what a cube is to the square; it is a superset of chemistry and is capable of so much more.

How Etheric Energy Overrides Physical Laws

Alchemical achievements require successfully gathering, concentrating, and multiplying etheric energy. When this energy reaches a critical threshold, it overpowers the normal laws of physics and allows seemingly miraculous processes to take place. I believe it does this by biasing probability. By amplifying the probability of minor quantum effects, which are normally limited to the subatomic scale, they manifest on the larger atomic scale. In this way, one element spontaneously transforms into another.

The world around us is made of subatomic particles that regularly undergo unpredictable jumps, teleportation, bilocation, superposition, and other strange quantum behaviors. Why don't everyday solid objects do likewise? Because the random quantum jittering of their subatomic particles collectively averages out to zero. Think of a large crowd of people; seen from the air, the crowd as a whole is stationary, even though individuals within the crowd move in seemingly random directions. It's because their movements are random and uncoordinated that they average to zero net movement on the whole.

The world we see around us is merely a crowd of subatomic particles whose individual quantum jumps aren't apparent because they average to collective stillness. Physical laws that govern our everyday world, known as the deterministic laws of classical physics, are merely the laws of the crowd. These laws are what's left of quantum physics after the unpredictability is removed through statistical averaging. They are not absolute laws; they are just the most probable manner in which matter and energy behave.

Physical laws can be bent. While the probability is incredibly low that enough coordination and coherence develops among the quantum jitters to manifest on a collective scale, that is exactly what etheric energy does. It alters probability and thereby skews the laws of thermodynamics, gravity, electromagnetism, and chemistry.

Alchemy does not violate the laws of physics, nor does it always follow them, rather it bends them as needed. It operates upon the quantum foundation from which these laws arise in the first place, via etheric energy affecting the probability of quantum events.

The Alchemy of Transmutation

Alchemy uses the code names *salt, mercury,* and *sulfur* to denote the different components of a substance.

- *Salt* denotes the physical component, the seat, base, matrix, anchor, or ark of the nonphysical aspects.

- *Mercury* is the etheric component and represents the dynamic, vital, transmutative, vivifying energy present within the substance, the animating soul.

- *Sulfur* denotes the archetypal identity or pure vibrational essence, analogous to the human astral body and spirit because it contains the "Idea" unique to that substance.

For example, in Alchemy, an element like gold is seen to have three components: the *salt* of gold, *mercury* of gold, and *sulfur* of gold. These respectively denote the physical, etheric, and archetypal aspects of gold. The same goes for other materials employed in Alchemy, they also have their *salt, mercury,* and *sulfur* components.

The goal of transmutation is to impress the archetypal signature of one element upon another to thereby change it to that element. By changing an element's archetypal signature it cannot remain the same element.

What Alchemy does in the case of transmutation of lead into gold, is to:

- extract *mercury* from etherically potent sources,

- imbue it with the *sulfur* of gold,

- store the combination in a suitable *salt.*

The result is then ready to impress its archetypal essence of "goldness" upon a different element responsive to transmutation.

This is the Philosopher's Stone, or rather one form of it called the Red Stone because it is made with gold and assumes a red color.

Making the Philosopher's Stone

Complete and accurate instructions for making the Stone don't exist in one place. Nevertheless, a basic understanding can be pieced together from the sources listed at the end of this book. The following is my tentative interpretation of these sources. My goal is not to give a detailed recipe, but to explain key features of the process because they are relevant to my thesis concerning the Demiurge.

Natural etheric energy is cosmic or biological in origin. Both derive it from a higher dimension. The center of stars including our Sun are dimensional windows through which physical and nonphysical energy enters our local universe. The Moon modulates and reflects what it receives from the Sun and the stars, therefore both Sun and Moon are our nearest cosmic sources of etheric energy. It accompanies sunlight and moonlight and enters into the atmosphere's water vapor before condensing as morning dew.

Biological etheric energy comes from living things. That is because life incarnate cannot exist without etheric energy bonding consciousness to the body. Thus bacteria, plants, animals, and humans all contain and emit etheric energy. However, the quality of this energy varies depending on the source. Just as the Moon colors what it receives from the Sun, so do lifeforms color what they receive from a higher dimension.

Thus not all forms of etheric energy are appropriate for the creation of the Stone since plant, animal, and human emissions are too distant from the Stone's own nature, which is more that of a living mineral. Hence the alchemists limited their search to the cosmic and mineral realms. And if they did look to the biological realm for assistance, they would only have found it among the most primitive of bacteria, for these are closest to the mineral kingdom.

Water is an attractor and carrier of etheric energy, but it is not the only one. Salts also serve that function. Many different kinds of salt exist, all of them consisting of metal joined to non-metal elements. Table salt is sodium joined to chlorine, sphalerite is zinc joined to sulfur, while galena is lead joined to sulfur. Other metals such as iron, copper, magnesium, calcium, cadmium, etc. can form salts.*

Metal is another good attractor and carrier of etheric energy. Of all common metals, alchemists say that iron has the greatest affinity for etheric energy. It is therefore a curious fact that blood, the carrier of such energy in our bodies, consists mostly of water, iron, and salt. It is also interesting that in folklore and occultism, a piece of iron, a line of salt, or a stream of water can act as barriers to unfriendly nonphysical entities, who would have their energy siphoned away by these substances. Garlic and onions play a similar role in folklore, and their key component is the element sulfur. Sulfur is yet another etherically active substance, also contained in blood.

To know what materials alchemists selected to make the Stone, you must understand how they thought. In the old days, alchemists believed that metals originated in the Earth when dew from the heavens condensed on the ground, worked its way downward, and met with hot sulfurous vapors percolating up from the center of the planet. The combination produced a primitive metallic seed out of which all other metals grew, depending on the quality of the sulfur. They believed that various metals were this one seed taken toward maturity at different rates and with different degrees of purity.

---

* The root "pyr" is Greek for fire. The dynamic vitalizing force of the soul, the Demiurgic energy so to speak, was called *sacred fire* by the ancients. Therefore the root "pyr" is bound with the concept of demiurgic technology. Hence terms like pyramid, Pyrenees, and pyrite, three terms that are very closely related to demiurgic technology. As will be explained in another chapter, the Great Pyramid is a channeler, collector, and amplifier of etheric energy. The Pyrenees are the mountain range between France and Spain, where a conclave of powerful alchemists allegedly reside. And pyrite is a salt of sulfur and iron that sparks when struck, and thus contains within it latent fire, or so it appeared to the ancients. This brass or bronze-colored mineral, or rather its starry variant known as marcasite, was the raw material preferred by Fulcanelli for production of the Philosopher's Stone. Note that pyrite is also known as "Fool's Gold." It is the true gold of Fools in the esoteric sense, for they value it more than real gold; through it, they can make as much gold as they require and produce the Elixir of Life.

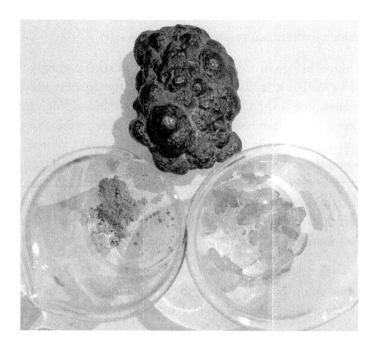

Gold was considered to be the oldest and most perfect of the metals, the final state toward which other metals were evolving. But in its old age, gold had expended all of its etheric energy. What was left was a dead body (salt) carrying the image (sulfur) of gold, but lacking the youthful vitality (mercury) that younger metals still possessed. Thus the goal of Alchemy was to take the noblest of metals and reinvigorate it, thereby taking it to a state of evolution higher than anything achievable in nature.

In practice, this meant starting with the youngest of metallic products that would act as the donor, one so early in its evolution that it wasn't yet a robust metal but rather more of a primitive metal-like mineral. It had to have an affinity for gold and be a potent source of etheric energy. It had to contain the secret fire of the cosmos and be capable of attracting and storing more of it when imbibed with external sources of etheric energy. Alchemists chose a mineral that resembled gold but appeared darkened by impurities. This raw matter they crushed to a fine powder and fed with dew. Dew contains the etheric energy of the cosmos, which is of the same nature as the etheric energy contained within the mineral.

They aimed to induce decomposition of the mineral via repeated wetting and drying. This would break down the material and unbind the matter's mercury, salt, and sulfur components, just as death unbinds the human physical, etheric, and astral bodies. This was difficult because decomposition takes a long time in the mineral kingdom and the speed depends on the electrochemical qualities of the mineral which varies from mine to mine, as well as the presence or absence of bacterial catalysts and the size of the powder's particles.

In any case, when the appropriate factors are present, the mineral decomposes as intended and the soluble products comprise the mercurial salt needed for the next part of the process. In successfully extracting the mercury and salt from the starting mineral and leaving behind the impure sulfur, they now had a youthful body and soul that could be joined to gold's ancient spirit and dead body.

This mercurial salt they called their *secret fire*, Universal solvent, the "water that does not wet the hands", common mercury, and alkahest. Alchemists believed it was the one thing by which the whole work could be accomplished, the one agent that could dissolve gold and acquire its sulfur.

In the so-called "Dry Path" of making the Stone, this salt and gold leaf or filings are placed in a crucible and heated to glowing temperature for several days, thereby joining them into one. This path is the quickest but also the most dangerous due to the high temperatures and potential for explosions.

In the "Wet Path," gold leaf or filings are mixed into the water-solubilized mercurial salt, then sealed in a glass flask and heated until the gold is fully disaggregated by the Universal solvent. The mercurial saline body dies and transfers its mercury to gold, whose body is vivified and tinged with the sulfur of gold. The result is a white buttery substance some have called "animated mercury" or "philosophical mercury," and this is the Philosopher's Stone in its nascent form.

After putrefying this white substance to blackness, heating until its impurities are driven away and it turns white once more, then repeating the process with some variation, a red oil arises on the surface. This red oil is the sulfur of gold completely fused with youthful mercury. Further evaporation and heating, eventually to hundreds of degrees, coagulate this oil into a solid.

This solid is the Philosopher's Stone in finished form unless one wishes to multiply its power by dissolving it in more fresh Universal solvent (which is a refined donor of etheric energy) and repeating the previous operation, except using the Stone instead of gold this time. This can be repeated any number of times, and each time a fresh dose of etheric energy impregnates the solid or oily remains and takes the Stone to its next order of power.

Upon attaining success, the final result is a dense stone, red and translucent like a ruby. It is said to be water-soluble, melts like wax, flows like quicksilver when melted, does not burn at any temperature, yet volatilizes when thrown into the molten metal it aims to transmute. It is a physical substance supersaturated with etheric energy and imprinted with the vibrational fingerprint of gold. When pulverized, mixed into beeswax, and cast into molten lead, it transmutes a certain multiple of its weight of lead into gold. It can also transmute quicksilver in the same way. The lead or quicksilver atoms are overwhelmed by the etheric potency of the Stone and become malleable at the quantum level, allowing the fingerprint of gold to reconfigure them accordingly, thereby converting these into gold.

Alchemists emphasize that to succeed in this work, one must be of the highest ethics, have a deep mind capable of penetrating the mysteries of nature, and be a good observer and experimenter. Prayer and purity are essential to receive the intuitive insights and synchronistic guidance needed to discover the right steps in the right order. This is important because the less one understands about Alchemy, the more hidden variables there are, and the lower the chances of success by trial and error. But if you are decreed so by destiny, or if you attain sufficient spiritual purity that higher forces deem you responsible enough to handle it, then you will be synchronistically and intuitively guided to success. But that won't happen if you are driven by greed, skepticism, or other anti-spiritual motives, or if it goes against your karma and destiny. You don't find the Stone, the Stone finds *you*.

The secret is synchronistically encrypted from those who would use it to cause trouble for themselves or others. Even misguided help can be a form of damage, thus in addition to purity, wisdom is needed. And if by chance someone did discover it and attempted to cause trouble, they would likely die suddenly, as already happens to people who try to bring antigravity and free energy technology into the world. The Philosopher's Stone is of that same vein. That's why no alchemist has ever revealed the full picture. They not only realize the terrible implications of its misuse but fear what harm might come to themselves if they facilitate that by giving knowledge without sufficient discretion.

Again, here I only give a general and limited estimation of the process for the sake of illustrating the underlying dynamics involved, as they are pertinent to my exposition on the Demiurge.

Other Applications of the Stone

At the first order of multiplication, a minuscule portion of the Stone may be dissolved in water or wine, and thereof a small portion ingested daily. This "Elixir of Life" or "Universal Medicine" is claimed to strongly energize one's etheric body. With a reinforced etheric body, the physical body is less impacted by the degrading effects of linear time and may even reverse aging. Additionally, psychic powers begin to manifest as a function of increased etheric energy current output. So you can imagine what became of alchemical masters who succeeded in producing the Stone and made full use of it. They became more than human. However, they presumably had the spiritual maturity to handle this. Any ordinary person, being more psychically fragile, would go crazy, get sick, and die from being unable to handle the increased etheric current load.

This "Universal Medicine" takes on great importance in Alchemy, because it represents a true panacea, something that cures all ills by charging the diseased organs with vital energy so that rightful health is regained. This goal is far more important than the transmutation of metals. Actually, the transmutation is done primarily as a test to see how strong the Stone is, and thus whether it is safe for ingestion because beyond the first power it is no longer safe to use as a medicine.

In another application, by the seventh or eighth order of multiplication, the Stone remains liquid and begins to physically glow, even more brightly if multiplied again. It glows continually without exhaustion. This is what powers the fabled "eternal lamps" in occult lore, per Trithemius. And if multiplied beyond a certain point, it is said to eat through glass and even dangerously explode in something akin to a matter-antimatter reaction. This shows that etheric energy concentrated beyond a certain point may initiate an outpouring of electromagnetic energy. This makes sense because ether is the precursor and precipitator of matter, energy, space, and time.

Thus the Stone, in its full application, potentially provides wealth, health, psychic power, and light. No wonder it has been kept so secret through the ages, mainly to keep it out of the hands of unscrupulous individuals whose misuse of these powers would bring catastrophic consequences upon the world. That is not to say such catastrophes haven't happened.

Alchemy as Demiurgic Technology

What we have here is a *demiurgic* type of technology. How so? Recall that the Demiurge has an astral and etheric body. The etheric shapes matter according to the archetypes or "vibrational patterns" contained in the astral.

Well, the Philosopher's Stone is a physical object charged with etheric energy, carrying the vibrational pattern of gold. It can reshape physical matter like lead or mercury into conformance with that vibration. Thus the Stone is a physical object imbued with demiurgic power. The technology of using etheric and astral energies to reconfigure matter is hereby called *demiurgic technology*.

The most remarkable thing is that it's made by human hands, which is the closest thing to hyperdimensional technology that one person in an attic laboratory can produce using everyday materials and uncommon techniques.

But even with all its purported greatness, the Philosopher's Stone is only an elementary demonstration of a science with far greater potential. Alchemy as we know it is a primitive form of hyperdimensional science. Producing the Stone is like wrapping a wire around a nail, connecting it to a battery, and rejoicing in it becoming an electromagnet. But higher forms of demiurgic technology exist that can produce something more like a billion-dollar supercollider. Both the wire-wrapped nail and supercollider employ the same basic principles of electromagnetism, but the first is a trivially simplistic version of the latter.

In the Philosopher's Stone, we have proof, through circumstantial evidence and logicality of its existence, of what can be scaled up to an even higher level. Remember, the power of the Stone lies in its etheric potency, and its potency determines the degree to which it can bias probability and influence physicality. The archetypal fingerprint determines the nature of this biasing.

The weakest etheric fields can only nudge an electron this way or that. A bit stronger can nudge neurons and living cells. Even stronger it can influence synchronicity. Stronger, it can override chemical laws and allow for elemental transmutation or psychic spoon bending. You can scale this up higher and higher until you reach a point where the entire world, our entire timeline, can be shifted, reconfigured, reprogrammed, and transmuted. Etheric energy does all this at the quantum level, which is the foundation of our physical reality.

That Alchemy can only produce these effects on the chemical scale, places it in the category of Low Demiurgic Technology. So what, then, is High Demiurgic Technology? It is that which does to the universe what Alchemy does to gold leaf and lead ingots. It can manufacture an artifact charged with such unbelievable amounts of etheric energy as to dissolve and reconfigure the world according to the artifact's programmed archetypes.

This object is a kind of "World Philosopher's Stone", the macrocosmic equivalent to the Philosopher's Stone. Two well-known examples of such High Demiurgic Technology will be discussed in the chapters to follow.

3 THE HOLY GRAIL

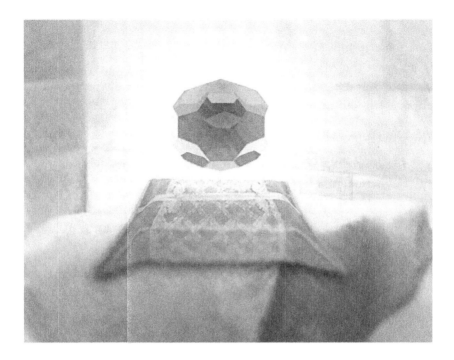

In the last chapter, I explained how the Philosopher's Stone is an actual object manufactured through the principles of *Low Demiurgic Technology*, better known as Alchemy. I call it "demiurgic technology" because it employs the energies of the Demiurge — etheric and astral energies — to reshape matter at the quantum level, and "low" because the Stone's reach of influence is localized: it can only transform the lead or mercury it is cast into, and can only biologically regenerate the individual who ingests it.

In this chapter and the next, I will discuss two examples of *High Demiurgic Technology*: the Holy Grail and the Ark of the Covenant. Both operate on the same principles as the Philosopher's Stone, just taken to a higher degree of power and sophistication and having a more global reach.

The Grail is an object with supernatural powers brought to our world by otherworldly forces. The Ark of the Covenant was a container constructed by ancient Hebrews, during their flight from Egypt, to house a powerful artifact.

Since descriptions of the Ark's capabilities closely parallel those of the Grail, what the Ark contained may have been the Grail. As to their ultimate purpose, both the Grail and Ark were generally portrayed as physical embodiments of a god-like intelligence.

The Grail subject has several complementary aspects:

1. *The technology.* What it is, and what it does. Its physical nature, function, and purpose.

2. *The history.* The events that lead to its creation and introduction to our world. Who is responsible for it. What it has done, and will do, to our world.

3. *The spiritual metaphor.* What it represents within all of us. What is indicated about a proper course of spiritual development.

I will explore these in sequence over the coming chapters, reserving the spiritual aspect for last because it concerns the solution to a problem I have yet to delineate. If it seems like I'm getting hung up on technology, it's only because I find it a prerequisite for understanding the reasons behind the historical aspect, which then underscores the gravity of the spiritual aspect.

I will begin by addressing the functional characteristics of the Grail and in the next chapter follow up with those of the Ark. From this, it will become clear how competition over, and the abuse of such immense power can, has, and will have catastrophic consequences for our world.

Medieval Literature Describes the Grail

The original Grail legends preceded Christianity. Later the Church retrofitted these pagan tales with Biblical symbolism and context. From that retrofitting we get the popular notion that the Holy Grail was the cup from which Jesus Christ served wine at the Last Supper, which later caught his blood as he died on the cross, or the notion that it was a platter carrying the decapitated head of John the Baptist.

Of all medieval authors who wrote of the Grail, Wolfram von Eschenbach seemed most privy and sympathetic to the pagan/gnostic stream of Grail lore. He was a wandering knight, scholar, poet, and singer — the German equivalent of troubadour — who associated with secret societies like the Templars or was a member himself. In his book *Parzival*, he tells the tale of a foolish boy named Parzival who leaves home to become a knight. This boy is destined to become Grail King but out of timidity fails miserably when eventually offered the opportunity. Cursed for his failure, he spends several years in utter dejection undergoing numerous hard trials before developing the inner strength to fight for his destiny regardless of the failure. And only by this inner resolve and being true to his Self does he earn his second chance and finally become Grail King.

Embedded within this plot are periodic references to the Grail, its origins, and functions. These are set within a Christian context that, upon closer inspection, disguises a more gnostic, pagan, pre-Christian core. In other words, Wolfram may have had the inside scoop on the Grail and inserted what heretical truths he could between the obligatory religious veneer, as is evident from the odd details about the Grail that fit poorly within the Biblical context.

That is not to say the other Grail books are worthless because their retrofitting occasionally kept the original meaning relatively intact. For instance, if Jesus Christ was the incarnation of a personified extension of the Logos, which is the spiritualized aspect of the Demiurge, then you can see how a cup holding his blood is identically a physical vessel holding demiurgic energy. You have already encountered one example: the Philosopher's Stone, of which the Grail is a higher order relative. Or consider the platter holding the head of John the Baptist; John poured "living water" upon Jesus and baptized him, indicating his symbolic function as the conferrer of that which made Jesus more than a mere man, that is to say, he symbolized the Logos, and "Logos" being associated with mind/intellect may explain the head-on-a-platter visual. These are examples of ecclesiastical steganography.

In Wolfram's *Parzival*, the Grail was neither cup nor platter, but an otherworldly stone. It was called neither "Holy Grail" nor "Holy Vessel" but simply the "Graal." It was treated as a strange and marvelous non-terrestrial artifact. To avoid redundancy, I will call it "Grail" instead of "Graal." Here is how Wolfram characterizes it:

- *It was paradisaic and transcended all Earthly perfection.* This implies it was more than just a hunk of rock. Rather its perfection extended beyond the Earthly material level.

- *It was cared for by a woman of perfect chastity and purity, and all who served the Grail must forego carnal love.* This means spiritual integrity was of vital importance for those who interacted with it.

- *It would only let itself be carried or moved by a perfectly chaste woman.* This implies it has some level of volition to choose whom to let itself be carried by.

- *It would instantly materialize whatever food and drink were desired by those who held their cups and plates before it.* This means it could turn thoughts into reality and function as a stone of plenty.

- *It could only materialize what the Earth already yields in terms of food and drink.* This means it cannot just materialize any thoughts, only foodstuffs that already exist. This carries shades of an uncreative demiurge.

- *It receives its power to materialize from a Dove that flies down from heaven every Good Friday and leaves a white wafer on the stone.* This is a mix of pagan and Christian symbolism. Aside from the religious aspects, it also has to do with raw energy charging the stone at a specified time. Take note that Good Friday is the Friday following the first full Moon after the vernal equinox. The date is entirely astrological/astronomical and may signify maximum cosmic etheric inflow.

- *It would impart vitality to any who looked upon it, restoring youth, delaying death, and curing illness. One could live for hundreds of years without growing old this way, save for hair turning gray.* This means the Grail emits very strong lifeforce energy, a.k.a. etheric energy, just like the Philosopher's Stone.

- *It would give written messages via mystical letters appearing on its surface. These letters would vanish after being read. Messages included the names of children in the world who would be called to serve in the Grail castle, and other dictates.* This indicates the Grail possessed intelligence or relayed communications from some intelligence with a preference for letters and writing. It also means the Grail served as an oracle.

- *It was invisible to those who were not baptized.* This means it takes an infusion of divine energy into one's consciousness, an opening of perception, to be able to see the Grail. Otherwise, it remains invisible before one's eyes. This is a very gnostic concept, to have one's third eye opened through divine grace or initiation. It implies the Grail is tangible but not necessarily always fully here in the world, rather shifted slightly from our reality and requires expanded perception to see.

- *By its virtue, the Phoenix burns to ashes and is born anew more splendid than before.* This metaphor is alchemical symbolism, though more generally it indicates the transformation of something, like a person or the whole world, into a more perfect form through dissolution and reformulation.

There is a question of how close Wolfram stuck to the original tale, and how close the original was to the truth. Eschenbach says he was told the story by one called Master Kyot, who came across it in an old book written in Arabic by a "heathen" astronomer named Flegetanis. Flegetanis himself was somehow privy to the truth concerning the Grail and its origins, having written, "A troop left it on Earth and then rose high above the stars, if their innocence drew them back again. Afterward, a Christian progeny bred to a pure life had the duty of keeping it. Those humans who are summoned to the Grail are ever worthy." Kyot went looking in the literature of Britain, France, and Ireland for mention of this "Christian progeny" and at last found a tale of their existence in Anjou, France, of which the *Parzival* story is a second-hand recounting by Eschenbach.

Not mentioned by Wolfram, but claimed by other books of the period:

- *The Grail could glow as bright as the Sun and impart enlightenment to those who looked upon it.* Recall the Philosopher's Stone glowing when multiplied beyond a certain point, and that its potent etheric energy output assists with psychic activation.

- *It was carried by cart or ship from castle to castle instead of being home to just one.* This meshes with the Grail leaving a breadcrumb trail from location to location throughout history, from ancient Egypt to medieval France and other places.

- *It could unleash a fiery energy surge capable of knocking someone out.* The Ark of the Covenant possessed the same trait.

- *Only those qualified to wield the Grail could sit in a special seat called the Siege Perilous, all others would be swallowed by a vortex that opens beneath them, should they attempt to sit in that chair.* While figuratively underscoring the necessity of utmost spiritual strength and purity in those who seek the Grail, the vortex/whirlpool is a peculiar detail that may stem from a literal observation of the Grail's destructive behavior in the presence of unworthy individuals.

- *It was more often in the custody of heavenly beings, who would present it to humans according to circumstance and subsequently withdraw it back into their realm.* Sometimes it was in human possession, other times it was retrieved for safekeeping by its otherworldly guardians.

If these latter claims are valid and literal, they don't necessarily contradict Wolfram's account because his primary source concerned events from the time of King Arthur several centuries earlier. In the intervening period, more may have happened regarding the Grail from which additional streams of information besides his own could work their way into the books of his time. So I would append these details to the ones provided in *Parzival* to paint a more complete picture of the Grail.

Taken at face value, in the Grail we have a stone or crystal-like object of variable physicality that emits powerful lifeforce energy, can translate thoughts into material foodstuffs, has seeming intelligence and volition, functions oracularly, and requires high spiritual integrity from those who wield and serve it lest they be destroyed by it.

Is the Grail Real?

How do we know the Grail is an actual artifact and not just a metaphor for spiritual ideals or a veiled allusion to the Philosopher's Stone?

1. Because its footprints are found in actual history and not just literature. I will leave the tedious history of people like the Phoenicians, Egyptians, Celts, Cathars, and Templars for the books listed at the end of this work, but will say for now that for each of these a magical stone or crystal artifact with supernatural qualities played part in their origins, organization, and power. They were at some point in possession of something important, closely guarded, and endowed with the traits of demiurgic technology. It conferred to them special guidance and abilities without which their achievements would not have been possible.

2. Because its characteristics go beyond that of the Philosopher's Stone in a manner suggesting these extra features are not just arbitrary embellishment based on fantasy, but extensions made with logical adherence to the principle of demiurgic science. In other words, if Grail myths simply encoded alchemical knowledge, the described Grail functions would be limited to those of the Philosopher's Stone and anything beyond that would be made up and thus physically implausible. Yet these extensions, like materializing food out of thin air or functioning in an oracular manner, are perfectly plausible and in line with demiurgic science, as will be explained later. The Grail can do what the Stone cannot, but only because those who make the Stone lack the ability to take demiurgic science to the higher level of which the Grail is a product. If the Stone exists, then so ought the Grail by extension of that same science.

3. Because while anyone with the right knowledge and integrity can make the Philosopher's Stone, the Grail was something

sought and fought over as if there were only one. It wasn't something that could be made as needed. Therefore it was a unique artifact and not just a recipe. It was a real object carried around via carts, barks, and arks.

4. Because the medieval Grail was the surviving remnant of the ancient Ark of the Covenant, or at least another fruit from the same tree of demiurgic science. The Ark was undoubtedly a real artifact with real powers and not just myth and metaphor, therefore if the Ark of the Covenant with its alleged functions once existed, then the Grail with *its* purported powers can exist also, for both are of the same caliber.

Although it bears similarities to the Philosopher's Stone, it is not identically the Stone. Although its human seekers must undergo an arduous path of spiritual strengthening and purification to approach and serve it, the Grail is not just a metaphor for spiritual evolution. Although it employs etheric and astral energies in its operation, it is not just a visual metaphor for these energies but a vessel containing and radiating them. It is hyperdimensional, spiritual, demiurgic technology representing a union of all such interpretations.

What are the Origins of the Grail?

As will be shown later in this book, what medieval literature says concerning the origins and characteristics of the Grail deeply correlates with Celtic, Greek, Scandinavian, Persian, Egyptian, Mayan, and Indian mythology. The common origin of these myths explains who brought the Grail to our world many millennia ago: an advanced civilization possessing demiurgic technology. Further clues on their identity are provided by modern alienology, Fortean research, Rosicrucian studies, contactee culture, and quality channeling literature. This suggests not only that the Grail is as important today as it was in ancient times, but that its supernatural progenitors are still with us.

The Grail is a mysterious artifact with supernatural powers. What is such an *otherworldly* artifact doing in *our* world? Who made it, where did it come from, and how did it come into human possession? The angles of approach to these questions are diverse: medieval Grail legends, Indo-European mythology, occult literature, and the modern fields of Fortean phenomena and alienology; but they all converge upon the same answer.

In *Parzival*, the Christian hermit Trevrizent explains how it was brought to Earth by a group of "noble and worthy" angels after they were exiled from Heaven for refusing to take sides when Lucifer waged his rebellion. God commanded these neutral angels to bring the Grail to Earth and entrust it to a divinely appointed line of spiritually pure humans. That is to say, they were exiled and divested of the Grail. They are the so-called Fallen Angels.

As to what became of these exiled angels, Flegetanis said they "rose high above the stars" after dropping off the Grail. Trevrizent seems to concur, initially saying they returned to Heaven if their innocence called them to return and God willed it, which is a Gnostic concept concerning the redemption of evil, something the Church would find offensive since Fallen Angels were supposed to be eternal enemies of God without the possibility of redemption. Later in the book, Trevrizent admits this was a lie and that these exiled angels were actually eternally damned and eternal enemies of God and his appointed Grail guardians, that they had no hope for redemption. This recanting is thought to have been Wolfram appeasing the Church.

It's also possible that in the original streams from which the story of *Parzival* was derived, both are true: the neutral angels polarized into two groups, one rising closer to divinity, the other falling further. Some would therefore be higher guardians of the Grail cooperating with their human counterparts, while the others, having been fully divested of the Grail, would be their adversaries desiring to regain it for themselves. This would resolve the seeming contradictions in Grail legends concerning otherworldly beings both helping guard it from abuse and attempting to steal it from its rightful guardians. Thus the legends suggest that a duality exists among these higher beings. For instance, in *Lucifer's Court* (p. 21) Otto Rahn recounts a variation of the tale: the Grail was a gemstone knocked loose from Lucifer's crown during the fall of the angels, which his forces have since been trying to repossess.

Stripping the religious gloss from the above accounts, the basic story is that some catastrophe in another realm forced a group of beings to leave with a powerful artifact. They came to Earth and entrusted it to a line of spiritually elite humans through whom the artifact continued its function.

Wolfram called it *lapsit exillis,* meaning "stone of exile" in his garbled Latin, because it was taken from its home and brought to Earth by forces exiled by some cataclysmic event. This motif repeats itself throughout human history, whereby the artifact is endangered and must be moved to a new location. There it establishes its power for some time before peril strikes once more, forcing another relocation, and the cycle repeats.

One example is the Israelites fleeing Egypt under catastrophic conditions and taking the early Ark of the Covenant with them, through which they won victory, guidance, prosperity, and power. When the Temple of Solomon was sacked, the Ark was spirited away and disappeared from Jewish history. I will discuss the Ark in more depth in the next chapter because it gives further insight into the nature of demiurgic technology and introduces the historical turn of events that precipitated a negative deviation of our timeline.

To be Continued…

The above is just a quick introduction to the Grail subject. I have much more to say about the historical and mythological context of the Grail, but these issues will be covered in subsequent chapters as my thesis continues to build.

Next, I will address the technical aspects of the Ark of the Covenant, to show how they parallel those of the Grail. Putting the two together, we may arrive at a basic understanding of High Demiurgic Technology and what it can do.

4 ARK OF THE COVENANT

Like the Grail, the Ark of the Covenant was an object endowed with supernatural powers. The Ark is described in the Bible as a large wooden chest on carrying poles, gilded inside and out with gold, and having a solid gold lid surmounted by two golden winged figures.*

The Ark remains the most sacred artifact of the Jews despite their losing it long ago. Without it, their ancestors would not have overcome certain obstacles, vanquished their enemies, received guidance from it, or prospered into the eventual nation of Israel. *Therefore the entire Judeo-Christian paradigm owes its existence to the Ark of the Covenant.*

Is the Bible's descriptions of the Ark accurate? Well, the Old Testament is a fictional narrative sewn together from sometimes factual patches. These patches are eyewitness accounts passed down through the oral

---

* Exodus 25:10-22

traditions and documents of the various tribes that existed in Canaan when the Old Testament and its subsequent revisions were being drafted, around the 8th century B.C. By creating a single continuous narrative from these old stories, the diverse people in central Canaan could be united into what subsequently became the nation of Israel.[*]

The ancient history of Israel and the story of Exodus as told in the Bible are composited from separate historical episodes. Isolated parts are true within their original contexts, just that they may be out of order, superimposed, embellished, or borrowed from other cultures.

I haven't pieced together the complete history of Israel and the Ark, but my research over the years has given me some basic bearing. Since it's too lengthy and tangential to cover here in detail, I will just list some examples of what historical persons and events may have been reworked centuries later into the Old Testament narrative:

- The story of Moses being drawn from a river comes from an Akkadian legend relating the genesis of their king, Sargon the Great,[†] or else both draw from an even older myth. The old Akkadians allegedly existed from 2700 – 2200 B.C.[‡] Another theory says they were the Hyksos Dynasty from 1628 – 1550 B.C.[§]

- The two pharaohs of the Exodus were Pepi II and Merenre II circa 2200 B.C. They were the last pharaohs of the Old Kingdom of Egypt.[¶] This is almost a thousand years before conventional Biblical chronology places the Exodus.

- The cataclysm that ended the Old Kingdom and killed Merenre II in the "place of the whirlpool" occurred around 2190 B.C.

---

[*] *Who Wrote the Bible?* (Robert Beckford, 2004, video) ▪ *Who Wrote the Bible?* (Richard Friedman, 1997, book)

[†] *Sargon of Akkad* (Wikipedia) ▪ *Sargon vs. Moses* (JPH, article)

[‡] *Akkadian Empire* (Wikipedia) ▪ *Akkadian Language* (Wikipedia)

[§] *Who were the Hyksos?* (Gunnar Heinsohn, article) ▪ *Empire of Thebes* (John Sweeney, 2006, book, pp. 7-10)

[¶] *When was the Exodus?* (Brad Aaronson, article) ▪ *Is there evidence of the Exodus from Egypt?* (Gerald Aardsma, article)

and was an early contributor to the stories of Passover, the Ten Plagues, and the Parting of the Sea of Reeds.[*]

- In 1628 B.C., the Mediterranean super-volcano of Thera exploded, forcing migrations out of Egypt and inspiring further additions to the stories of Exodus, particularly the Israelites seeing a pillar of cloud and fire before and later behind their wandering procession.[†]

- The Semitic Hyksos were purged from Egypt in 1550 B.C. after being paid off in large sums of gold and silver to leave.[‡] From this derives the story of the Israelites being given gold, silver, clothing, and jewels by the Egyptians in preparation for their exodus. The walls of Jericho fell around 1550 B.C. according to archaeological dating, suggesting the Ark of the Covenant was en route to Canaan by that point.[§]

- The historical King Solomon lived in north-central Canaan in the decades following the Hyksos expulsion from Egypt. According to classical historian Flavius Josephus, the Hyksos founded Jerusalem.[¶]

- The historical Temple of Solomon was built around 1500 B.C. along with the megalithic temple complex at Baalbek

---

[*] *Escape From Planet Egypt Part 2* (Christian Media Research, article) mentions the El-Arish inscription where the pharaoh perished in the "Place of the Whirlpool."

[†] *Exodus to Arthur: Catastrophic Encounters with Comets* (Mike Baillie, 1999, book). Baillie studies tree ring evidence to date major historical climate events. He confirms that the Thera explosion happened in 1628 B.C. And he also proposes that its plume was visible from Egypt, see pp. 105-106 and was incorporated into the Exodus accounts. If so, then Exodus merged the volcano plume with the vortical Shekhina into the same pillar of fire and cloud.

[‡] *The Biblical Exodus Inscribed on an Ancient Egyptian Stele* (Ralph Ellis, article)

[§] *Jericho* (Wikipedia) ▪ *Is Bryant Wood's Chronology of Jericho Valid?* (Gerald Aardsma, article) ▪ *Jericho Chronology Dispute* (Conservapedia, article)

[¶] *Manetho and Josephus on the Hyksos* (Manetho, Josephus, article) ▪ *Osarseph and Exodus: Literary Reflections in an Egyptian Mirror* (Gary Greenberg, 1997, article)

located in modern-day Lebanon.* Both were constructed by the Phoenicians using advanced technology; they were familiar with the Ark of the Covenant.†

• Queen Hatshepsut (1508 – 1458 B.C.) was contemporary with the historical King Solomon and may have held personal relations with him and/or the Phoenicians and/or the Mitanni. Some believe she was Queen Sheba of the Bible.‡

• After Hatshepsut died, her nephew and successor Thutmose III waged military campaigns into northern Canaan and sacked Solomon's Temple just four decades after it was built.§ He then defaced Hatshepsut's statues and attempted to erase her from history. Thutmose III was the historical basis for the Biblical pharaoh Shishak.

• Pharaoh Akhenaten, who reigned from 1353 – 1336 B.C., imposed a tyrannical form of monotheism upon Egypt consisting of worship of a single solar deity and suppression of all others. His reign lasted almost two decades, after which the Egyptian traditionalists who were loyal to the old ways fought to purge Egypt of this radical monotheism and its followers, who may have been related to the Hyksos. According to Manetho, among them was a high priest of Akhenaten named Osarseph who led the exiled Semitic monotheists in an uprising against

---

Baalath (Wikipedia) ▪ 1 Kings 9:15-19 ▪ *Baalbek, Lebanon* (Martin Grey, article) ▪ *Baalbek* (World Mysteries, article) ▪ *Baalbek – Lebanon's Sacred Fortress* (Andrew Collins, article)

† *The search for Osiris takes Isis to Astarte in Phoenicia* (Carnaval, article) ▪ *Ancient Coins Showing Sacred Stones: The Shrine of Astarte* (Bill Welch, article) ▪ *Baetyl Stones* (Livius, article)

‡ *Ages in Chaos: From the Exodus to King Akhnaton* (Immanuel Velikovsky, 1952, book) ▪ *Ages in Chaos* (Velikovsky Encyclopedia, article) ▪ *Hatshepsut and the Queen of Sheba. Answering Dr. John Bimson's Challenge* (House of Gold, article) ▪ *Yemen as it is...* (Viewzone, article) ▪ I believe Velikovsky was wrong in his dating; Solomon needs to be moved back to circa 1500 B.C., not Egyptian chronology moved forward to circa 1000 B.C.

§ *Thutmose III* (Wikipedia) ▪ *Thuthmosis III* (Jimmy Dunn, article) ▪ *Thutmose III, Shishak, and Menelik* (Emmet Sweeney, article) ▪ *Pharaoh Thutmose III* (Specialty Interests, article) ▪ *Ages in Chaos* (op cit. pp. 143-148)

the Egyptian traditionalists. In the end, he was forced to flee Egypt with his followers, and he subsequently became the historical model for the Biblical Moses.[*] In Canaan, they became the final wave of Egyptian exiles incorporated into the story of the Israelites.

I could go on, but right now it's more important to focus on the purported technical capabilities of the Ark to show how similar it is to the Holy Grail and what all this says about the nature of High Demiurgic Technology. What follows is a list of key aspects of the Ark and my interpretations of them.

Ark: Etheric and Electric Fields

The Ark is infamous for its deadly energy discharges. Those unqualified to touch, approach, or even look at the Ark would be struck dead:

- Uzzah was struck dead by a burning flash of energy from the Ark as he reached out his hand to steady it. The Ark was being transported on an ox cart and one of the oxen had stumbled.[†]

- Seventy people from the town of Beth Shemesh were killed when they opened the Ark and looked inside. The Ark was temporarily stationed there on its return from Philistine custody.

- Aaron's sons died when, against permission, they attempted to offer incense to the Ark and fiery energy sprang forth and consumed them.[‡]

- Those of the Kohathite branch of the Levites, who were assigned to carry the Ark and associated items once they were securely wrapped for transport, were instructed never to touch or look at these items directly, or they would die immediately.[§]

In attempting to explain this, others have noted that the gilded wooden box resembles a capacitor, something that stores electric charge. In

---

[*] Manetho and Josephus on the Hyksos (op cit.) ▪ *Osarseph and Exodus: Literary Reflections in an Egyptian Mirror* (Gary Greenberg, article)

[†] 1 Chronicles 13

[‡] Leviticus 10, Numbers 3:4

[§] Numbers 4

this case, the capacitor is two electrodes of gold sandwiching a wood insulator. Since the Ark could accumulate and store high voltage electricity, some conclude the Ark was nothing more than a big capacitor.

A large enough capacitor can indeed electrocute a person. But according to my calculations, the capacitance of the Ark is only around 3-5 nF at most, giving barely enough energy to kill one person under ideal conditions if charged to 300,000 Volts.* That kind of voltage is very difficult to reach, let alone maintain without flashover between inner and outer gold layers. To throw a spark long enough to hit someone just a few yards away, millions of Volts would be needed. There is no way a wood-based capacitor by itself can accumulate enough power to kill a crowd, let alone surround itself with a glowing energy field and perform the more miraculous feats ascribed to it.

The Ark alone cannot do what the Bible says it can, at least not according to conventional science. The top mistake fringe researchers make is limiting their interpretation of the Ark's function to the perspective of conventional physics and engineering. Thus they propose it was merely a spark gap radio, electrical capacitor, seismic energy transducer, algae food grower, or some other mundane device.† While each of

---

*Ark capacitance calculation assumes dielectric constant = 2.9, wood thickness 1/2 inch (.0254 meters), dimensions = 2.25 × 2.25 × 3.75 feet. Capacitance is 3.3 nF for a box without lid. Gives 15-20 Joules if charged to 100 kV, 200 Joules (minimum to kill a person, or jump start a heart per defibrillator devices) at 350 kV. 2) To be struck just by touching or nearing the outside, capacitance of outer surface must be considered instead, not capacitance between inner and outer conductors. Total surface area is 4 square meters, giving capacitance around 60 pF. The 200 Joule threshold requires 2.5 million Volts. Spark length in that case is 2-3 meters. 3) If carried on poles, then spark length is less than height of shoulders otherwise it would discharge to the ground, suggesting a potential around 1 million Volts. Such potentials cannot be produced by mere picking up of stray charges from the environment. More likely internal electron precipitation from ether and/or a diverging magnetic vector potential altering the local charge density and thereby creating high voltages between center of the Ark and the environment.

† Ark Stone as seismic energy transducer: *Opening the Ark of the Covenant* (Frank Joseph and Laura Beaudoin, 2007, book, pp. 61-74) • Ark as biological manna machine: *The Holy Grail – Chalice or Manna Machine?* (Johannes and Peter Fiebag, translated by George Sasoon) • Ark as electrical accumulator and

these may explain a few alleged Ark traits, they cannot account for them all.

High Demiurgic Technology, however, explains everything. Just as in Alchemy, conventional scientific principles may enter into the equation but are not the only ones involved. While the Ark may be a capacitor, that is only a small aspect of its total function. One has to go beyond regular physics to understand it.

For instance, it's worth noting that, topologically speaking, the Ark is a spherical capacitor, where one electrode is nested inside the other. According to my fringe physics research, what makes spherical capacitors special is that they can receive, transmit, absorb, and emit gravity waves. It has to do with changes in charge density coupling to changes in the gravitational potential.[*] If the Ark was a spark gap radio, it would have had to intercept gravity waves and convert them to electrical arcing between the two winged figures. But I doubt that was its primary function.

Further, anyone familiar with orgonomy will realize that the Ark is constructed like an orgone accumulator, which is a box whose walls are made of alternating layers of organic and inorganic substances.[†] It's said to attract and store orgone energy, which appears to be a grade of etheric energy closest to the material plane. Wilhelm Reich also observed a connection between negative ions and orgone energy, although the two are distinct. Their relation may be like the one between water drops and water vapor; one is a condensation or evaporation of the other. The electrical effects of the Ark may therefore be side-effects of etheric processes. Still, no orgone accumulator has ever built up enough energy to fry someone.

Since it was a chest with a lid, the Ark presumably carried something, and that object may have been responsible for its purported powers.

---

spark gap device: *Ark of the Covenant, Return to Eden* (Hutchison, article) • *Ark as spark gap radio: How to Build a Flying Saucer* (T. B. Pawlicki, book pp. 143)

[*] See the "Science" section of my Research Notes, and also <scalarphysics.com>

[†] *Orgone Accumulator Handbook* (James DeMeo, 2007, book) • *What is Orgone Energy & What is an Orgone Energy Accumulator?* (Orgonics, article)

The Bible says that the first item it carried was the stone tablet(s), also known as the Covenant or Testimony, that Moses brought out from Mount Sinai.* This fictional story has elements of truth, namely that a stone-like object was retrieved and placed in the Ark, after which it brimmed with energy. Therefore the Ark served more as a container, shield, and/or transceiver for the mysterious object placed inside it. It was also called Ark of the Testimony, as it contained something relating to the covenant between Hebrews and their Lord: a stone artifact called the Testimony. (From this point on, when I refer to the Ark, I mean the Ark with its power source installed and not just the wooden box alone).

That the Ark radiated energy is further supported by the detail that, when it was being transported, it was thoroughly wrapped in shielding material and its carriers were forbidden from touching or looking directly at it.† And when encamped, it was kept inside a structure known as the Tabernacle. The Tabernacle was a portable tent system designed to safely contain and surround the Ark. The first tent around the Ark was made of flax linen, the second of woven goat hair, third and fourth of dyed animal skins.‡ This great redundancy in layer upon layer appears to be additional shielding. And shielding of this type is only necessary if the Ark were putting out an intense non-electromagnetic energy field.

The choice of construction materials is significant. Flax fiber has a spiral crystalline structure.§ Hair and wool strands are nonlinear dielectrics because the medulla, sheath, and cortex of the strands have different dielectric constants, which makes them excellent attenuators or reflectors of gravitational, scalar, or longitudinal waves.¶ And Baron

---

* Exodus 19

† Numbers 4

‡ *Mosaic Tabernacle as an Aaronic Temple* (Bryce Haymond, article)

§ *Influence of kink bands on the tensile strength of flax fibers* (C. Baley, article)
• *What are the optical and physical properties of flax fibers (linen)?* (Raymond Rogers, article)

¶ *On the Meaning of Field Shaping* (Townsend Brown, article) • *Electrokinetic Apparatus* (Townsend Brown, patent #3187206) • *Soviet Weather Engineering Over North America* (Tom Bearden, 1985, video) • *Microscopy of Hair Part 1: A*

von Reichenbach found through extensive experimentation that wool could attenuate etheric energy the same way metal shielding attenuates electromagnetic waves.*

Copper, silver, and gold were the only metals used in constructing the Ark and the Tabernacle.† They are all non-magnetic, have only one valence electron, and share Group 11 on the periodic table. Iron was strictly forbidden. Even later, in the construction of Solomon's Temple, supposedly well into the Iron Age, no iron nails were used. Solomon's Temple being built around 1520 B.C. means it was still in the Bronze Age, but there's another reason iron wasn't used back then. Folklore says that fairies and other supernatural beings have an aversion to iron.‡ Physically it is magnetic and has two valence electrons, but etherically it may have undesirable effects upon etheric entities and technologies. Therefore we can infer that ferromagnetic materials interfered with the Ark's operation, save iron-containing blood that played an important role in its function.

From the above, we can already see that the Ark's operation included both etheric and electric elements. Again, the gilded wooden chest was not the source of the Ark's power, rather the object it contained was what radiated an intense energy field of an etheric, scalar, and/or electrogravitational nature. This energy field could precipitate electrical effects as well, but these were side effects rather than the primary ones. Proof of this is in the construction of the Ark, Tabernacle, and Solomon's Temple, which incorporate principles of etheric/scalar manipulation and shielding. They would be designed differently if mere electrical effects were intended.

Practical Guide and Manual for Human Hairs (Deedrick, Koch, 2004, article)

* *Luminous World – Baron Karl von Reichenbach* (Gerry Vassilatos, article)

† Exodus 25 (no mention of iron) ▪ Deuteronomy 27:5 "Build there an altar to the LORD your God, an altar of stones. Do not use any iron tool upon them." ▪ Exodus 20:25 "If you make an altar of stones for me, do not build it with dressed stones, for you will defile it if you use a tool on it." ▪ *Solomon's Temple Copy of Phoenician Temple of Melqart in Tyre* (Phoenicia, article)

‡ *Iron in Folklore* (Wikipedia) ▪ *Explorations of the Jinn Descriptions in Islam* (OkarResearch, article) "Jinns fear iron and steel so some people wear steel rings or put steel daggers or knives where the protection from Jinns are needed. Iron is similarly used."

Although the Ark has electrical properties, that is insufficient to say its function was merely electrical. This parallels reports of human encounters with alien crafts, whereby the ship exhibits strong electrical and electromagnetic interference effects, but these alone are not enough to explain how the ships can levitate because their primary propulsion fields are non-electromagnetic.* We are dealing with demiurgic technology here, not human technology.

Ark: Vortical Plasmic Intelligence

The Ark's lid was called the "Mercy Seat" because a luminous cloud perceived as the Lord would station itself upon it, between and above the winged gold figures.† This luminous cloud was known as the "Glory of the Lord" or "Shekhina," the latter being a Hebrew term meaning dwelling, settling, or presence of the Lord.‡

It would seem at first that the Shekhina is just an electrical corona emanating from the golden winged figures, were it not for the detail that the Shekhina was mobile and independent of the Ark. For instance, the Shekhina accompanied the Biblical Hebrews out of Egypt even before the Ark was built. It led them as a pillar of cloud by day and fire by night as they crossed the desert.§ It settled itself on Mount Sinai.¶ It appeared in the desert when food was about to manifest from the heavens.** Even after the Ark was built, the Shekhina could leave it and freely travel about of its own volition.††

---

* *Unconventional Flying Saucers* (Paul G. Hill, 1995, book). Analyzes UFO reports to determine the method of propulsion: pulsed gravitational waves. I take it a step further: gravitational wave synthesis through phased arrays to allow for solid state directional propulsion.

† Exodus 25

‡ *Shekinah* (Wikipedia) ▪ *Shekinah* (Jewish Encyclopedia, article) ▪ *The Shekinah* (Fred Miller, article, excerpt from *Zechariah & Jewish Renewal*) ▪ *Yehova's Shekinah Glory* (John D. Keyser, article)

§ Exodus 13:21

¶ Exodus 19, Exodus 24:16-17

** Exodus 16:8-12

†† Exodus 33, Leviticus 9:23-24

The Shekhina is described as looking like a "pillar of cloud" during daylight, suggesting condensation of water vapor into a visible tornado-like structure.* This makes sense because, according to orgonomy, sufficiently dense orgone energy concentrations cause water vapor condensation.† At night it glowed like a "pillar of fire" possibly indicating ionization of air, which is identically plasma. Therefore a very dense etheric energy field accounts for both the condensation of water vapor into visible mist and the glowing field of ionized gas.

The Shekhina could also diffuse into, or was simply accompanied by, a general glowing aura around the Ark. When kept in an enclosed shielded place like the inner Tabernacle tent or inner chamber of Solomon's Temple, the Shekhina would fill the space like a luminous fog.‡

Solomon's Temple was built to house the Ark permanently. Like the Tabernacle, the Ark rested within its central chamber known as the Holy of Holies surrounded by numerous shielding walls. The energy field diffused and filled the space surrounding the Ark, creating a glowing atmosphere testifying to the power residing in Solomon's Temple.§ The first Temple was eventually destroyed and the Ark went missing. The second Temple of Solomon completed in 516 BC lacked both the Ark and its Shekhina. While the people rejoiced that their temple was back, the priests lamented because they knew it was missing the most critical component.¶

Note that all these characteristics don't support the notion that the pillar of fire and cloud was an alien spaceship. It's something else. That the Shekhina could localize upon the Mercy Seat and give messages or travel about freely suggests that it possessed intelligence and volition. Enough so that the Hebrews were convinced it really was their Lord dwelling in their midst.

---

* Exodus 13, Exodus 33, Numbers 12

† *Cosmic Orgone Engineering* (Wilhelm Reich, 1954, book) ▪ See my *Cloudbusting Resources* article.

‡ Exodus 40:34

§ 1 Kings 8:10

¶ *Second Temple: Missing Articles* (Wikipedia) ▪ *The Second Temple* (Rabbi Ken Spiro, article)

Ark: Water Influencer

When the Hebrews fled Egypt under pursuit by the Egyptian army, the "Lord" went ahead of them and parted the Sea of Reeds so that they could cross. Water piled up into vertical walls and allowed passage over dry ground as though a solid force field had materialized left, right, and underneath them. The waters congealed beneath their feet and kept them dry, which contradicts mundane explanations of wind patterns, gravitational tugs from passing planets, or tidal effects being the cause, because the latter would still leave a wet muddy mess to slog through. Dry ground and congealment indicate either a solidification of water or a firm force field upon which one could walk.[*]

Later the Ark was used to part the Jordan River. Levite priests carried the Ark into the river, causing water to pile up on both sides some distance away and allowing the Israelites to once again cross over what they perceived as dry ground. When the priests carried the Ark to the other side, the river resumed course.[†] Again, mere weather or seismic explanations don't account for this. Note also that while the water was pushed away, the people crossing were not; therefore it wasn't just an outwardly blowing antigravitational field but something acting selectively. Either the powered Ark created a shell-like force field or else it had direct control over water itself.

In another curious detail, cast metal basins were installed both in the Tabernacle and in Solomon's Temple. In the Tabernacle, it was a smaller bronze basin filled with water, said to be for washing. It was kept between the inner tent and a sacrificial altar in the courtyard where the Shekhina could pass over it.[‡] In Solomon's Temple the basin was circular, fifteen feet in diameter, and almost eight feet high.[§] Presumably, it was also filled with water, but something that large and deep excludes a basin solely for washing, especially since smaller ones for that purpose were included elsewhere in the Temple.

---

[*] Exodus 14

[†] Joshua 3-4

[‡] Exodus 30:17-20

[§] 1 Kings 7:23-24

Therefore one could speculate that the Ark, its power source, or the Shekhina had a proclivity for water and the basins served a functional purpose toward that end. Wilhelm Reich wrote about the great affinity that orgone and water have for each other. A circular basin like that at Solomon's Temple is the optimal shape for a whirlpool, and water scientist Viktor Schauberger indicated that whirlpools infuse water with etheric lifeforce energy.[*]

There is a strong water-vortex motif here. The vortex is an archetype that repeatedly accompanies the Grail and the Ark, and I will say more on this later. Recall the Siege Perilous, the seat upon which only the worthy champions of the Grail could sit lest they be swallowed by a vortex. Recall the Shekhina manifesting as a tornado-like pillar of cloud. And recall that Merenre II, Egyptian pharaoh of the first Exodus, was said to have perished in the "place of the whirlpool."

Ark: Soul Frequency Selectivity

The Ark was selective with what effects it had upon whom. Generally speaking, those with high spiritual purity, meaning etheric and astral integrity, who obeyed protocol were left unharmed. This included the Levite Priests in charge of operating the Ark, first in the Tabernacle and later in Solomon's Temple. In the Temple, only ones with the highest spiritual training had access to the inner chamber where the Ark was located.

Those who disobeyed protocol or were spiritually tarnished were struck dead or afflicted with sores, boils, and other symptoms of biological disintegration mimicking leprosy. The leper factor appears several times. When Moses encountered the Burning Bush in the desert, which was an early appearance of the Shekhina, his hand briefly turned leprous.[†] When prophetess Miriam was summoned to the Tabernacle for making a transgression, she became leprous after the "pillar of cloud" descended upon her.[‡] In Egypt, the Hebrew immi-

---

[*] *Implosion: Rethinking the Basis of Technology* (Dolly Knight, Jonathan Stromberg, article) ▪ *Living Energies* (Callum Coats, 2002, book)

[†] Exodus 3

[‡] Numbers 12

grants and slaves were known as the "polluted ones" because of their rampant leprosy problems, which Frank Joseph and Laura Beadouin hypothesize was due to their local proximity to the Ark power source when it was still stationed in Lower Egypt.

When the Philistines (Pelasgians) captured the Ark, wherever they moved it among their territories, there broke out death, boils, and in one case mice.* This illustrates what happens when the Ark is brought in the midst of those who have not been sufficiently trained and purified. It seems to amplify and bring into outward manifestation the quality of their psychic energy, which in the case of decadence could manifest boils and mice for instance. This, in contrast to the Ark's enriching and fructifying influence when stationed in Biblical Jerusalem.

Only the Levite priests could openly handle the Ark without getting harmed. Moses and his brother Aaron were said to be Levites. Not only did they have to wear special clothing and follow certain safety protocols, they also had to be of sufficient spiritual purity. Compare this to the Grail, which would only let itself be cared for by a woman of perfect chastity and purity.

It wasn't enough to simply "keep one hand in the pocket while wearing insulating shoes" because the Ark wasn't just a high voltage device, but a Demiurgic one that translated astral/spiritual qualities into physical manifestation.

Ark: Manifesting Food

Further indication of the Ark's demiurgic power is given in Exodus 16, where the Israelites run out of food while crossing the desert to Canaan and the Shekhina manifests food for them. It covered their camp with quail to provide meat in the evening and coated the bare ground with dew that turned into edible granules called manna. The latter may have had alchemical qualities.

Manna is referred to as the "grain of heaven", "the bread of the mighty" in Psalms; it was ground up and made into cakes that tasted like "wa-

---

* 1 Samuel 5

fers made with honey" or "as the taste of fresh oil".' The substance melted in sunlight. This manna was pure in the sense of not producing any waste products in a person.† It ceased to fall once the Israelites arrived in an area and ate its grain. This shows it was not a natural phenomenon, but that there was intelligence behind it.

In Exodus, the appearance of manna was cyclical, with twice the quantity raining down on the sixth day of the week and none on the Sabbath, which was a holy day of rest and worship. If true, this suggests the Ark was being operated by someone who obeyed the weekly Sabbath system, thereby implying that one or a few operators manifested food for the entire camp. Contrast this with the story told in *Parzival,* where the Grail Stone manifested food and drink according to the visualized desires of each knight who held his empty plate and cup before it.

If this account is taken literally, then the Shekhina had the power to manifest or attract particular animals, like quail in this case. When the Philistines captured the Ark, a plague of mice broke out in one city where it was stationed, thus another case of specific animals being manifested or attracted. And according to Jewish oral tradition, King Solomon had the power to draw specific wild animals to his Temple because he knew their "names".‡ A name in this context is a type of word unique to a thing, basically its spiritual archetype, astral signature, or Logoic template.

---

* Grain of Heaven, Bread of the Mighty: Psalm 78:24-5 • Taste of honey: Exodus 16:13 • Taste of fresh oil: Numbers 11:8

† *Manna: Use and Function* (Wikipedia, Sifre on the Book of Numbers) • *Manna* (Jewish Encylopedia, article) • Compare with alchemical nourishment in *Comte de Gabalis: Discourse II* (Abbé de Villars, 1670, book pp. 65-67)

‡ *The Legends of the Jews, Chapter V: Solomon* (Louis Ginzberg, 1905, book): "When Solomon was of good cheer by reason of wine, he summoned the beasts of the field, the birds of the air, the creeping reptiles, the shades, the spectres, and the ghosts, to perform their dances before the kings, his neighbors, whom he invited to witness his power and greatness. The king's scribes called the animals and the spirits by name, one by one, and they all assembled of their own accord, without fetters or bonds, with no human hand to guide them."

The quail and manna manifestations are reminiscent of modern Fortean phenomena in which anomalous objects and animals rain down from the sky. It's always one type of object (like river stones) or one animal species (like fish or frogs). This specificity precludes their cause being water spouts picking up aquatic life and dumping it onto land. Some of what rains down aren't even known species. Thus they appear to have been projected into this dimension. Perhaps these are natural dimensional glitches following similar principles that the Ark employed intentionally to materialize food.

Ark: Loosh Transducer

In Robert Monroe's book *Far Journeys,* "loosh" is defined as metaphysical energy, encompassing everything from the crudest etheric energy produced by plants to the most refined astral energy produced via human love and suffering.[†] Loosh is equivalent to demiurgic energy.

It appears the Ark of the Covenant was powered, triggered, or catalyzed by externally supplied loosh. One example is the profuse level of animal sacrifices that the Israelites performed before the Ark in order to please their Lord, "sacrificing so many sheep and cattle that they could not be recorded or counted".[‡] Another example is King David dancing half-naked before the Ark after its homecoming from Philistine capture.

David dancing before the Ark has stumped many. But if you know anything about Native American rain dances, or the technical dances of the Sufis, or Rudolf Steiner's Eurythmy, you know that dance is a motional ritual that is highly active on an occult level and generates specific patterns of energies. The more intense the dance, the greater the energy output. "David, wearing a linen ephod, danced before the Lord with all his might".[§]

---

[*] *Raining Animals* (Wikipedia) • *Strange Rain* (Bobette Bryan, article) • *Strange Storms – Frogs, Spiders, and Fish* (Epoch Times, article)

[†] *Far Journeys* (Robert Monroe, 1985, book, pp. 160-172)

[‡] 1 Kings 8:5

[§] 2 Samuel 6:14

Animal sacrifices are convenient loosh sources. Slaughter liberates astral energies via the emotional experience of dying, while fat and blood provide rich sources of etheric energy. As naturopaths and occultists know, fat and oil are good mediums for storing and transmitting subtle energies, hence the ancient practice of anointing with blessed oil.

As for blood, that it carries lifeforce is obvious. Even the Old Testament says as much: "For the life of a creature is in the blood" and "But be sure you do not eat the blood, because the blood is the life, and you must not eat the life with the meat".* So a distinction was made between blood and meat; the latter could be eaten, while the blood contained the lifeforce and had other uses. The Levite priests sprinkled the blood against the Tabernacle altar on all sides and burned the fatty carcass upon it, which would entice the Shekhina to exit the tent and consume the remains.† "It is a burnt offering, an offering made by fire, an aroma pleasing to the Lord".‡ This practice of sacrificing bulls, rams, and sheep was repeated regularly.

When the Ark was installed in the first Temple of Solomon, animal sacrifices were prohibited everywhere else in Jerusalem other than the Temple.§ This would make sense if sacrifices absolutely had to be done in the Ark's presence to be utilized, further supporting the idea that the Ark was affected or even powered by the loosh emitted by a dying animal and its blood. Manna not falling on the Sabbath may be connected to animal sacrifice being forbidden on that day.

The Jewish practice of ritual slaughter is known as Shekhita and its techniques are used to produce kosher meat. The practice involves precise cutting of the animal's throat to ensure a calm but conscious death. Afterward, the animal is fully drained of its blood. As a side note, it's worth noting that cows and bulls are by definition the main targets of cattle mutilations. They are killed while fully conscious and later found completely drained of blood. The aliens who do this leave

---

*Leviticus 17:11-14, Deuteronomy 12:23

† Leviticus 8-9, also see Exodus 24

‡ Leviticus 1:9

§ Deuteronomy 12:8-14 • *Why do Jews no longer sacrifice animals?* (The Straight Dope, article)

behind the carcass and only take certain organs, as well as the 5-10 gallons of blood per cow, bull, or horse.[*]

The Egyptian word for bull is "Ka" which is identically the Egyptian name for lifeforce energy.[†] This suggests lifeforce was the primary concept associated with bulls. The symbol of "Ka" is two upright arms raised in reverence, possibly stemming from a ritual pose conducive to the reception and transmission of etheric energy. The symbol is also reminiscent of bull horns, the crescent Moon, and the two winged figures atop the Mercy Seat. Ka is said to determine one's destiny, habits, and vitality. It's clear that Ka translates to etheric body. The other subtle parts of a being, what the Egyptians called "Ba", translates to astral body. The Ba, depicted as a flying stork with a human head, is said to wander around during the night but had to return to the body by morning. Further, the Ba was said to indulge in pleasures, which fits the emotional and passionate nature of the astral body. The final component, "akh" was reached only after death when the deceased made it to the celestial realms, and this translates in occultism to "spirit."

Hence the Egyptians sacrificed bulls, as early as the Second Dynasty of the Old Kingdom if not earlier. These so-called "Apis Bulls" were held as divine, treated with reverence, mourned at their death, and buried with honor. The bulls would be ritualistically slaughtered at the age of 28, which ties symbolically into the Moon cycle, and the meat eaten by the priests and king.[†]

---

[*] *Major New Evidence In The Cattle Mutilation Phenomenon* (rense.com, article) ▪ *Cattle Mutilation/Predator Kill Comparison Pictures* (Chuck Zukowski, article) ▪ *Human Mutilation* (Tim Swartz, article)

[†] *Apis Bull* (Ancient Egypt Online, article) ▪ *Apis* (Wikipedia)

[‡] *La Mort De Philae, Chapter VI — In the Tombs of the Apis* (Pierre Loti, article) ▪ Not all bulls made it to age 28. Some died or were killed in their 17th, 25th, or 26th year, depending on circumstances. The "28" year is symbolically significant since that is how old Osiris was when he was murdered by his evil brother Set. Jews also have a ritual performed only once every 28 years called Birkat Ha-Hammah when the Sun is said to return to its location in the sky at the time of Creation. Of course, astronomically that isn't true. However, Saturn has a 29.5 year cycle, which plays significantly into the Parzival tale. Saturn is also Chronos, the god from whom we get the etymology behind words relating to linear time. All of this ties into the Mayan calendar as well, with the first

If Apis bulls were once slaughtered for loosh harvesting, eventually that purpose was forgotten but the ritual continued anyway. During later dynasties, mummified bulls were buried in the stone coffers of the underground Serapeum complex. As Christopher Dunn writes, these coffers were exquisitely carved to perfection using advanced technology equaling or surpassing anything we have today and originating from a much earlier time.* They were likely built by the same advanced pre-Egyptian civilization that constructed the Great Pyramid. Either those ancients who created the coffers also sacrificed bulls, or else the coffers were created for more utilitarian reasons, and only later were they repurposed by the Egyptians to house mummified bulls.

The Apis Bull was considered a manifestation of the Egyptian god Ptah, a deity who called creation into existence, and who was considered a god of craftsmen. He is said to have spoken creation into existence. Thus Ptah is equivalent to the Logos or Demiurge. "Ptah" means "opener of the mouth", and opening the mouth is the first step to saying a word or name.[†]

As you can see, much connects here: Logos, Demiurge, animal sacrifice, etheric energy, and Ark of the Covenant. Bulls supplied etheric energy through their blood to power Demiurgic processes. That is the function of the etheric body anyway, to demiurgically ensure the continuation of form in a biological system prone to entropic decay. Just that this same energy can be repurposed toward non-biological applications through ritual slaughter. According to Christian theology, the practice of animal sacrifice ended with the coming of Jesus

---

day of Creation being 4 Ahau, and the Jewish ritual having to do with the Sun being created on the 4th day. ▪ *Apis* (Wikipedia): "When Osiris absorbed the identity of Ptah, becoming Ptah-Seker-Osiris, the Apis bull became considered an aspect of Osiris rather than Ptah. Since Osiris was lord of the dead, the Apis then became known as the living deceased one. As he now represented Osiris, when the Apis bull reached the age of twenty-eight, the age when Osiris was said to have been killed by Set, symbolic of the lunar month, and the new Moon, the bull was put to death with a great sacrificial ceremony."

* *The Amazing Boxes of the Serapeum* (Christopher Dunn, article) ▪ *Lost Technologies of Ancient Egypt* (Christopher Dunn, 2010, book)

† *Ptah, God of Craftsmen, Rebirth and Creation* (Caroline Seawright, article) ▪ *Ptah* (Crystalinks, article)

Christ because his dying on the cross fully atoned for our Original Sin; he was the ultimate sacrifice to end all sacrifices.[*] I don't believe this exoteric interpretation for a second, but as usual, there is truth lingering behind the symbolism.

Notice that, whereas the ancients resorted to animal sacrifice and other crude means to activate the Ark, the Grail knights merely maintained a state of spiritual transcendence to activate the Grail stone by thought alone. The Grail knights were burning with a Christ energy, not in a religious sense, but in the sense of their being vessels for the positive personification of the divine Logos. In other words, they were connected to the highest, purest, most vibrationally elevated loosh source in existence — the face of God. Further proof is seen in reality creation: you manifest quickest when you are attuned with your Higher Self, heart, or spirit. There is no greater demiurgic creational power than this, but there are certainly lesser ones.

The means to achieve such a state of connectedness has been taught by the greatest sages of the ages, one of whom was the historical character forming the nucleus of the Jesus Christ mythos, whose surviving teachings may be found in the *Gospel of Thomas* and the *Q Source*.[†] The *Gospel of Thomas* was a 2nd-century reconstruction of the original teachings. Note where the New Testament differs from the *Gospel of Thomas* and the *Q Source*, and there you will see what the Church added to hijack and corrupt the genuine teaching. The Biblical Jesus versus the historical Jesus is like Sunny Delight versus Fresh Orange Juice; fundamentalists believe Sunny Delight grows on trees; the skeptics refuse to believe oranges exist. The truth is between and beyond both.

Christian theology is correct that Christ ended the need for animal sacrifice, though not for the claimed reasons. Rather, his core teachings provide a superior alternative to harvesting energy from the environment to fund demiurgic creation. Theology is also right that

---

* *Why did God require animal sacrifices in the Old Testament?* (Got Questions Ministries, article) ▪ *Why did Jesus shed his blood?* (Jesus is Lord, article)

† *The Gospel of Thomas Collection* (Gnostic Society Library, article) ▪ *Gospel of Thomas* (Wikipedia) ▪ *Q Source* (Wikipedia) ▪ *The Gospel of Q; All sides to the controversy* (Religions Tolerance, article)

this relates to Original Sin and mankind's Fall from Paradise, though it's because the spiritual transcendence embodied in the Grail knights is identically a non-Fallen state of consciousness, which Christ termed the Kingdom of Heaven.

Those who cannot tap into this higher energy/intelligence must resort to lesser methods and sources to trigger their desired demiurgic effects. These include ritual, dance, sexual energy, animal sacrifice, and human sacrifice. Even today, black magic and voodoo still make use of animal sacrifice. Synchromystics and conspiracy researchers know how the global occult elite perform mass rituals through current events, media, and entertainment, and how they engage in ritual killings through staged accidents, manipulated wars, and induced disasters. There have been tribes and cults throughout history, from Meso-America to the Mid-East to South India, who performed human and animal sacrifices in exchange for power, abundance, security, and prosperity. In all these cases, loosh energy bought desired physical manifestation.

When loosh cannot be tapped from an infinite source, cruder grades must be harvested from finite sources; the Israelite and Egyptian use of animal sacrifice illustrates this.

Ark: Sound and Pyramid Connection

Sound consistently accompanies the Ark's operation and effects.

One example is the fall of Jericho, where the Israelites were told how to breach the city walls: "March around the city once with all the armed men. Do this for six days. Have seven priests carry trumpets of rams' horns in front of the Ark. On the seventh day, march around the city seven times, with the priests blowing the trumpets. When you hear them sound a long blast on the trumpets, have all the people give a loud shout; then the wall of the city will collapse and the people will go up, every man straight in."[*]

Another example is the sound associated with the Shekhina's activities on Mount Sinai: "Mount Sinai was covered with smoke because the Lord descended on it as fire. The smoke billowed up from it like smoke

---

[*] Joshua 6

from a furnace, the whole mountain trembled violently, and the sound of the trumpet grew louder and louder."*

There are other examples of shouting, music, and trumpet blasts being present during Ark and Shekhina activities. It seems that sound, like loosh, played an important role. Frequency and amplitude are the main variables defining a sound. That volume is emphasized as a factor in the above accounts suggests that the Ark translated sonic energy into something else in proportion to its intensity, and vice versa.

In *Tempest and Exodus,* Ralph Ellis makes a convincing case that Mount Sinai of the Bible was actually the Great Pyramid. For instance, Mount Sinai is traditionally described as the tallest of three mountains, each of which contained deep "caves." Moses was commanded to go into Mount Sinai. It was named for the sharpness of its peak and infamous for the steepness of its sides, and an alternate name places its location in the desert. The base of Mount Sinai was encircled by armed guards, which is unfeasible for an actual mountain, but not the Great Pyramid. Another name for Mount Sinai is Mount Horeb, meaning "glowing mountain." These are just a few examples. There are many indicators that the Ark had something to do with the Great Pyramid. When Moses emerged from Mount Sinai, he descended with the stone Testimony, which he subsequently placed into the Ark. Hence the Ark's power source was retrieved from within the Great Pyramid, whose granite sarcophagus correlates with the stated dimensions of the Ark.

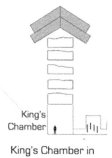

King's Chamber in the Great Pyramid

Entrance to the Great Pyramid.
[engraving by Vivant Denon, 1808]

Apis Bull Hieroglyphs
(Wikipedia)

---

* Exodus 19

In another connection, the hieroglyph for "Apis Bull" is two gabled roofs over a box, exactly resembling the entrance to the Great Pyramid.* With the bull already linked to etheric energy via its name "Ka" also being that of the etheric body, linked to the Ark of the Covenant via animal sacrifice, and linked to the Demiurge via the bull being associated with Ptah, it's fitting that a pyramid connection exists here as well.

The Great Pyramid today is a gutted machine with all its active components missing. The modern Pyramid versus its original form is like a bullhorn versus a megaphone; one is just a passive sound shaping funnel, the other an active sound amplifier with powered electronics. We know from experiments that even a cardboard pyramid produces strange negentropic effects, meaning the shape itself influences the ambient etheric field, but such passive structures are weak in comparison to the Great Pyramid in its original working state.† The Pyramid is currently a passive remnant of its original self and all its associated exotic phenomena are nothing compared to what it once could do.

The technical operation of the Pyramid has been well investigated by Christopher Dunn, author of *The Giza Power Plant*. I agree with his data, but not necessarily his conclusion that it was merely an electric power plant. I also disagree with Frank Joseph and Laura Beaudoin that it was a piezoelectric attenuator of seismic energy designed to protect the region against earthquakes. Earthquake activity certainly accompanied the Ark, but perhaps more as an effect than a cause of its function.

According to Dunn, the Pyramid's function depended on several critical aspects: the Queen's Chamber into which chemicals were dumped to produce hydrogen gas, the Grand Gallery serving as a sound production and amplification chamber via its hypothesized network of acoustic resonators, the antechamber with its movable vertical stone slabs that could fine-tune the sound coming from the Grand Gallery, and lastly the King's Chamber where the sonic energy was focused

---

* *Apis* (Wikipedia)

† *Secrets of the Pyramids—Experiments in Energy-Form, Part One* (Joseph Robert Jochmans, article)

to vibrate the granite stones in order to piezoelectrically produce electromagnetic waves that energized the hydrogen gas filling these chambers.*

If you look carefully at the Grand Gallery and the antechamber according to Dunn's description, you will see that they respectively mimic the human larynx and tongue/teeth/lips.

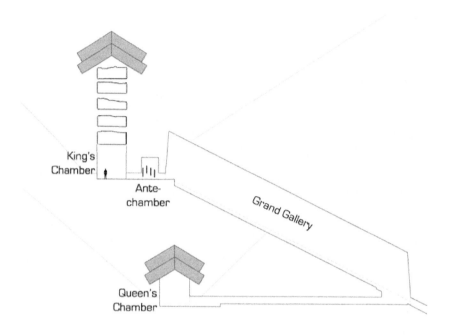

If the Grand Gallery produced sound, it might have been through a collection of installed tuning forks and the Helmholtz resonators that converted their vibrations into a loud and focused beam aimed toward the King's Chamber.[†] This mass of sound enters the antechamber and

---

* The so-called "air shafts" in the Great Pyramid have been hypothesized by researchers like Robert Bauval to point to certain ritually significant stars. Evidence says otherwise; for example, the shafts are bent when viewed from above and don't have a continuous line of sight; some end within the Pyramid. See *The Great Pyramid and the Axis of the Earth – Part 1* (Scott Creighton, Gary Osborn, article). Chris Dunn's analysis fits the evidence better, and he proposed a strictly utilitarian purpose behind the shafts.

† *Fourier Synthesis* (Kenyon College, article) shows a setup using tuning forks

is modulated by the series of adjustable granite gates. In other words, the Great Pyramid functioned as a vowel resonator.[*] Thus a vowel sound would have been pumped with great intensity into the King's Chamber.

In the King's Chamber, there is a granite chest whose dimensions are similar but not identical to those of the Ark of the Covenant. Accordingly, it's been proposed that the Ark slid into this chest, but considering the narrow entrance to the room, it's more likely that the smaller stone-like power source was placed therein, with the Pyramid itself serving as the original Ark/Tabernacle/Temple. Moses bringing back the stone Testimony from inside "Mount Sinai" and then placing it inside the Ark supports this.

One can imagine the "Ark Stone" being stationed in the King's Chamber and saturating the connecting spaces with its luminous energy field. Plasma is ionized gas, and if the chambers were filled with pure hydrogen as Dunn proposes, then it would have been a hydrogen plasma. The entire vowel resonator may have been filled with hydrogen plasma through which tunable sound was pumped from the Grand Gallery through the formant-synthesizing antechamber. And when you pump sound waves through a charged plasma, you get longitudinal ion-acoustic waves, which produce longitudinal EM waves, which are identically gravity or time waves.[†] Etheric energy would have accompanied it as well, which the Pyramid by virtue of its shape alone can bias and amplify.

The five ceilings above the King's Chamber consist of loose granite crossbeams, polished on the bottom to reflect coherent energy from below, and intentionally uneven on top to disperse incoherent energy from the top, thus functioning like a one-way mirror capable of cohering and directing the energy like a laser. These ceilings might also be

---

and Helmholtz resonators to make composite soundforms • *Egyptian Tuning Forks* (Keelynet, article) • *Tuning Forks and Megalithic Technology* (Montalk Research Note, article)

[*] *The Great Pyramid of Khufu* (Guardian's Egypt, article) shows internal structure to the Pyramid and the antechamber with its sliding gates • *Vocal Vowels* (Exploratorium, article with sound clips) • *Formant* (Wikipedia)

[†] <scalarphysics.com>

mimicking the human sinus passages for additional resonance activity. Vibration of the granite beams would have produced longitudinal electric waves as well via the piezoelectric effect. The gravitational, etheric, temporal energy produced in the King's Chamber would have been made coherent and unidirectional, aimed either up to the sky or down to the center of the planet – more likely the latter since the center of the planet is always directly below a level structure on the surface. It's also possible that the Pyramid was not designed to do anything outwardly, but rather focus all its energics inward upon the King's Chamber to charge, initialize, and/or program the Ark Stone.

The Pyramid is a physical representation of the human body. Even the underground chamber, which seems to have functioned as a beating hydraulic ram pump, is located where the human heart would be.

If you keep in mind that the Ark responded to sound, that Ptah (who is the Demiurge or Logos) means "opener of the mouth", and that loud

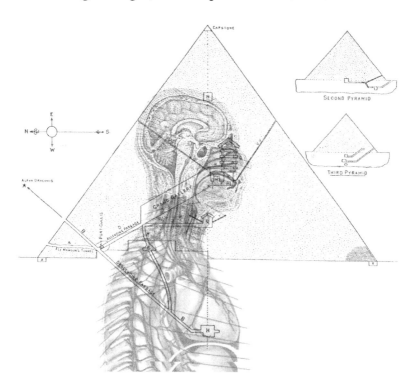

vowel sounds were likely pumped into the King's Chamber from the larynx/mouth-like structures, you begin to see that the Great Pyramid must have had a truly awesome purpose.

Ark: Physical Terrain Transformer

Jewish oral tradition ascribes several additional powers to the Ark not mentioned in the Old Testament: 1) as it was being carried by the Isra-elite vanguard, the Ark cleared the path of scorpions and snakes via a burning ray issuing forth from the Mercy Seat, 2) the Levites carrying it would also be carried by it, meaning levitation. 3) the Ark could level hills and mountains in the way.[*]

The third claim that the Ark could alter geography and terrain seems tenuous, but there are a few potential points of correlation.

First is that the Nile River may have been intelligently engineered, as explained by Goro Adachi in his book *The Time Rivers*. You would have to read his book to be convinced there is something to it, but in short, the features, proportions, alignments, lengths, bends, etc. of the Nile are too synchronous to be mere natural formations. The only problem is that something so large cannot be created through physical digging like with the Panama Canal (4132 miles versus 51 miles). Adachi doesn't really explain who did it, but they must have possessed god-like power to directly transform geography.

The second point of correlation is the Glastonbury Zodiac, a circular collection of zodiac images spanning ten miles in diameter, impressed upon the landscape of the Isle of Avalon where legend says the Grail was once kept. The zodiac images are made of streams, dykes, roads, and other landscape features. The center of the zodiac is the famous Glastonbury Tor, a stone tower built on a sacred hill.[†]

The third is the French town of Rennes-le-Château. Like the Glaston-bury Zodiac, the position of landscape features and markers including mountain tops and churches trace out a meaningful pattern, the pen-

---

[*] *Ark of the Covenant* (Jewish Encyclopedia, article)

[†] *The Glastonbury Zodiac* (Frances Howard-Gordon, book excerpt) • *The Glastonbury Zodiac* (Pauline Ross, Morgana West, article)

tagram in this case. Rennes-le-Château is famous for its association with secret Templar activities and later the priest Saunière who struck it rich after discovering secret documents pertaining to Templar treasure or perhaps a method for making the Philosopher's Stone.*

These alleged landscape geometries include some features not placeable by human hands. While they bear enough ambiguity to support the skeptical view that people are just reading too much into things, they also display enough order and improbability to look like "graffiti tagging" by some hyperdimensional intelligence. Seems like everything deeply connected to the Grail, Ark, and Philosopher's Stone bears the fingerprint of intelligent design or synchronistic orchestration, down to the prophetic codes in the Torah and Hebrew gematria.

Or consider the Moon's association with the sacred Bull, that the Hebrew calendar is based on Moon cycles, and that Good Friday and other key days associated with the Grail and Ark are timed to the Moon. Not surprisingly, the astronomical parameters of the Moon indicate some heavy synchronistic orchestration. Books have been written on its anomalous nature including *Who Built the Moon* by Butler and Knight and David Icke's *Human Race Get Off Your Knees*.

What all of these environmental geometries have in common is that they seem *synchronistically* rather than *mechanically* formed. So instead of the Moon being towed in via tractor beams, or the Nile river being dug with antigravity bulldozers, it may have originated through intelligently guided or selected natural evolution via intentional probability biasing (timeline switching or probable past selection). Thus these geometries seem both natural and unnatural at the same time. Natural enough to please the skeptics, unnatural enough to convince the believers. The religious might just call it the handiwork of God, but it's not that simple. I'll talk more about this later when I get into the timewar idea, and how High Demiurgic Technology is capable of reality reconfiguration and timeline selection. For now, I just want to mention that the Ark may very well have leveled hills and mountains and that this isn't without supporting context.

---

* *The Secret of Rennes-le-Château* (Robert Richardson, article) • *Rennes-le-Château Research and Resource* (website)

Just to speculate, what would happen if the Ark Stone's terrain-transformational power is amplified and channeled by the Great Pyramid, whose coherent energy beam points down to the center of the planet? In the Biblical story of Mount Sinai, the entire structure was quaking and trembling while a trumpeting sound grew louder and louder. It's interesting that the Pyramid is aligned almost perfectly with True North, skewed a little today due to crustal shifts since the time of its construction. If it was built after the last pole shift, which occurred around 10,500 B.C. (or possibly 3200 B.C.) then it was simply positioned in alignment with the new pole. This is the most plausible case. If, however, it was built *before* the pole shift, then either its builders knew clairvoyantly what the new pole alignment would be, or *the Great Pyramid was used to shift the planet's axis.* It's impossible to say whether it was built before or after the pole shift, so I'll leave this as food for thought.

Putting it All Together

I began this book by explaining the nature of the Demiurge, the universal intelligence responsible for shaping physical reality according to given archetypes. Its etheric component biases probability at the quantum level while the astral component carries the archetypal signature that directs that biasing. Together, etheric and astral energies may be called "demiurgic energies" because they have the power to intelligently alter matter, energy, space, and time — precisely the function of the Demiurge.

Demiurgic technology makes use of these energies to affect the physical universe. One example is the Philosopher's Stone, a saline substance impregnated with dense etheric energies and tinged with the astral signature of gold, thereby being capable of transmuting lead or mercury into gold by reconfiguring their atoms at the quantum level in accordance with that signature. By logically extending the principles of the Demiurge and Philosopher's Stone, I can also explain the purported characteristics of the Holy Grail and Ark of the Covenant. The latter are higher applications of demiurgic technology.

The central tenet of Alchemy is to imitate Nature, not only the mineral aspect upon which all of modern science is fixated but also the biological and spiritual aspects. In producing the Philosopher's Stone, Alchemy is imitating the process of mineral-to-plant evolution. Notice that the Philosopher's Stone is primarily a combination of physical and etheric bodies, with only the slightest astral component to impart a specific "flavor" to its transmutative power. Unlike ordinary minerals, it possesses lifeforce by virtue of its intrinsic etheric energy. This places it above the rank of chemicals and closer to the vegetable kingdom. Both plants and the Philosopher's Stone have physical and etheric bodies but not much of an astral body. Just like a plant, the Stone is passive and immobile.

What separates animals from plants is that their physical bodies are more complex, their etheric bodies more intense and developed, and they have an actively functional astral body. The animal level is where sentience and volition begin, where the first semblance of independence develops. The more complex physical body is what allows a higher order of life to inhabit it. If Alchemy were more refined, it could mimic this process of plant-to-animal evolution and take the Philosopher's Stone beyond the vegetative level. Then the physical body of the Stone would be more ordered and perhaps crystalline, its etheric body would likewise have to be greatly intensified, and an actively functioning astral body with volition could develop.

What separates humans from animals is that, on average, humans have egos and personalities that allow them to be independent reasoning individuals. As explained in the first chapter, the ego is a higher order structure that develops in the soul thanks to more sophisticated environmental programming made possible through the body being evolved enough to allow for it. Likewise, if Alchemy were taken to an even higher level, it could produce something that not only has an etheric and astral body but also possesses an independent sentient intelligence.

The above can also be explained from the perspective of thought-forms. The most basic thoughtforms are just passive etheric energy constructs comparable to sponges or fungi. The more developed ones have an astral body as well, and like animals, they are hungry critters; astral succubi are an example. But the most evolved thoughtforms possess ego and personality.

The quintessential point is this: *not only does demiurgic technology make use of etheric and astral energies, but it also creates artificial physical bodies to house any order of soul or thoughtform, from the lowliest etheric constructs to the highest individualized intelligences.* (This technology is alien; I can see it being used nowadays in Gray worker drones and alien ships, whereby the physical vehicle is made autonomous by a resident etheric/astral thoughtform, a literal ghost in the machine).

What is the Grail Stone, what is the Ark Stone? My current theory is that it's an advanced crystalline object housing an equally advanced thoughtform; and not just any thoughtform, but an *entitized* one. The Ark and Grail Stones are the pinnacles of High Demiurgic Technology, at least of what has *fallen* into human hands. The entitization is what makes it oracular and volitional. The intensified etheric field is what produces the various electromagnetic emissions. External etheric, astral, and archetypal inputs modify its behavior. The probability biasing effects of its etheric field can be amplified to allow for the manifestation of physical matter according to the entered archetypes and energies.

The Ark of the Covenant, as described in the Old Testament, ought to consist of the following components: 1) the Ark Stone as the physical body, 2) the Great Pyramid, Ark box, Tabernacle, and Temple of Solomon as housing for the body, 3) the vortical Shekhina as the soul (etheric and astral bodies), and 4) Yahweh, the Lord of the Israelites, as the residing ego. In mysticism, the soul is feminine relative to spirit, thus the Shekhina is of feminine gender in Judaism since it is identically the soul of Yahweh. When the Shekhina leaves the Ark and travels about, that is comparable to astral projection.

In summary, the Ark Stone is a physical matrix possessed by a powerful entitized thoughtform created or invoked according to the operator or priest's instructions. The Stone itself pre-existed the original Jews, but for a time it was in their possession and they came under its control. If it seems belittling to call Yahweh a thoughtform, bear in mind that the universal Demiurge is a thoughtform also, and so are our souls. Thoughtforms are not always insignificant things. The bigger question is whether the Demiurge, thoughtform, or soul in question is subordinate to spirit/Creator or acting independently out of selfish motives. If the latter, then it exists only to perpetuate its own survival and carry out its prime directive through energy feeding and probabilistic control. Hence, at the beginning of this book, I talked about the Corruption of the Demiurge and how its development of a lower ego divorced it from the harmony of Creation, turning it into a World Parasite. Gnostics equated Yahweh to the Corrupt Demiurge.

In the next chapter I will discuss how the misuse of High Demiurgic Technology explains why the entitized intelligences communicating through the Ark and Grail were so unlike in their temperaments and goals, and what this means for our future. I will also get into the origins of the Grail and its role as a fulcrum in a grand chess game spanning ancient feuds to future timewars.

5 MOSAIC ABUSE OF DEMIURGIC TECHNOLOGY

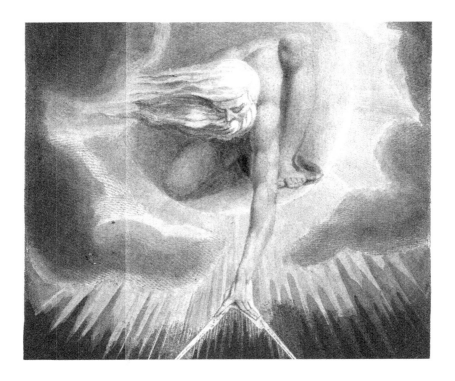

Acquisition of the Ark Stone by the proto-Israelites was a critical turning point in history. Under the direction of the entitized thoughtform manifesting through the Ark, these exiles conquered and prospered into what eventually became ancient Israel and the Jewish people. High Demiurgic Technology inserted a new religious, political, and economic power into the timeline.

History would have turned out very differently had the Israelites never acquired the Ark Stone, if they faded into history like other tribes of the past. First and foremost there would be no Judaism, and hence no Islam or Christianity. Thus the Catholic Church would not exist either, nor the Inquisition. There would be no anti-Semitism during the Middle Ages, which forced Jews to take refuge in the financial industry since other occupations were barred to them.* Without anti-Semitism, there would be no Nazis, World War II, or Holocaust. After the war, the Nazi scientific intelligentsia was transferred to the USA to work in black ops projects.† From their influence arose the Military Industrial Complex.‡

And because of the Holocaust, Israel exists once again as a nation, though only through the oppression of the Palestinians. This has further increased anti-Zionism and anti-Semitism in the world, especially among Israel's Arab and Persian neighbors. This conflict is bound to erupt in regional warfare, possibly nuclear, which would drag other nations like Russia, China, America, and the European Union into World War III.

Organized religion, international bankers, Military Industrial Complex, and World War III are the key factors that will bring about a New World Order, the reign of the Antichrist. As you can see, the

---

* *Secular Jewish culture: Banking and Finance* (Wikipedia) ▪ *Usury:Medieval Doctrine* (Jewish Encyclopedia Entry)

† One example of Nazi scientists being transferred to America: *Operation Paperclip* (Wikipedia). This was not the only project, just one that made it into the history books.

‡ See Eisenhower's farewell speech of January 17, 1961 in which he warns of the burgeoning Military Industrial (and Congressional) complex. I suspect this came after an important turn of events around 1959-1961, when American territories fell into negative alien jurisdiction after the U.S. Government made treaties with them in exchange for technology. During that same time period, the government rejected the benevolent alien factions who only gave warnings and advice but refused to share technology. This is obvious if you closely study UFO and alien contactee history. On September 19, 1961 the Betty and Barney Hill abduction happened, which kicked off decades of widespread Gray alien abductions. It's worth noting that during the abduction, a humanoid figure reminiscent of a Nazi officer was seen in a supervisory position. The Military-Industrial complex has a Nazi/Alien/Black-Ops nucleus, which is responsible for the joint military-alien abductions occurring around the world today. This cancerous structure ascended to power by 1961 and Eisenhower was the last president of the old guard, thus his farewell warning. Ever since, the alien disinformation campaign has been in full swing. See my book *Discerning Alien Disinformation* for an in-depth exposition of the campaign's methods and intentions.

Ark Stone being taken out of Egypt initiated events that contributed to the potential advent of global totalitarianism. On another timeline, different players and events could have produced similar ends, but there's no denying that our particular history reached this point with extraordinary speed and efficiency thanks to special assistance by nonhuman forces.

In Jewish origins, we have an example of otherworldly forces and technologies shifting the direction of history. Without the Ark, the impossible would not have become possible and our timeline would not have deviated to the degree it did. This and other deviations to the timeline have ensured that mankind is now religiously, psychologically, politically, technologically, and militarily primed for global self-enslavement.

Who is responsible for this grand orchestration of history? The lead conspirators are aliens. This fact is detailed in my book *Discerning Alien Disinformation* and the works of William Bramley, Michael Tsarion, David Icke, Jordan Maxwell, and Marshall Vian Summers. Hopefully, it's clear by this point that the Ark/Grail Stone is alien in origin. Is it so surprising that alien technology helped propagate alien agendas?

But the alien presence is not the *raison d'etre* behind it all. Their agendas are just subplots in a bigger story. Consider how aliens reside somewhere between the level of humans and divine spirits, or between humans and demonic entities, depending on their spiritual orientation. Just as the human sphere is surrounded by the alien sphere, so is the alien sphere encompassed by the divine and demonic. Therefore, alien dynamics occur against the backdrop of occult, cosmological, and spiritual dynamics, namely the battle between the Corrupt Demiurge and the Creator. It seems that all other conspiracies and agendas follow, in one way or another, from this primordial schism.

On a scale of power, humans occupy the lower levels, aliens the middle, and cosmic intelligences like the Demiurge the higher. With that in mind, it looks like:

- the Ark/Grail is alien technology (middle)

- that has fallen into human hands (lower)
- yet allows human interaction with personified extrusions of the Demiurge (higher)
- resulting in a deviation of human history (lower)
- toward the fulfillment of various alien agendas (middle)
- that stem from the primordial schism between Demiurge and Creator (higher).

This system of interactions between multiple levels gives a preliminary sketch of the kind of "game" humanity could be caught within. To make it more complete, I would need to add feedback loops between warring time travelers or interdimensional beings and our alternate pasts, presents, and futures. More on that in the next chapter.

For the moment, let's explore the interaction between human and Demiurgic levels by revisiting the subject of the Ark of the Covenant, specifically the intelligence manifesting through the Ark and why it differed so greatly from the one manifesting through the Holy Grail.

The Advent of Yahweh

It all goes back to the Hyksos expulsion (1550 B.C.) and the Osarseph Rebellion (1320 B.C.) in Egypt. One or both of these events involved the transport of the Ark Stone out of Egypt into Canaan. In both events, the Semitic leadership in Egypt was ousted and exiled. According to ancient historians Manetho and Josephus, a High Priest of Akhenaten named Osarseph, who held allegiance to the Semitic people of Lower Egypt, led his monotheistic followers out of Egypt after a failed rebellion against the Egyptian traditionalists. As the story goes, this heretic priest and his people became Moses and the Israelites.[*]

There may be more to the story. In *The Stellar Man,* Hermetic author Dario Salas Sommer (John Baines) relays a parallel account of what happened in Egypt, based on his research and inside sources as a

---

[*] *Manetho and Josephus on the Hyksos* (Manetho, Josephus, article) ▪ *Osarseph and Exodus: Literary Reflections in an Egyptian Mirror* (Gary Greenberg, article)

member of the Hermetic brotherhood. Because of its importance and relevance, I quote it here in full:

> Why do we designate Christ as the symbol of spirituality? Because Jesus was the most distinguished member of the *Magician's Fraternity*, prepared specifically for his mission to make Christ incarnate in himself. Jesus and Christ were two different persons; one human, the other, divine.
>
> Christ is a superior being who is on an advanced level on the scale of evolution, which a human being could reach in perhaps millions of years of evolution. Let us conceive of him as an extraterrestrial spiritual power, which we could call an *Archangel*. This *Archangel,* due to his very lengthy evolution, possessed perfect and powerful spirituality. This is why Jesus went through a long preparation for this role, for he had to be able to withstand an extremely high vibration in his physical body. This vibration could only manifest itself for brief moments, as its intensity could destroy the nervous and cellular system of Jesus' body. Christ was the one who performed miracles through Jesus, who provided the matter for his manifestation.
>
> The *Magician's Fraternity* remains well hidden, as it has a right to its own privacy, but some of its members have intermingled with ordinary people, motivated by the wish to show *sapiens* the road to a higher life. The magicians know, however, that knowledge of *The Hermetic Art* as an instrument to reach spiritual heights, is only for the "elite" and is not to be divulged. Nevertheless, the fraternity of initiates provides the opportunity for any person with sufficient merit to join the Hermetic elite of *Magicians* or *Stellar Men,* if the scope and intelligence of his efforts permits him to do so.
>
> The science of the Magicians is called *Hermetic Art* in honor of Hermes Trismegistus. According to tradition, he arrived on earth from outer space approximately thirty thousand years ago, anointed as Supreme Grand Master of the Initiatic Fraternity. Inspired by his light, Egypt became great and wise, and the sacred science of its priests was called *Hermeticism*. In those days, only by means of huge sacrifices and trials was it possible to belong to a Hermetic Initiatic School. The great majority who succeeded in entering such a school faltered along the way, lacking the moral and spiritual courage to overcome the multiple obstacles, temptations, and trials by which

ISIS, mistress of the mysteries of Nature, evaluated the true worth of those who aspired to the supreme knowledge of the absolute truth.

It was in one of those schools that Jesus himself became a Hermeticist and reached the highest degrees of initiation.

Because the time is right, we will divulge the mystery of Jesus the Christ and the causes for the moral suffering of humanity, according to the teachings of the *Magician's Fraternity*. This moral mystery stems from the *adoration of the golden calf;* from the submission of the human being to the god of money. In honor of this god, he must give up or sacrifice his spiritual possibilities in order to be able to subsist. Those who possess adequate means of subsistence generally pervert their potential spiritual values in the foolish game of gaining social position on the consumer market. The spiritual or moral quality of an individual is worth very little, as the need for money leads him to lower and prostitute him self for the vile metal, which buys honor, respect, love, fame, and power. The money god is sitting above the world, and whoever wishes to enjoy his gifts must adore him. The real power of money is not only material, but it is principally a hidden force, as the coin is not worth anything in itself; it is only symbolic for human effort or work. By a strange paradox, although work is intrinsically noble, money, the result of this effort, is under the control or influence of a satanic or diabolic power.

We invite the reader to meditate on what he could do to corrupt human beings if he was Satan; what means or tools would he use to instigate crime, greed, war, fratricide, and decay of moral values? It would be difficult to imagine anything more perfectly suited for this than gold; neutral in its own condition, but diabolical when handled perversely.

Does Satan really exist, or is he only a myth created by the masses to explain certain things? If a person believes in the existence of God, then he must believe there is a devil or Satan as a counterpart of the Supreme Creator. Because absolute unity does not exist in life, the mere existence of something leads us to the affirmation that its opposite is also real. There is no light without darkness, no good without evil, no truth without falsehood. Death follows life, and life follows death.

God would thus be the supreme creative intelligence, and the "devil," the destructive intelligence. In the ancient Kabbalah, the devil has been symbolized as the shadow of God. Therefore, just as the Great Creator has his angelic hosts, the devil also has his infernal legion. William Blatty, in his book *The Exorcist,* refers to this legion when he presents the phenomenon of "demonic possession." After the following explanation we can continue our story.

The tradition transmitted by the great Hermetic Masters affirms that at a crucial moment in the history of humanity, a powerful *diabolic Archangel,* if we are allowed to call him thus, succeeded in penetrating the earth's occult defenses and entered its atmosphere, provoking extreme disturbances. To be able to imagine such a being, we suggest reading the book *The Lurker at the Threshold* by H. P. Lovecraft. According to Hermetic tradition, the direct, albeit unwilling cause of this catastrophe which affects us to this day, was Moses.

Everybody knows that Moses appeared floating in a basket down a river and was subsequently adopted, deceiving the Egyptian priests of the time. They took him for an Egyptian and initiated him into the mysteries of ritual magic, which is a method for making the key notes of Nature vibrate, and thus produce certain phenomena which the operator wishes to achieve. The study of atomic physics shows us that it is theoretically possible to produce changes or transmutations in matter; therefore, there is nothing miraculous about these mutations being achieved by means of secret procedures. In spite of his esoteric identification with Egyptian magic, Moses was always loyal to his ancestral blood. Thus, his most powerful wish was to make himself the leader who would free his people from enslavement, leading them to the promised land. Guided by this desire, and conscious of the powerful forces he had learned to control, Moses had a daring idea: to make a magic pact or alliance with an angel, a divine creature charged with the task of providing him with power and assistance from heaven to save his people.

After lengthy preparations done in deep solitude, he performed the ritual ceremony with magic words and corresponding invocations. In the midst of amazing atmospheric and terrestrial phenomena, an impressive being appeared, making Moses tremble with fear and panic, due to the tremendous force it projected. It will never be possible to know or even imagine the conditions under which the pact between man and heaven was made. The angel agreed to everything. Moses requested and promised his help, demanding the strictest obedience in return. He revealed his name as Y., and requested that as a sign of union, all his followers should undergo a small ritual surgical operation, with a light discharge of blood. Every man who underwent this would come to be a son of Y. The blood that was shed sealed the pact.

From that day forward, Moses was invested with superhuman powers and started doing all kinds of magical feats, converting the Ark of the Covenant into the center of his power. Plagues and calamities fell over Egypt, and non-believers and rebels were struck down by the wrath of Y. In this manner, Moses' people started the Exodus that would last forty years. Later, Y., the occult power behind the leader, suddenly started to change his procedures by formulating strange demands, all of which had the shedding of blood as the common denominator.

Moses was overcome with fear and started to become aware of the magnitude of the error he committed. He then understood that the *divine angel* was in truth an *angel of darkness,* the complete opposite of the luminous power he had intended to invoke.

This *infernal angel* was a member of the host of shadows. In order to maintain its power and strength, this vampire needed to feed on human blood, an essence charged with the vitality conferred by the divine spark. This is why all through the Exodus, so many blood-shedding incidents occurred, provoked by the occult dictator.

In reality, who was Y.? One could say he was a very ancient being whose evolutionary origin is unknown. Through long periods of cosmic time, this being kept his individuality, but unfortunately his evolution was directed toward negative, dark, and destructive aspects; much like a human being who grows bitter with the passing of time and adopts a negative and destructive concept of life.

Many beings similar to Y. exist in the Universe. Fortunately, the magnetic defenses of the planet constitute an impenetrable barrier against those beings. However, Moses' magic ritual opened a door and cleared a pathway through which Y. was able to penetrate into the Earth. It is possible to see this as the most transcendental, but unfortunately harmful event in the occult history of humanity. To justify this statement, it is necessary to digress in order to clarify exactly what the planet Earth really is.

One can affirm, without fearing any sarcastic mockery from the ignorant or the semi-wise, that the planet Earth is a human being. It is not something equivalent to a human being, but a man in all aspects of the word.

Hermetic philosophy upholds the truth of reincarnation, but affirms that this takes place only with some people who possess, or have developed within themselves some qualities or characteristics apart from the physical body, which are capable of resisting death. The term "people" refers to human beings, even if these beings may present physical characteristics different from terrestrial man. Regarding reincarnation, Hermeticism teaches that a Hermetic initiate of a high degree can achieve the power to reincarnate consciously, that is, changing physical bodies while maintaining his individuality and a certain degree of memory. Gradually, in the course of successive lives, the initiate grows in spiritual power. His essence or divine spark grows successively more powerful.

In this way, the moment will come when the body of man, in the dimension and shape we are familiar with, is no longer capable of containing or supporting such a vast and powerful essence. For this reason, such a spirit or super-developed essence must seek an adequate physical body that corresponds to his tremendous energetic force. Thus he *reincarnates* in the body of a new or young planet, and continues his development there, in ways and conditions that are difficult for us to conceive. This is how an extraordinarily evolved human being took the body of the planet Earth and made it his own, in the most perfect shape in the Universe: the sphere.

This sphere is formed by the same basic materials as the human body, which are, in brief, the materials of the Universe. This sphere breathes, moves, thinks, and feels. It has a circulatory, digestive, procreative, and respiratory system. Petroleum is its blood, and it feeds on vegetable, animal, and mineral matter. Sexually, it is hermaphroditic, with a masculine and a feminine hemisphere. It breathes through plant life, and receives its etheric or magnetic nourishment through emitting and receiving antenna, that is, through *Homo sapiens.*

Once this clarification has been made, and in order to grasp the magnitude of the catastrophe accidentally brought about by Moses with the arrival of Y., we can reveal that this ancient, vengeful, and malicious being expelled the young spirit from the Earth, incarnating in his place. With this act, a dark and bloody era commenced for humanity. A period of suffering, torment, and pain started for the Jewish people as they were converted into the innocent victims of the negative forces of Y. This is the explanation for the great afflictions which the Jews have had to suffer.

Imagine Moses' despair when he realized the calamity which had occurred and the suffering created for those he had wanted to help. As time passed, Moses understood that nothing had power over Y., as he possessed incalculable malignity. Convinced of this, Moses brought together the wise men of his people and instructed them in the great mystery of the Messiah. These men, using magical rituals, could create a god and fulfill the mystery of theurgy, in the hope that this god could liberate them and save the world from the destructive influence of Y.

Once his instruction was given, Moses climbed Mount Nebo and was never seen alive again.

The wise men who inherited the patriarch's instructions followed them faithfully, carrying out the Messianic ritual according to the instituted rules. As a result, hundreds of years later, Jesus appeared. He was the "Son of Man" (consider this expression carefully) and the Savior expected by the wise men initiated by Moses.

This is how Jesus was born, under the circumstances that are familiar to all. Hermetic teaching maintains he was the son of a Jewish woman and a Roman father, his progenitor being a Roman soldier and merely an instrument of higher occult forces.

Why is it said that Mary remained a virgin? This mystery really does not refer to physiological virginity, but to the fact that actually there was no physical contact between Jesus' real father and Mary. In effect, his spiritual father was a great Hermetic initiate who etherically used the physical body of the Roman soldier to procreate a son. The spiritual seed was transmitted by the occult Master; the physical sperm by the Roman. In this manner, Mary conceived "without losing her virginity." In those times the term "virginity" was not used to designate maidenhood; it was used to distinguish those women initiated in the secret of the "virgule" as Mary was. The magic rod used by Moses was known as the "virgule."

Those who have "eyes to see and ears to hear" will understand this. For others, it will produce a dismal silence in their interior, and they will remain in the realm of ignorant sarcasm, suffering the mental emptiness of those who do not want to understand, or worse, the unconscious blindness of those who do not want to see.

Jesus, the god created by man and incarnated in the body of man, was consecrated by the great initiate John the Baptist, otherwise known as the *Antechrist*. Jesus' baptism in the river was the means that permitted the first manifestation of Christ in Jesus, the man-god, whose mission was destined since his birth.

From the time of Moses, the *Fraternity of Magicians* had been attentively observing these events without being able to alter them. The *magicians* were connoisseurs of the Messianic mystery and had the knowledge that certain wise men were working on this. They decided to help the wise men try to correct the serious anomalies explained before. They were awaiting Jesus' birth, and they were his occult godfathers who protected and educated him so he could fulfill his double mission.

His first mission was to liberate the *chosen people* from their occult killer. His second mission was to save the world in general from the invisible vampire who called himself Y. In order to begin a new era on Earth under the Christian motto "love one another," replacing the dictum of "an eye for an eye and a tooth for a tooth."

At the same time, Jesus was an active member of the *Fraternity of Magicians,* receiving support and inspiration from all of them. However, the great Masters maintain that Jesus failed in his mission, or more accurately, that he only achieved partial success, since he did not reach his goal. This refers only to Jesus, however, and not to Christ. In order to truly understand Jesus, it is necessary to consider his triple personality: 1. Jesus the man, 2. Jesus the God (created by man), and 3. Christ (who manifested himself through Jesus). Christ was an angel, a solar spirit who *descended from Heaven* to manifest himself as the supreme power of the *Father* on earth.

Jesus and his twelve disciples are the symbol of a solar and cosmic mystery. Hermetic science teaches that our solar system is composed of twelve planets plus the sun, an analogy for the twelve apostles and Christ, and that the unknown planets will be discovered in time.

We will speak no more of Jesus; we have perhaps already said too much. We will only add that the crucifixion was an expected drama in which Jesus' blood had to be shed so that Christ could in turn incarnate in the planet Earth and displace Y., definitively casting him out of our atmosphere. However, as we have already mentioned, this mission had only a relative success. Christ incarnated in the planet Earth, but Y. could not be expelled. Since then, both govern the planet.

Christ's force acts in the world through the representatives of the *Fraternity of Magicians.* These men direct Hermetic schools in which the student can develop his spiritual force to the point of disintegration of his animal soul and liberation from the influence of Y., who can only act through primitive and animal instincts such as hate, envy, lust, greed, pride, and vanity.

In this way, the Spiritual Beacon is kept alight to illuminate the select spirits who are potentially capable of converting themselves into fully developed human beings and abandoning their *sapiens* condition.

Every person who reaches this condition is converted into a center of Christic irradiation and is therefore another obstacle for Y.'s influence. The naive say that Christ will return to the planet Earth. But Christ is on Earth! He needs only to be removed from the cross by the same humanity who nailed him to it.

Until that time, wars will continue. Great numbers of people will die and their vitality will be absorbed by Y., the great occult force behind these conflicts. None of this will end until this being is conquered.

The real Antichrist is Y., and he has spread his negative influence throughout his followers, those of bestial instincts, who in turn have incorporated this vibration into the multitude. The multitude is composed of amorphous and blind entities, receptors of any force of sufficient power. In this way, Y.'s principles incorporated in the collective unconscious of humanity motivate the philosophy of "an eye for an eye, and a tooth for a tooth." Trapped by this malignant force, people live diabolically: hating, destroying, stealing, killing their brothers, returning evil with more evil, selling out their honesty and honor, enslaving the weak, exploiting the unprotected, and denigrating the just. Luckily, there are many who act contrary to all this. If this were not so, life would be unbearable. They are the ones who somehow have received a true Christian influence (not necessarily religious) and have higher values than usual.

Religions have a positive family and social influence, but unfortunately on solely spiritual grounds they do not have much to offer, and generally they try to check this deficiency with the indiscriminate use of the banner of Christ.

The *Fraternity of Magicians* does not derive its power from Christ, nor speak in his name. The Fraternity only exalts his values and shows or narrates events which the world should know, so that the *chosen* (the true humans) can reaffirm their conviction and loyalty to a superior spiritual life. The power of these *Magicians* comes from their harmony with, respect for, and obedience to cosmic laws, and the profound and serene spiritual condition they have reached. Their spirituality places them in a magical relationship with God, the *Great Universal Father,* who is recognized by the Hermeticists as the first cause of the origin of all and the great force of order and creation.

To speak about Christ is to explain the esoteric side of the psycho-social phenomenology of the world today. In its innocence, *sapiens* believes that everything in life is as it appears on the surface, and that things must surely be as the vast majority say they are. When some people hear of the esoteric side of events or the occult causes of different phenomena, they smile unbelievingly, arguing with infantile logic that "if that were true, it would be made known by the press" or, "it would have been taught at school or in the university" or, "well documented books would exist on the subject." That way of thinking nullifies all progress, because if everyone's belief was the same, no one would bother to study or investigate little-known phenomena.

Despite obstacles already mentioned, *sapiens* in his individual manifestation (not as a species) can have latent superior qualities and characteristics, which may lead him to partially understand Hermetic truths. Motivated by this knowledge, sapiens can awaken to a superior reality. The *sapiens* individual can save himself from the lethargic destiny of humanity and eventually reach the world of the Hermeticists, *magicians,* or *awakened men.*

Moses, a man of strength and wisdom, was driven by his yearning for freedom to commit an error of cosmic magnitude. According to the great Hermetic wise men, this error nearly destroyed the solar system. To clarify this statement, the solar system can be compared to the composition of an atom, borrowing on the Hermetic theme of "as above, so below." In this case, Y.'s rise to power could be seen as an arbitrary substitution of an electron, which changed the spiritual nucleus of the Earth.

This is one of the many lessons, which oblige the *Fraternity of Magicians* to strictly guard Hermetic secrets. The Fraternity will only give instruction in higher knowledge to those who have demonstrated their strength, their moral and spiritual purity, and the rectitude of their intentions. (John Baines, *The Stellar Man,* pp. 5-23)

In the context of earlier *Gnosis* chapters, the core of what John Baines says should make *profound* sense. His explanation closely parallels my conclusions, except my research has given me a different take on certain points.

The Ark of the Covenant was not just a religious ornament installed after the fact, but the very conduit through which Yahweh gained major influence in our world and further corrupted the timeline. Such powerful and chthonic a being cannot be created or invoked without the use of High Demiurgic Technology. Occult rituals and sacrificial slaughter alone are not enough, otherwise people like Aleister Crowley and Jack Parsons could have brought them in by the dozens. Thankfully they lacked the amplification technology to breach our reality's defenses to the extent that Moses did.

The Ark Stone being used by the Mosaic priesthood to invoke Yahweh was a blatant abuse of High Demiurgic Technology. It shifted history in favor of negative forces. As Baines said, "It is possible to see this as the most transcendental, but unfortunately harmful event in the occult history of humanity." The mindset of those who invoked this entity perfectly explains the angry, jealous, wrathful, commanding, and malefic nature of that entity. Recall that thoughtforms act in line with the emotional energies and conscious programming that went into them. The Mosaic ritual was performed during a time of great distress for the Egyptian Semites, who needed a liberator to smite their oppressors and lead them toward their homeland. The situation is similar to someone who makes a desperate pact with the dark side to exact vengeance, even if it means giving up freewill to the demons assisting him. Anyone familiar with demonology and black magic knows that demons operate through pacts or covenants. Such contracts are how the solicitor is bound and owned by the entity providing the service. Nothing is free when it comes to favors from the dark side.

Moses entering the Great Pyramid to retrieve the Ark Stone was accompanied by the Pyramid trembling, bellowing fiery smoke (or plasma), and generating an intensifying trumpet sound. This suggested the Pyramid was active at that time.* One of its functions may have been to charge, program, and initialize the Ark Stone according to the conscious intent of the operator. At least that's what it sounds like when the Bible states Moses stayed inside "Mount Sinai" for many days before emerging with the Stone. If he were only there to retrieve something, he would have emerged in hours. But the ritualistic creation or invocation of a powerful entitized thoughtform would take considerably longer. In other words, the Mosaic invocation ritual was technologically assisted black magic whose tragic consequences have cascaded into modern times.

Yahweh as Interloper

To recap the first chapter, once let loose, a thoughtform pursues its objective with single-minded determination. It exists solely to bend the timeline toward the fulfillment of the original intent. Astral archetypes at the beginning become physical manifestations at the end; that is simply a Demiurgic function. A thoughtform is the "Alpha and the Omega, beginning and end."

When thoughtforms become entitized, however, they acquire an ego. This can be a lower ego if generated from base emotions and ignoble intents, or higher ego if generated by spiritual emotions and divine will. In the case of Yahweh, much suggests it was lower ego. All the characteristics that we commonly assign to egotism are present in Yahweh: narcissism, anger, wrath, jealousy, control, insecurity, hunger,

---

* Exodus 19

bloodlust, intellectual abstraction, xenophobia, binary thinking, and intolerance. Even the seemingly redeeming qualities such as paternal concern are rooted in egotism, like how a mafia boss might act with charity toward others only to break their knees if they disobey. The *Ten Commandments* only apply to the Israelites amongst themselves, not between Israelites and outsiders, who were freely massacred. Yahweh's love is conditional and limited to the Israelites, the people bound to him via the Mosaic covenant.

An entitized thoughtform has a self-preservation instinct. If strong enough, this instinct overrides the original intent behind the thought-form's creation. The thoughtform can even use the original intent as a means to its own survival. In other words, if Yahweh was manifested to liberate the Israelites and bring them into political supremacy, self-preservation would mean they quickly become its tools, lured into serving the unchecked growth and power of that entity. They become hosts for a demonic parasite that exploits them toward its own ends, which is the way demonic pacts always turn out: first they serve you, then they own you.

We see this dynamic depicted in science fiction stories where artificially intelligent robots gain sentience, self-preservation instinct, and turn on their creators. The masters become the mastered. One doesn't have to be malicious to come under the control of malicious forces, just ignorant of the consequences. Therefore the followers of Yahweh may be pious, devout, and upstanding but still play into a negative agenda out of sheer naïveté. As always, "the road to hell is paved with good intentions."

The conspiracy is too big to invest itself in just one people. Therefore I don't adhere to anti-Semitic conspiracy theories that place all blame on Jews. Like other shapers of history — Merovingians, Anglo-Saxons, Greeks, Romans, Nazis, etc. — they are but tools in an agenda being run by *non-human* forces. If anything, Jews have been used as decoys to distract and provoke other manipulated people into furthering the Antichrist or alien agenda. In that case, they function like a matador's red cape directing a charging bull. The true enemy is of another world, another time, another dimension, and we would do well to keep our eyes on this root instead of blindly whacking at the branches. No single vector of manipulation should be criticized to the exclusion of all others. Rather, everyone deserves equal scrutiny because the true enemy works through everyone it can.

That said, the Corrupt Demiurge (a.k.a The Adversary) achieved significant advancements in ancient Egypt during the Hyksos and Amarna periods, which severely screwed up the timeline by introducing further imbalance in the state of things. It's an imbalance that wouldn't have come about had the Ark Stone never been misused.

Christ as Intervention

Otherworldly technology creating an otherworldly problem invites an otherworldly intervention. As explained earlier, the Logos is responsible for planning and upholding Creation. Part of that function includes correcting errors and imbalances. With the Corrupt Demiurge causing imbalance, it only makes sense that an equal and opposite force would be introduced by the Logos to help restore balance. A lower ego would have been countered by the intervention of a higher ego. If the Universal Lower Ego was personified in Yahweh, then the Universal Higher Ego was personified in Christ.

Baines relays that after regretting the invitation of Yahweh, the Mosaic priests set about creating a counter-deity. Historically, that was when Jews first acquired the notion of a Messiah who would come and save them. It took centuries for their created Messiah to incarnate in person and begin the work of undoing the damage. This involved the introduction of spiritual teachings that, like those of Buddha and the other great avatars, showed the way out beyond lower egotism. Egotism is what allows the Corrupt Demiurge to manipulate us.

If the Ark Stone was used to manifest Yahweh, could the Ark Stone have been used to manifest Christ? Indeed, and that's when it becomes the Grail Stone... again. Same object but different entitized thoughtforms manifesting through them. In the Ark Stone, it was the Universal Lower Ego, in the Grail the Universal Higher Ego. Both are entitized thoughtforms pulled deep into our world, our timeline, via technologically assisted ritual. Whether the Ark Stone created a new deity or opened the door to an existing one is a matter of perspective;

either way, it created a new manifestation, presence, or avenue for pre-existing ones.

The non-human, non-physical, divine Christ is an extension of the Logos. His assigned purpose is to restore imbalances and fallen conditions brought about by the corruption of the Demiurge. In other words, Christ is "tech support" for a reality gone awry. Like any entitized thoughtform, he pursues this objective with single-minded determination.

But as the story goes, the Jewish Pharisees rejected the teachings, the Romans and Greeks perverted the message, and the world remained in the grip of dark forces. John Baines and Rudolf Steiner explain how Christ's mission was a partial failure because it remained incomplete. Hence we have both Yahweh and Christ currents active in the world today, one representing the force of spiritual enslavement and deception, the other of spiritual liberation and awakening.

The legacy of Christ was largely absorbed and inverted toward the fulfillment of the Antichrist agenda. From this usurpation sprang organized Christianity as a political institution responsible for the murder and mental enslavement of countless millions. Whereas Christ was the fountainhead for a gnostic stream of wisdom, the Church suppressed and replaced this with a counterfeit that locked its followers into serving the Matrix Control System instead of becoming free from it.

Real and False Dichotomies

In reality, Yahweh and Christ stand in dualistic opposition, for they are opposite extrusions of the same Demiurge, one worldly and the other divine. One was called Kosmokrator by the Greeks, meaning dark World Ruler, and the other Pantokrator, the divine Universal Ruler. Modern Christianity fails to distinguish between these two. Fundamentalists who try to reconcile the wrathful, jealous, tribal side of this chimera with the universal, loving, and compassionate side suffer a dissociative psychological split. They pay lip service to the spiritual teachings of Christ while allowing ego to express the jealous and wrathful side of Yahweh.

The external duality between Yahweh and Christ is paralleled by our internal duality between lower and higher ego. When one equates these opposites and fails to see their differences, lower can imitate and displace the higher. The lower ego dressing in saintly clothing mirrors the Church portraying itself as divine appointees, which mirrors the Corrupt Demiurge masquerading as the Infinite Creator. It's elegant because the impostor usurps the throne and thereby prevents a return of the rightful king; when the lower has been mistaken for the higher, the return of the higher is rejected for being some kind of foreign intrusion. This is how the true Christ is kept out of Christianity, how intellectual arrogance leads to self-imprisonment through rejection of better ideas, and why the majority of humanity sees Matrix values as strength and spiritual values as weakness. There has been an inversion between reality and illusion, truth and lies.

For those who object to dualism, understand that there are real and false dichotomies. Even though a real one exists between the Logos and the Corrupt Demiurge, the latter employs its own set of false dichotomies. Obvious examples of false dichotomies can frustrate people into throwing away dualism altogether, but that blinds them to the real dualities. This mistake is common in the New Age field.

Both real and false dualities exist. Thus at the most basic level, we have a trinity instead of a duality: two false choices and a third transcending them. The transcendent choice is symbolized by Christ, the false ones by the Adversary. The latter uses false dichotomies because that is all it can create, and because it works so well on the human psyche.

Through false dichotomies, the Adversary offers seemingly "good" and "bad" choices that end up producing the same outcome. Hence these opposites are not freewill choices themselves. They are illusory traps that, together as one, represent the choice for illusion made as soon as one believes they are valid options.

Due to intellect being the seat of lower ego, intellect has a strong affinity and vulnerability to the Corrupt Demiurge. The first is just a microcosmic version of the latter; both are of the same essence and speak the same language. The human intellect has a terrible tendency for binary thinking that allows these false dichotomies to work so successfully. Binary thinking means reacting blindly and mechanically, instead of thinking intelligently and creatively toward paradigm-shifting conclusions. It means taking one of two false choices instead of the third transcendent one. It keeps people in opposite corners of the same box. Pretty much all human stupidity traces back to binary thinking. Even the sharpest intellectuals can suffer this flaw, because like the Corrupt Demiurge, the intellect is ungrounded in the greater Reality. It merely builds upon what it blindly accepts as given, like a wind-up robot marching methodically in whatever direction it's been placed.

It takes some connection to the greater Reality to transcend false opposites. One needs a connection to spirit via intuition and the higher intellect. But humans generally default to binary thinking, a flaw that may have been engineered into the human neural physiology by our Archontic alien progenitors who serve the Corrupt Demiurge. Through binary thinking, blind reactions to one deception become further deceptions, and reactions to those become yet more. To get out of this mess, *genuine dualities must be seen as separate and distinct, and false dualities as one and the same trap.* The inverse is what allows the Adversary's agenda to propagate.

The Unholy Trinity

Given the obvious problems with organized religion, some turn to satanism, science, or mysticism because these seem like better alternatives. But each can serve the Adversary all the same. Satanism puts the lower ego on a throne, same as organized religion; science is preoccupied with matter to the exclusion of spirit. And mysticism can inspire false illumination and spiritual imbalance.

These three false alternatives are not random errors, but reflections of the physical, etheric, and astral components of the debased Demiurgic system:

- The physical component is expressed through materialism, atheism, hedonism, transhumanism, socialism, and nihilism. This matter-centric force is at the root of the Demiurge's corruption. It ultimately leads to disintegration, entropy, and spiritual death because those are the properties of matter. Its personification was named *Yaldabaoth* by some Gnostics, meaning "Child of the Void." Rudolf Steiner called it *Sorat* and termed its demonic agents the *Asuras.* Their momentum is to extinguish consciousness, freewill, and spirit, and replace it with pure machine-like materialism. The impending alien deception and transhumanist agenda, with its goal of genetic and cybernetic assimilation of the human race, represents this impulse.

• The etheric component is expressed through organized religion, ritualism, intellectualism, satanism, conservatism, bureaucracy, corporatism, racism, ecclesiasticism, and theocracy. This follows from etheric energy's affinity for patterning and repetition. This component is associated with intellectual abstractions, formulas, preoccupation with laws, blind obedience within hierarchies, self-preservation, preservation of the past, plant-like expansionism, maintaining the status quo to the point of atrophy, and exploitation and discrimination against foreign patterns. The Gnostics called this force *Samael,* "God of the Blind"; Steiner termed it *Ahriman.* Yahweh of the Old Testament belongs to this category.

• The astral component is expressed in New Age Mysticism, Nazi occultism, black magic and voodoo, anarchism, Luciferianism, Christian Revivalism, and entheogenic escapism. This follows from the astral flitting about in delusional reveries when not held in check by spirit. What these expressions have in common is that they seek to rebel against current conditions and escape enthusiastically into another, being led astray in the process. It is the force of transcendence without restraint, like a rocket without a guidance system, bound for false destinations in the land of fools. For instance, this may entail escaping the *dead* world of matter or the *restrictive* world of ether, and getting lost in some metaphysical rapture. Or it may entail the opposite, falling from the divine realms into the world of matter out of misguided desires for physical existence. Gnostics called this force *Sakla,* the fool; Steiner called it *Lucifer,* in this case the bearer of false light.

These are the heads of the hydra, the triple aspects of the Matrix Control System, that bubble of illusion isolated from greater Creation. One devolves, one atrophies, and one leads astray. False dichotomies that afflict humanity are various permutations of this unholy trinity set in opposition against each other.*

The Holy Trinity

Countering these corrupting influences is the trinity of Creator, Logos, and Christ. In Christianity, these are known as the Father, Holy Spirit, and Son. The Holy Spirit, also termed Advocate or Paraclete, is called "Sophia" by some Gnostics who view her as the embodiment of wisdom and facilitator of awakening, but really she is just another personification of the Logos. As for the Mother archetype, curiously missing from the Trinity, remember that "mother" comes from Latin *mater,* root of "matter" and "matrix." The Mother is the all-encompassing matrix that allows for our existence.

When one is filled with the genuine Holy Spirit, and not its Luciferic counterfeit that only induces delusion, one is filled with the impulse of the Logos. This means one becomes Christ-like, in the sense of being repurposed toward the correction of the timeline. This infusion of Logoic energy activates the higher intellect and reorients the astral body to the divine impulse of spiritual love and the best of all possible futures. Through gnostic revelation, wisdom, and love, one becomes a willing agent of the Universal self-correction mechanism. That is the

---

*Followers of the Grail, gnostic, occultic, mystic, and pagan streams may see Judaism and/or Catholicism as wicked forms of spiritual oppression and deception. But in doing so, they may err on the side of Luciferianism, which emphasizes transcendence, willpower, and individualism to the point of imbalance and egotism. One example is Grail researcher Otto Rahn who ranted against the Catholic church and didn't have anything good to say about Judaism either. But through binary thinking, he found favor in the opposite fallacy of Luciferianism. As Steiner explained, the Luciferic and Ahrimanic forces have their positive qualities. Those qualities extracted and held in higher balance is what comprises the third Christ path. Binary thinking results in imbalance either way by taking one to the exclusion of the other, or worse, synthesizing the worst of all the forces, which is what our world is approaching via the Antichrist / alien deception.

true meaning of baptism, not the Ahrimanic ritual done in Churches, but the pouring of Logoic energy from above. In *Parzival,* the Grail could not be perceived without baptism.

The two trinities are represented by upright and inverted triangles. The central emblem of Israel, the Seal of Solomon / Star of David, depicts these forces locked in struggle.

Conclusion

Demiurgic technology acted as a powerful fulcrum throughout history, shifting the balance according to its use and misuse. Misuse drew negative forces deeper into our world, affording them stronger deviations of the timeline. In turn, this error called for equal and opposite intervention by positive forces. The conflict between positive and negative manifests at all levels. It is part of a cosmic battle being waged within us, outside us, across space, across dimensions, and across time.

6 NORDIC ALIENS AND THE GRAIL RACE

Who forged the Grail? Who brought it to Earth? What is their role today? Mythology, folklore, history, religion, esotericism, occultism, and alienology all contain clues declaring the existence of superhuman beings who seem deeply invested in our affairs but prefer to remain hidden. Those among them with the most consistent historical presence are human in appearance, yet far beyond human in their knowledge and abilities.

Regardless of what human groups came into possession of demiurgic technology before and after the Israelites, none of them truly owned it. Instead, the supernatural artifacts were ultimately borrowed, licensed, or stolen from the so-called "gods" who originally manufactured them. It seems these "gods" bestow and retrieve such artifacts according to circumstance, finding it necessary to entrust them to chosen human proxies at certain times. In doing so, they risk such power occasionally falling into wrong hands. The rebel priesthood fleeing Egypt with the Ark Stone is one example.

Mankind is unwittingly caught in a war between hidden superhuman factions who select, train, and equip their human agents to participate in that war. Demiurgic technology enables major shifts in the balance between their competing agendas.

In this chapter and the next, I will speculate on the nature, origins, and motivations of these superhuman beings and their human proxies who, in modern times, surreptitiously coexist alongside humanity as a hidden parallel civilization. This will widen our perspective for understanding current and future world events.

The Grail Company

In *Parzival,* Wolfram von Eschenbach describes the "Grail Company" as a preternatural outfit of divinely appointed individuals who exist beyond our world but have a very close relationship with it:

> As to those who are appointed to the Grail, hear how they are made known. Under the top edge of the Stone an inscription announces the name and lineage of the one summoned to make the glad journey. Whether it concerns girls or boys, there is no need to erase their names, for as soon as a name has been read it vanishes from sight! Those who are now full-grown all came here as children. Happy the mother of any child destined to serve there! Rich and poor alike rejoice if a child of theirs is summoned and they are bidden to send it to that Company! Such children are fetched from many countries and forever after are immune from the shame of sin and have a rich reward in Heaven. When they die here in this world, Paradise is theirs in the next.

> God ordained concerning the Grail that it should be kept by virgins ministering before it. The Grail chooses lofty servitors, thus knights are appointed to guard it endowed with all the virtues that go with chastity.

> [...] Fortune often faces those of Munsalvaesche [the Grail castle] with win-and-lose. They receive handsome children of high degree:

but if a land should lose its lord, and its people see the hand of God in it and ask for a new lord from the Grail Company, their prayer is granted. Moreover, they must treat him reverentially, since from that moment on he is under the protection of God's blessing. God sends the men out in secret but bestows maidens openly.

[...] Writing was seen on the Grail to the effect that any Templar whom God should bestow on a distant people for their lord must forbid them to ask his name or lineage, but must help them gain their rights. When such a question is put to him the people there cannot keep him any longer.

[...] As I say, maidens are given away from the Grail openly, men in secret, in order to have progeny (as God can well instruct them), in the hope that these children will return to serve the Grail and swell the ranks of its Company. Those knights who are resolved on serving the Grail must forego woman's love. Only the King may have a spouse in wedlock, and those others whom God has sent to be lords in lordless lands. (Hatto, p. 251)

Does Wolfram's version of the Grail Company have any real analogs? Some say it's an allusion to the Templar Knights or the Cathars, but these were only human attempts at emulating the real thing. Regular secret societies and religious orders don't fit the description because they lack the supernatural qualities, distinguished genetics, and the curious need to draw upon the human gene pool through interbreeding. The ascribed traits of the Grail Company indicate a transcendent elite who are nonetheless somehow dependent on mankind. If nothing else, this description matches the modern alien phenomenon. Extracting the key elements from the above passage:

- Their men are sent into our world to take up leadership positions without revealing their true identities. The implication is that our world is being directly influenced by superhuman males pretending to be ordinary humans.

- Their women may enter our world for sexual procreation. They do this without disguising their identity. In other words, human males are used for breeding purposes by superhuman females who make no secret of their otherworldly nature.

- Their children are of superhuman pedigree, seeded into human society until they are called to return to the realm of their progenitors.

Framed in this way, all three elements are found in modern alienology, specifically regarding the alien types who look human. From ancient to modern times, accounts exist of human encounters with such beings, their disguise as humans placed in influential roles, and their seeding of hybrids into human families.

That is not to say all are necessarily divine Grail guardians. The latter may only be a small faction among them who ultimately serve the Logos. Those same general traits could equally apply to humanlike alien groups bent on malevolent domination. All that's indicated is an otherworldly elite who, despite being more advanced, are dependent on us and/or heavily invested in our affairs.

For this chapter, I will focus on aliens who could pass for human, have supernatural abilities, and have shaped the course of history. They are the best candidates for the otherworldly forces involved in the demiurgic tug of war. Why is this important? Because the competing alien forces from our ancient past are still with us today, actively influencing the world. Those who were there for the beginning may be there for the end. It appears their cold war has been underway for several thousand years, and based on current trends it could become an open hot war in our near future. Therefore the study of these alien groups, how they relate to the human race, their role in history and our future provides the deeper context needed to fully appreciate everything discussed so far in *Gnosis*.

Provisional Summary

Based on my research, correspondences, and personal experiences, I have come to several conclusions concerning them:

- There is warring among these beings, indicating they are not all unified. At the very minimum, they are polarized into opposing sides, if not split into numerous independent factions. Some factions have a strong fascist orientation.

- They walk among us pretending to be human. Some are integrated into society and hold strategic positions, whether to influence or simply observe.

- They are genetically compatible with us, and some of their females have engaged human males for sexual encounters and even long-term relationships. Through interbreeding, their genes can enter our gene pool and vice versa. Therefore some human individuals and bloodlines would have more of their DNA than others, and their alien DNA would likely show under analysis to be basically human, albeit rare and unusual.

- Through genetic manipulation, they can insert alien DNA as a third-party contributor to a developing human fetus, so that the child resembles both human parents while also being somewhat hybridized. Whether artificially hybridized, naturally conceived between human and alien, or fully alien, such a child born and raised in a human family will mostly pass for human, except they will be of a caliber beyond their peers. The greatest heroes of myth and ancient history were popularly viewed as cross-breeds between gods and men.

- Throughout history, they have selected certain humans, or perhaps their own offspring/hybrids raised in human society, for privileged education, training, and guidance, so that these human proxies can function as vectors for their agenda, be it benevolent or hostile to mankind at large. This may include modern-day contactees and abductees, ancient prophets and magicians, and the founders of mystery schools and secret societies like the Rosicrucians. Note that such secret societies are just larger, more powerful, institutionalized versions of individual contactees, that is, they are both under the guidance of aliens, given privileged knowledge, and charged with a mission fitting the agenda of their alien benefactors.

- Considering that some of the esoteric knowledge communicated to humans is positively helpful, not all alien influences are selfish. It seems some are genuinely interested in raising humanity's potential in the areas of discernment, chivalry, ethics, and spiritual integrity.

- They are all secretive and known to lie, even if only by omission, regardless of their spiritual orientation. Benevolent reasons could involve a law of non-interference, complications with timeline dynamics arising from unscrupulous contamination of the past, the need to ensure that privileged and powerful knowledge is entrusted only to vetted parties who will use it responsibly, or self-protection to avoid discovery and persecution. Malevolent reasons could include the hiding of hostile agendas and hoarding of knowledge for leveraging purposes.

- They are extremely telepathic. They can read thoughts with minute precision, implant thoughts, scan the soul for its level of integrity or weakness, induce hallucinations, manipulate emotions, and steer a person's dreams. The human proxies they train can achieve these skills at a lower power level.

- They use technology to augment their innate superhuman abilities. This technology is demiurgic, can control time and gravity, affords them invisibility and antigravity, and allows them to walk through solid objects, meaning they can inhabit solid mountains in a dimensionally shifted condition, for instance.

- Their native environment is dimensionally shifted beyond ours, i.e., we cannot find their bases through mere physical searching. Like the Grail castle, which appears only to the chosen, their abode only becomes visible and accessible to us at their choosing. For example, a contactee may be psychically modified to perceive it, or dimensionally shifted to enter it.

- Like an angel losing its wings, under certain conditions they can lose their abilities and become "mortal" without the ability to return to their superhuman state, at least not within this lifetime. They get stuck here. If an entire group of theirs undergoes such a fall, they would enter into human history as an already developed and highly advanced culture that gradually undergoes decline upon becoming naturalized members of a primitive planet.

- The members of their civilization are not all homogeneous in standing or understanding. Composition ranges from a two-tier system of "lower retarded ones" and "higher advanced ones" to caste-like systems with many tiers similar to the Indian caste system.

- The retarded members of their kind are the ones who interact with the most advanced of humans. Why? Maybe because of their evolutionary closeness, and also because such an interaction could be mutually beneficial. Despite their seemingly superhuman qualities, those aliens who interact most with select humans may surprisingly just be the most flawed of their race.

- The apex of their leadership extends beyond the physical and semi-physical, into the domain of divine and demonic forces. In the case of positive alien groups and their angelic or spiritual superiors, the relation may not be so much of commanding and obedience, but oracular guidance and respect. The ancient human practice of consulting the oracles, consulting the gods, etc. may be a lower echoing of this relationship.

- The lower of their kind seem more physical, technological, and tactical while the higher tiers seem more esoteric, astral, and judiciary. The problem, however, is that their most flawed ones are not only the creators and users of demiurgic technology, but they are also most involved in human affairs. This means we suffer their errors, which are graver in consequence than any mistake we could commit, just as our errors are more severe than those possible by animals.

- The consequences of these errors and grave transgressions have cascaded back and forth throughout the timeline. They are now converging toward a nexus point representing the potential for a cataclysmic shift. Alien factions who were responsible for initiating these consequences are likely the same ones who are now involved in the final outcome. A thread of continuity exists between the most ancient and modern human-alien encounters. The alien disinformation campaign is an effort by one set of such factions to prepare mankind for enthusiastic acceptance of their overt control.

Since it would take a whole book to lay out the supporting research, here I will select excerpts from a few key sources to show that the superhuman presence is ubiquitous and hidden in plain sight.

Tony Dodd

First consider the Project Camelot interview[*] with Tony Dodd, a "highly respected British UFO investigator who died [in early 2009] of a brain tumor. He had always suspected that his illness was engineered and was directly related to his work." In his own words:

> I'm now much closer to the complexities involved in the UFO field and the government involvement. There's certainly a serious threat by some visiting UFOs and further problems caused by alien visitors who are integrated into our society, possibly holding high positions in government. These aliens – who look like us – are here for unknown reasons and this is causing many problems for those trying to find them.
>
> There's very little doubt they've been here for many years and they have occasionally had meetings with certain very high ranking people. One very high ranking military officer wrote about one such meeting. These meetings are far and few between and the individual is chosen by the alien for such meetings which take place under extreme secrecy.
>
> These aliens operate above normal government knowledge and they are pursued by highly trained hunter killers of several nationalities who operate to eliminate them. Normal people getting close to the truth of what is happening are getting into very dangerous areas and will quickly have a fatal accident. They will not permit anybody to rock the boat. I was warned I would be killed because of some of my work.
>
> The aliens are highly intelligent and have possibly obtained positions at a very high level and this is of great concern to senior authorities. My information is that the only way they can be recognized is by a deformed finger on one of their hands. To hide this they usually wear gloves or a bandage on the finger as if they have had an injury.

---

[*] <projectcamelot.org/john_robie.html>

The fact that they look like us and mingle amongst us secretly begs the questions: Why are they here and what are their intentions? Why are they so secretive? There are people in very high places who consider them a threat and have squads out looking for them with intent to kill. This is no doubt why they stay secret. The truth is that we fear what we don't understand.

It's not known what their true form is. The deformed finger strongly suggests that do not look like us in their true form. Either way they're obviously highly intelligent and far ahead of us technically. It is not known their planet of origin... or if they are time travelers, they've never disclosed this as far as we know.

Are there any well-known public figures, anywhere in the world, who you suspect or are suspected to be non-human?

I don't know. If it became known that there was one such person, he would certainly disappear in very quick time. The authorities would immediately subject him to interrogation in an effort to find out how many of them were here and what their intentions were. This is why they remain secret. But once again, we must question what they're here for and what their intentions are. Always remember: throughout the course of history, a more advanced race has always enslaved a lesser advanced race. This is what worries the authorities.

While the detail about the deformed finger seems dubious, here is a veteran UFO researcher investigating and speaking about human-like aliens in our power structure, and dying soon afterward.

Mac Tonnies

Later that same year, Fortean philosopher Mac Tonnies died in his sleep at age 34, only a few weeks before he was to submit the final manuscript for his book *The Cryptoterrestrials: A Meditation on Indigenous Humanoids and the Aliens Among Us,* which was posthumously published in 2010. Excerpts from the book:

> I propose that at least some of the accounts of alien visitation can be attributed to a humanoid species indigenous to Earth, a sister race that has adapted to our numerical superiority by developing a surprisingly robust technology. The explicitly reproductive overtones that color many encounters suggests that these "indigenous aliens"

are imperiled by a malady that has gone uncured throughout the eons we have coexisted. Driven by a puzzling mixture of hubris and existential desperation, they seek to perpetuate themselves by infusing their gene-pool with human DNA. While existing at the very margins of ordinary human perception, they have succeeded in realms practically unexplored by known terrestrial science, reinventing themselves at will and helping to orchestrate a misinformation campaign of awe-inspiring scope.

We typically assume interdimensional travel must involve arcane cosmological machinery such as a wormhole or "stargate." But I became increasingly drawn to the idea that our visitors' method of travel is less flashy (from a technical perspective) and more understandable in terms of earthly — if bizarre — paranormal influences.

This led to my growing suspicion that the "aliens" typically attributed to extrasolar planets are less advanced than they lead us to believe. In fact, I think a case can be made that we're dealing with a surprisingly vulnerable intelligence that relies largely on subterfuge and disinformation to achieve its goals, a theme I attempt to address in later chapters.

And as outlandish as it may seem, I've been forced to wrestle with the notion that our relationship with these "others" is far more widespread and intimate than even paranoid dramatizations of the UFO spectacle would have us believe.

These dawning suspicions are borne out, at least in part, by world folklore (with its preoccupation with "little people" in our midst) as well as by recent discoveries that suggest the history of our species is more enigmatic than we'd like to admit. We may well share our planet with cryptohominids that have mastered the art of camouflage in order to coexist with us. More portentously, their agenda might be within our ability to grasp. But to do so, we must suspend the assumption that we're dealing with something as quaint as ET astronauts.

Given reports of humanoid beings "materializing" and "disappearing," it's tempting to speculate that our visitors have mastered a technology of consciousness, able to manipulate their own wave functions and skip back and forth between multiple universes at the speed of thought. This is one (admittedly colorful) explanation for the lack of physical evidence; "they" might lurk in "hyperspace" as well as familiar, 3-D space-time. Moreover, this form of travel might be accomplished without the need for energy-intensive machinery; if shamanic experiences are any indication, the ability to transcend space and time might be a more fitting subject for parapsychologists than theoretical physicists. [...]

Also intriguing are accounts of "tulpas," which are either objects or human-like entities crafted by pure thought, according to certain esoteric Buddhist beliefs. Capable of carrying out tasks on behalf of their creators, tulpas aren't unlike the maddeningly transient "occupants" seen in or around "spacecraft" (sometimes digging for soil specimens in an almost parodic reenactment of the Apollo Moon landings).

While a more conventional flesh-and-blood explanation remains my central proposal, we would be timid to avoid addressing the UFO phenomenon's parapsychological aspects. I find it likely that an indigenous population of "aliens" would have experimented along "occult" lines out of sheer need for secrecy; a "nuts and bolts" technology can go a long way toward ensuring anonymity in the face of an intrusive human civilization, but the ability to directly influence the fabric of Mind itself would be even more effective and perhaps less resource-intensive.

Like John Keel and Jacques Vallée, Mac Tonnies saw the idea of aliens being curious visitors from the stars as deliberate subterfuge. These authors explain why aliens have fronted lies about their true nature and origins. My book *Discerning Alien Disinformation* also addresses that issue. But does the bogusness of the Extraterrestrial Hypothesis mean they are instead native to Earth? Well, the line between indigenous and extraterrestrial beings gets blurred when the latter have existed on Earth for longer than we have, even if they once originated from elsewhere in space and time. Maybe the deception isn't so much about whether they are extraterrestrial, but about the extent of their entrenchment in our activities, that far from being merely "visited," humanity has been influenced by alien intelligences since the very beginning. By portraying themselves as recent visitors, the depth and scope of their manipulation remain hidden.

Contrary to what Tonnies suspects, their technology is more advanced than they are letting on. Aliens seem to hide their secret science behind a veil of plausibility made of more primitive but trendy concepts and imagery borrowed from human culture. In truth, not only are aliens telepathic and able to induce hallucinatory camouflage, but they have the technology to parallel their psychic prowess. This demiurgic technology operates via metaphysical laws as much as physical ones and seems paranormal only because it extends beyond human materialistic science into the realm of the occult, the latter simply being a science that makes use of etheric, astral, and conscious energies and principles.

If the "cryptohominids" seem closer to fairies and elves who use magick instead of aliens who use science, it's because demiurgic technology appears like magick to those who don't understand it, and superhumans seem like supernatural spirits to those who assume aliens are as deeply mired in three-dimensional physicality as we are. We should avoid the mistake made by proponents of the Extraterrestrial Hypothesis (ETH) and Ultraterrestrial Hypothesis (UTH) and not fall into the false dichotomy of physical versus nonphysical, because the solution to the riddle is that these beings live an amphibious existence between these extremes.

Jordan Maxwell

Jordan Maxwell is another researcher familiar with the phenomenon of human-like aliens living among us, having experienced it firsthand. Here is his account from a Project Camelot interview:

> But when I was 19, I ended up in Los Angeles – at 19 years old with seven bucks in my pocket, incidentally. I had no idea where I was going, where I was. I ended up in Los Angeles on a Friday night with seven dollars in my pocket. You know, I was a stupid kid, but I lived through it.
>
> Later on, a couple months later, after I got a job and things were working out for me, I was in North Hollywood one morning, on a weekend morning, and I went into a restaurant. The place was crowded and there was only one seat available and that was at the counter, so I sat at the counter. There was a young girl sitting next to me, so we started talking.

Come to find out she only lived about two blocks from me and I only lived about two blocks from town, so she had walked downtown and I had also. So we started hanging out together. I'd meet her downtown; we'd hang out together. This was back in '59 and I was 19 years old.

When we would walk home, I lived two blocks closer, so she had two blocks farther to go, so I never knew exactly where she lived, but she knew where I lived. One night she came over to my place and said: My dad wants to see you. He wants to talk to you.

And of course that put me on alert. I SAID: I don't want to talk to your dad.

SHE SAID: No, my father is a very important and interesting man. He wants to talk to you. He's got something to tell you.

That sounded interesting, so I went with her, and when we walked up to the house which was only a couple of blocks away, we walked up to the house, just by chance, he happened to be coming out of the house.

The moment I saw him, an incredible feeling came over me of some kind of a euphoric, strange [and] wonderful feeling that I got, being in his presence. It was as if I were in the presence of a great prophet or some spiritual man. I felt it, and I loved the feeling. I mean, I can't describe it, but I loved the feeling. It was an other-world feeling. I noticed that he was very much in control of himself; he knew exactly what he was doing.

He motioned for us to come in. We went in and the girls sat on the floor by the fireplace. They sat on the floor. He sat on one end of the sofa, I sat on the other end of the sofa. The wife was in the kitchen. I never did see her that whole night.

So we were talking and he was, you know, he was asking me how I liked living in California, and do you have a job and how do you like your job, and just small talk. And I was beginning to feel a little of the apprehension was going away. I was beginning to feel a little bit better being in his company, but I knew there was something about this guy that wasn't right, but I loved the feeling.

I'm 19 years old, so I'm not sure what I'm doing, but I'm just talking to this guy who's dazzling me with his presence of mind and the presence he presented.

And so we're talking about all kinds of things and then, when he felt that I was sufficiently at ease, he said to me very nonchalantly, he said: Remember when you were eight years old back in Florida and your father built the new back porch and your uncle helped him? And remember, your dad used green lumber that smelled funny? And he built the new back porch? You remember that?

Tears started to come to my eyes, and I didn't want to show tears in front of my girlfriend, but he was scaring me because he was right and he knew it.

AND HE SAID TO ME: Well, did that happen or didn't it?

I SAID: Yes, that happened.

AND HE SAID: Also, one night when you were in bed, you got out of bed and you went out on the back porch and you were looking at the Moon and the Moon was full. Do you remember that?

AND I SAID: Yes, I remember that.

AND HE SAID: And you were picking the wood because it smelled funny. It was green lumber; it smelled funny, and you were picking it with your finger. Remember how you picked a piece of it, and you were smelling it and tasting it? AND HE SAID: Remember doing that?

AND NOW I'M REALLY SCARED BECAUSE IT'S FRIGHTENING TO ME AND I SAID: Yes.

HE SAID: Well, did you do that, or didn't you?

I SAID: Yes, I did.

AND HE SAID: Well, how would I know that? How would I know what you did?

AND I SAID: I don't know how you'd know.

HE SAID: I know because we were there. You just didn't see us, but we were there watching you.

AND I THOUGHT: Well... [laughs]

AND HE SAID, BECAUSE HE COULD TELL I WAS NOT BUYING IT: Was I correct in what I said?

Yeah.

HE SAID: Well, how would I know if I wasn't there? We were there.

I SAID: Who was we?

HE SAID: That's not important right now. What's important for you to know is that you're in California, because we brought you here. We brought you here to Los Angeles.

I SAID: You brought me here?

HE SAID: Yeah. Why are you here?

I SAID: I don't know why I'm here. I just had to come to Los Angeles.

HE SAID: That's right. We brought you here, he said, because what did you say to God? You talked to God that night. The night you sat on the porch, you said something to God. What did you say?

I just sat looking at him.

HE SAID: I'll tell you what you said. You asked God to let you do something important with your life. You wanted to do something of value and importance with your life.

And I was about eight or nine years old, right?

I SAID: Yes, that's what I said.

HE SAID: Well, then we're going to give you an opportunity to do something with your life now because you did ask.

I'm still amazed, listening to him.

AND HE SAID: What we have for you to do will not happen until the later part of your life, and I'm not going to go into it right now.

HE SAID: I'm not going to go into explaining it to you now; however, when the time comes for you to do what we have brought you here to do — you will know what you have to do. By that time, you will be sufficiently knowledgeable on who you are and what you're doing and where you're going.

AND HE SAID: All you need to know now is that we brought you here and that we will protect you wherever it is that we put you.

AND I ASKED HIM, I SAID: I still don't understand what you're saying.

HE SAID: You don't need to, but one day, you will understand.

AND HE SAID: So I'm here to start you on your journey.

HE SAID: I have a book I'm going to give you and I want you to read the book and that will begin your journey.

And he pulls it off the shelf and gives it to me, and today you can still get that book in bookstores anywhere. It's called The Complete Works of Charles Fort. [spells name].

Even in England there's a Fortean Society dedicated to the work of Charles Fort. A fascinating book. It's a monumental work, very thick book: The Complete Works of Charles Fort.

And he opened the book indiscriminately, just put his hand on the pages, because it's a very thick book, and he opens a page and he reads a paragraph. He just opened the page and reads a paragraph – he knew exactly what he was doing, precisely what he was doing. I didn't know because it looked like he just indiscriminately opened it, and he read a paragraph that just blew me away. I was knocked out by what he'd just read. AND I THOUGHT: Wow! That's interesting.

AND HE SAID: Oh yeah, the book is filled with that kind of thing. Let me read you another one.

He opened it up again and just indiscriminately read something. Not indiscriminately! He knew what he was doing. I'm sure that he knew how to get your particular attention. What would be very interesting to you, I may not even see. But he knew how to play on my emotions, and he read about three little paragraphs, one after the other, and each one – to me – was absolutely mind-blowing.

I was fascinated with him, with my new girlfriend, [laughs] and with this book. AND THEN HE SAID TO ME: You've always been interested in UFOs and other-worldly things, right?

AND I SAID: Yes, I have.

HE SAID: Would you like to see some UFOs up close tonight?

AND I SAID: I'd love to.

HE SAID: Well come on. I can do that for you.

So I got up with him, and the two girls – my girlfriend and her sister – the four of us came out in the yard. It was about maybe midnight in North Hollywood, 1959, and he looks up into the sky and starts inaudibly talking. His mouth is moving as if he's talking to somebody, but you can't hear him.

And as I'm watching him standing there talking to the stars, I look over at my girlfriend and she's looking at me. AND THE LOOK ON HER FACE WAS LIKE: Yeah, this is my father, that's him. Told you he was strange, didn't I? [laughs] And that kind of thing.

And her sister was looking at me, and I could tell what she was doing. SHE WAS TRYING TO FIGURE OUT: How is he taking this? You know, what's going on in my mind? [was] what the little one was thinking, because she's seen this before. She wants to see how I'm going to react to this.

AND SO THEN HE LOOKS AT ME AND HE SAID: They said that they will be coming from Griffith Park in just a minute. There'll be three of them and they'll be coming from the Griffith Park area. They're going north and they said that they'll be here in a minute for you.

AND I SAID: Who's they?

HE SAID: You'll see.

Within a couple of minutes, three beautiful disk-shaped things, glowing, very faintly glowing, came over with no sound whatsoever, in a triangle formation, came over and stopped right above our heads and stopped.

And when they did, you could see they were disk-shaped and it looked and appeared like it was a pie cut in six or eight slices, and each slice was a different color. What I remember distinctly is each color was like a laser color: vibrant orange, vibrant pink, very vibrant colors, six or eight colors on each one – and they were circulating, not so fast as to blend the color, but circulating. They were beautiful. They were about the size that the full Moon appears, so they're not little lights. Full-Moon size. Three.

And I'm standing there looking at these gorgeous, beautiful, vibrant-color things spinning, and colors, and no sound, and I was absolutely mesmerized. I was just... I was enthralled by seeing this gorgeous, beautiful display.

AND I LOOKED AT HIM AND HE'S LOOKING AT ME AND HE SAYS: They're pretty, aren't they?

AND I SAID: Yes. They're beautiful.

AND THEN HE LOOKS UP AND TALKS TO THEM. HE SAID: They've told me to tell you that they're going now but they'll see you later. And they did. They started moving and they went out north.

AFTERWARDS, WE WENT BACK IN AND I SAID: What did I just see tonight?

HE SAID: That was us. We've been here for a long time, you just didn't know it. HE SAID: We picked you a long time ago when you were a small child. We have something for you to do.

AND I SAID: I'm not understanding exactly.

HE SAID: You don't have to. We will let you know what it is you're supposed to do later on in life, but just go on with your life, don't worry about it. Whatever you're supposed to learn, we'll see to it that you learn, and when it is time for you do what we have for you to do, you'll know. We'll let you know.

After that, I would go over there on the weekends to visit him and the mother and the two girls, and we would go out to the desert sometimes, go way out in the desert. The girls, with their mother, would go for a walk, and he and I would walk in the desert, and he would tell me about all the different alien lifeforms that are out there, where they have come from, the ones that are here.

AND HE TOLD ME: You have enemies here. You have some very powerful enemies here from other places that have come, and they know who you are, and they know what you're going to do. So just be careful in your life, but we'll protect you.

I didn't know what he was talking about.

And then one day I went over to the house one morning, and the house was totally open, and they're gone. Everything was packed and gone and the girl never told me she was leaving. They'd never come to tell me anything. They were just gone.

Now that I look back on that experience, I feel very secure in saying that he knew what he was doing. HE SAID: I'm starting you on your journey, and he did. But after that was done, then he moves on.[*]

In this example, Maxwell finds himself in an arranged meeting with a mysterious person who, in response to Maxwell's earnest request made earlier in life to be made useful, starts him on a path of independent research. The final result is that through writing and speaking widely about his discoveries, Maxwell has gone lengths toward exposing the negative alien agenda.

What does Maxwell think is their ultimate goal? To enslave mankind through hybridization, through genetic assimilation and crippling. This is basically what I concluded in *Discerning Alien Disinformation,* though I disagree with Maxwell's pessimistic view that we can do nothing but accept our doom with solemn awareness. If all hope were lost, there wouldn't still be attempts by certain benevolent alien forces to interfere with the negative alien agenda by seeding awareness and secretly training their ground contacts to perform strategic duties during a future breakdown situation. Evidently they believe the future is still open, otherwise they wouldn't be investing their energies.

---

[*] <projectcamelot.org/lang/en/jordan_maxwell_interview_en.html>

Anonymous Gulf Breeze Contactee

More information on subversive humanoid alien groups comes from an anonymous account titled, *UFOs in the Gulf Breeze-Pensacola Area: Contact Since 1955:*

> The first recall starts in early 1955, late February or early March. It is still cold in the Connecticut town where I was approaching my third birthday.
>
> I am sitting on the edge of the bed. There was a pulsating green glow coming in through the window of my bedroom. Everything was silent. I mean completely silent.
>
> I hear footsteps up the back steps and the back door open. I wasn't frightened. In fact, I was very calm, almost detached.
>
> The footsteps approach my room and the door opens. Enter a blond haired man and woman. They are wearing a one piece suit that reminds me of my pajamas with the feet built into them. The color is a dull silver. To my child mind, I think they are pajamas. They look about the size of my parents. The woman is somewhat smaller than the man.
>
> They are standing there looking at me and I am sitting on the bed looking at them. They approached no closer than 3 feet. When they first come in they said, "Hello," and they knew my name. They were talking like the New England people with the accent. That is what I was used to hearing.
>
> I don't know these people but they seem to know me. I asked them, "Who are you?" And the man says, "We are your friends." I tell them I don't know them. And the woman says, "You don't remember us, but one day you will." It seems that the woman did most of the speaking.
>
> The following is quoted from the hypnosis session transcript:
>
> The woman says that they have come to visit and they will visit from time to time to help me learn big things. It seems that they are talking in words that are understandable to my three year old consciousness. So they are being fairly basic. They say that they are here now because I have reached the triad age, that the age of three

is significant for our type and that multiples of three have significant meaning. They're not saying significant, they are saying, holding up three fingers and saying that, "This many is important." That it's an important number to remember.

I asked, "Why?" They say they can't tell me yet but that they are my friends and that we have been friends for a long time. They say that it is time for them to leave, that they wanted to visit and say, "Hello," and it is time for me to go back to sleep. They tell me not to look at the light outside.

So I lay back down and cover up. And, the man leading the way, they turn around and open the door and walk out, closing the door behind them. I hear them walk out the back door.

I don't go to sleep immediately. I hear kind of a hum and a bright green light momentarily shines through the window. Then it stops and it is dark again except for a dim streetlight. I got sleepy and went to sleep. [...]

By this time, it was late 1956 or early 1957. It was cold outside.

I received the beep signal and my consciousness activated. I dressed myself in blue jeans, long sleeve shirt, and my Buster Brown shoes. I went out the back and down the alley as the house had no backyard, it had a side yard. In the side yard was a ship sitting on three pads. It was pulsating orange. The man and woman were there standing out away from the ship with a ramp descending to the ground. There was a whitish-yellow light coming out of the doorway or opening at the top of the ramp.

The man and woman were waving to me. I walked up to them and recognized them. They said, "Hi, Hello." I said, "Hello."

They indicated that they wanted to take me somewhere. I asked where and they said that they wanted me to meet some people. This seemed all right with me; it didn't seem out of the ordinary. We walked over to the saucer, walked up the ramp and entered. The ramp then retracted and then blended with the side of the ship.

There were four aliens in the ship. Two women pilots, the man and the woman. They were all dressed in one piece gray suits with integrated boots. [...]

The extra-terrestrial craft was flying over an area that reminds me of the Smoky Mountains today. Soon the craft was flying over a big V type valley. One giant hill on one side and one giant steep hill on the other side. From the air, it looked like it went down into a big V.

Then the ship stopped in midair. In the console viewer was a 90 degree rock cliff. One of the ship's operators sent some sort of signal; they pushed a sequence of buttons. In the upper left hand screen of the console monitor, a window popped up. Then, on the side of the steep, rocky cliff, a black hole appeared.

It didn't look like a hole to me on the monitor, rather it looked like a large black spot. Before the signal was sent, there was terrain. From the air, this black spot looked oval with the elongated part of the oval being towards the top of the hill.

The ship started descending and they turned the floor view off. But I could see on the console monitor that they lined up with this black spot and traveled into it. What a surprise! [...]

This black spot was the strangest thing I have ever seen. Even with current day recall, I have never seen anything like it. The only way I can describe it is like jet black light. If you take a spotlight and shine it on a surface, you have a white beam with a white spot; make that a black beam with a black spot and it describes what it looked like. It is hard to describe but what it was and what it led to was even more difficult to explain.

This black beam created an opening through solid rock! It was of tremendous size because the 25' diameter ship was dwarfed by the opening. I watched the flat panel console monitor, obviously not an invention in 1956, as the ship entered the black spot. It was dark briefly like going through ink. Then from the center of the monitor out, an image reemerged opening out until there was a panoramic view.

What a view. We were inside a huge, and I mean HUGE, circular room with flying saucers of every size and configuration parked in various places. There were ships much larger than the one we were in and there were some smaller ones as well. The only analogy I can draw is an airport, or I guess you would call it a spaceport.

The room was cylinder shaped. The walls, floor and ceiling had a shiny black, glass like surface that had a faint orange glow to it. There were no sharp angles anywhere. It was the same in the flying saucer. Where surfaces met, it was rounded. This giant room was the same way.

The ship maneuvered through spaces between the parked ships and ultimately landed. The door opened. It was weird how that door worked because it seemed to not be there one minute and the next, it just materialized.

This was the first time I had ever been to this place although it appeared that the other passengers had been there before. Everyone, including myself, stood up except for the pilots. I knew I was supposed to stand up but didn't know why. There appeared to be routine to the other passengers. There were several people, three men actually, waiting outside for us.

The man and the woman extra-terrestrial stuck by me and the other kid, I suppose to assist us since we were rather small.

So we walked down the ramp. I was a little curious about everything there. Because well, the room was gigantic. It was HUGE! There was all different types of ships parked there. I could see some that were exact duplicates of the one we arrived in. Then there were other ones too, different sizes and configurations. My child mind was curious about all this.

But no one was really talking at this point. One of the three men seemed to be the spokesperson and he said, "Welcome. Let us go to the meeting room."

Before I continue the narrative of this extra-terrestrial contact experience, it is necessary to discuss an unusual but real phenomena that occurs around this group of E. T.s. This is the phenomena of consciousness expansion.

This was not explained to me until 1991 when it became necessary to understand why Missing Time occurs and also, why contact experiences with extra-terrestrials of any species are difficult to remember.

The life energy field of the least developed extra-terrestrial civilization is significantly greater than that of a human. Human beings, like all life forms in this Galaxy are electromagnetic in nature. If you consider the brain, and its corresponding consciousness as a light bulb on an adjustable dimmer control, it will be easier to understand the phenomena.

Under ordinary circumstances, the typical human is at the lowest setting. Rather dim compared to E. T. s. However, the potential for more exist. Some individuals have higher settings with corresponding talents that primitive human science labels as phony or, if being charitable, extrasensory perception. The extra-terrestrials, on the other hand, have their dimmer switch turned way up all the time. They perceive at what they call a tri-level. For humans with a philosophic or Theosophical orientation, that translates to the etheric, astral and mental planes of reality. The E. T. s have a 360 degree field of conscious perception that is spherical in nature. The only analogy I can make about it is that they are aware of EVERYTHING at once, constantly.

When a human gets around an extra-terrestrial, the enhanced energy/electromagnetic field of the E. T. has the impact of turning up the human's dimmer so that the consciousness is "brighter". This pushes the individual's consciousness into areas that normally are relegated to the "Subconscious." This produces a duality effect. The person is "themselves" but they are "more". I won't digress into the sorts of things that are stored in every individual's subconscious. I will say that the normal individual is incomplete without access to this information. Being around an extra-terrestrial brings out this completeness and the extra-terrestrials respond to the total individual, not the limited view of self that everyone sees in the mirror.

It is necessary to understand this in order to understand what happened when this group of human passengers finally reached the meeting room. To understand how two 4 year old kids were functionally equal to two teenagers and a young adult.

As I mentioned, the wall, floor and ceiling of this gigantic cylindrical room were shiny black with a strange orange background glow. There were no obvious light sources but everything was brightly illuminated. There were ships of various sizes around but the largest appeared to be only twice as big as the one we arrived in. The 25 foot model seemed to be the most common but there was a mixture of larger and smaller craft as well.

There were different colored striped lines on the floor. My interpretation of them were parking zones.

The three extra-terrestrials that greeted us were standing by a rectangular vehicle, a bit larger than a golf cart. [...]

[At this point he mentions being put into a chamber that transforms his body into that of a grown adult, similar to the aliens, or perhaps his soul was simply transferred into such a body]

The extra-terrestrials at the meeting had their individual distinctions. There are four of them; two men and two women. Three of them have that ageless quality but one of the men doesn't. He looks more mature and appears to be the group leader.

One of the extra-terrestrial women is blond, one has black hair; both with a page boy type shortness. The other extra-terrestrial male has sort of a sandy colored hair. Those three look like the bodies we were transformed into.

As I mentioned, they asked how we liked the form we were in and the general consensus was that it was too limiting. They told us that they were working to improve the physical situation, to provide enhancements, but had to work within parameters so that we would not be detected. That we had physical enemies that must not know who, or I suppose what, we were.

Then they started talking about how we would contribute to a new generation from the genetic materials contained in our current body cells and how the new generation, literally our offspring, would have greater, enhanced capabilities. These new "people" would enter the world in a time when things were different and it was safe to do so.

[...] After the topic of the next generation of us, whatever we are and whatever that is, the extra-terrestrials began talking about their concern about the genetic breakthrough that the gray aliens had made in Nazi Germany. They said the gray extra-terrestrials had succeeded in contriving a way to make their alien gametes work with human gametes. The goal was a half human-half gray alien with the superiority of the extra-terrestrial portion.

It was obvious that the gray extra-terrestrials did not have the best interest of humans in mind.

Of note from this account: human-looking aliens in bodysuits, the blond and black-haired women with pageboy haircuts, the alien base inside a mountain, the use of hyperdimensional technology to phase an entire ship through solid matter, that via some proximity effect aliens induce a shift in a person's consciousness ("assemblage point shift" in Toltec jargon), their moving about human society while evading detection, the idea of future humans having enhanced abilities, and their wariness of the Gray hybrid breeding program.*

Orfeo Angelucci

An important but lesser known contactee is Orfeo Angelucci. His encounters also took place in Los Angeles in the 1950s. Excerpts from his main book *The Secret of the Saucers* (Amherst Press, 1955):

> About a mile further along the disk swerved to the right, away from the road, and hung motionless over an unfenced field some distance below the road level. I drove off the pavement about thirty feet to the edge of the declivity. From there the glowing red disk was directly in front of me and only a short distance away. As I watched it in bewilderment it pulsated violently; then shot off into the sky at a 30- or 40-degree angle and at very great speed. High in the sky to the west it decelerated abruptly, hung for a moment; then accelerated and disappeared like a meteor.
>
> But just before the glowing red orb vanished, two smaller objects came from it. These objects were definitely circular in shape and of a soft, fluorescent green color. They streaked down directly in front of my car and hovered only a few feet away. I judged each to be about three feet in diameter. Hanging silently in the air like iridescent bubbles their green light fluctuated rhythmically in intensity.
>
> Then, apparently coming from between those two eerie balls of green fire, I heard a masculine voice in strong, well-modulated tones and speaking perfect English.
>
> Because of the nervous tension I was under at that moment, amounting almost to a state of shock, it is impossible for me to give a verbatim account of the conversation which followed. The invisible speaker obviously was endeavoring to choose words and phrases

---

* <geohanover.com/docs/contact1.htm>

which I could understand, but there were several things which even now are not clear to me. I can only make a poor approximation of the gist of his words.

I do, however, remember the first words spoken which were: "Don't be afraid, Orfeo, we are friends!" Then the voice requested that I get out of my car and "Come out here." Mechanically, I pushed open the car door and got out. I didn't feel fear, but I was so weak and shaky that I could scarcely stand. I leaned against the front fender of my car and looked at the twin pulsating circular objects hovering a short distance in front of me.

The glowing disks created a soft illumination, but I could see no person anywhere. I remember vaguely that the voice spoke again calling me by my full name in words of greeting. It further stated that the small green disks were instruments of transmission and reception comparable to nothing developed on earth. Then the voice added that through the disks I was in direct communication with friends from another world.

There was a pause and I dimly remember thinking that I should say something, but I was stunned into utter silence. I could only stare in fascination at those fantastic balls of green fire and wonder if I had lost my mind.

When the voice spoke again I heard these startling words: "Do you remember your eighteen balloons and the mold cultures that you lost in the skies back in New Jersey, Orfeo?" I was astounded to hear the strange voice recalling an incident out of the past which had happened so long ago that I had almost forgotten it. "Yes .... yes sir, I do!"

"Do you also remember the strange, wingless craft that appeared to be observing your activities?"

Suddenly the entire scene came back to me crystal clear in memory. I remember Mabel, my wife, my father-in-law and our friends and neighbors with me as we stared at that strange, disk-shaped object in the sky. I recalled how the object had appeared to follow the balloons bearing my precious cultures of *Aspergillus Clavatus* mold. I had been quite an experimenter in those days. It was then it dawned upon me that the fluorescent disks were similar in shape and behaved in the same erratic manner as had that mysterious craft back in New Jersey.

The only difference was that I had seen the craft in daylight when it glistened like metal whereas the disks glowed in the darkness.

"You do remember us, Orfeo," the golden voice stated. "We were observing your efforts that day as we have watched you since then."

Like with Maxwell, these beings employed the very direct and personal "do you remember..." method to quickly prove their superhuman awareness about those whom they address. Due to their monitoring and telepathic abilities, they may come across as omniscient.

The twin disks were spaced about three feet apart. Now the area between them began to glow with a soft green light which gradually formed into a luminous three-dimensional screen as the disks themselves faded perceptibly. Within the luminous screen there appeared images of the heads and shoulders of two persons, as though in a cinema close-up. One was the image of a man and the other of a woman. I say man and woman only because their outlines and features were generally similar to men and women. But those two figures struck me as being the ultimate of perfection. There was an impressive nobility about them; their eyes were larger and much more expressive and they emanated a seeming radiance that filled me with wonder.

Even more confusing was the troubling thought somewhere in the back of my mind that they were oddly familiar. Strangely enough, the projected images of the two beings appeared to be observing me. For they looked directly at me and smiled; then their eyes looked about as though taking in the entire scene.

I had the uncomfortable feeling as they studied me that they knew every thought in my mind; everything I'd ever done and a vast amount about me that I didn't even know myself. Intuitively, I sensed that I stood in a kind of spiritual nakedness before them. Also, I seemed to be in telepathic communication with them, for thoughts, understandings and new comprehensions that would have required hours of conversation to transmit, flashed through my consciousness. Before those two incredible Beings I felt that I was only a shadow of the shining reality I sensed them to be. It is difficult to express my feelings in words, for my understanding of them through intuitive perception.

The large eyes, notable physiognomy and physique, peculiar radiance, and telepathic intensity are details that didn't become generally accepted in alienology regarding these alien types until decades later. In a subsequent incident, Angelucci goes further into their appearance and nature:

> As I cut across the vacant lots the Hyperion Avenue Freeway Bridge loomed huge and dark ahead of me. The sky was overcast and the dense, oblique shadows from the vast concrete structure were heavier and more eerie than usual. Yet in the shadows of the dark archways of the bridge I had come to feel a kind of warmth and welcome, a spiritual communion with a vastly greater and more kindly world. For it was in the shadows of the huge bridge that I had come upon the saucer which had carried me out of this world.
>
> I was thinking of these things when I suddenly became aware of someone approaching from out of the darkness. I was startled for I'd never before met anyone taking the short-cut beneath the bridge so late at night. I was about to call out a word of greeting when it dawned upon me that the stranger was coming from the dead end of the bridge. My first thought was that someone was lying in wait for me, possibly to rob me. But before I could become alarmed, I heard the stranger call: "Greetings, Orfeo!"
>
> My heart almost stopped beating, for immediately I recognized the vibrant, beautiful voice of the being who had spoken to me in the saucer. I stopped in my tracks, utterly speechless, and stared at the approaching figure. But then a wave of joy and gratitude flooded over me, and I finally replied falteringly: "Greetings ... to you ..."
>
> He laughed pleasantly. "I know that in your mind you have given me a name — I who have remained nameless to you," he said gently. "You may call me by that name, Orfeo — it is as good as any other and has more inner significance to you than any name I might give you."
>
> "Neptune..." I spoke the name slowly and reverently. For it was indeed the name I had given to this great and mysterious being. Then I added: "At last you have come to give me strength and faith."

These beings conceal their real names and identities, that much is invariant. When pressed, they might give simple symbolic nicknames drawn from our mythology, planets, stars, and constellations to convey the gist of what they are about. Even on an individual level, this might apply; for example, a female member might use the alias "Andromeda" if she is burdened by punitive limitations, just as Andromeda was chained to a stone in Greek mythology.

> He was near enough then for me to see that he was several inches taller than I and similar in outline to a well-built man. But the shadows were so heavy that I couldn't make out the details of his figure. But just to be in his presence once more was to sense again a tremendous uplifting wave of strength, harmony, joy and serenity.
>
> "Come, Orfeo," he said gently, continuing on past me. "We have many things to discuss tonight." I followed him as he strode ahead of me through the dense shadows. I could hear his solid footsteps upon the graveled path which convinced me beyond the shadow of a doubt that he was no phantom or illusion.
>
> He led me to a better lighted area near the bend of Glendale Boulevard where it goes up and over the bridge. I was actually trembling in anticipation of my first actual look at the mysterious visitor from another world.
>
> When he turned I saw his face, the same wonderful, expressive countenance I had seen on the luminous screen. I again noticed especially his extremely large, dark and expressive eyes and nobility and beauty of his features which actually seemed to radiate warmth and kindliness.
>
> Then I noticed that he was wearing a kind of uniform, bluish in color, perfectly tailored and tightly fitted to the outlines of his body. But it was apparently without seams, buttons, pockets, trimmings or design of any sort. In fact it fitted so perfectly that it was almost like a part of his body.
>
> But as I studied him I became aware of an astonishing phenomenon: I could see his uniform and figure clearly, but it wavered occasionally, as though I were viewing it through rippling water. And the color did not remain solid and uniform, but varied and changed in spots, which reminded me of an imperfectly tuned television set. Only his face and hands remained immobile and stable as though not partially obscured by a film of rippling water. [...]

For a time he was silent and I was acutely conscious of a tremendous vibrational field about him; a tangible emanation of serenity, brotherly love, and ineffable joy. At last he said: "You sense and understand intuitively many things I cannot say directly to you, Orfeo. You have just fully realized that we are not like earthmen in that we function in dimensions unknown to your world. Earth is a three-dimensional world and because of this it is preponderantly false. I may tell you that to the entities of certain other worlds Earth is regarded as 'the accursed planet', the 'home of the reprobate, fallen ones'. Others call your Earth 'the home of sorrows'. For Earth's evolution is evolution through pain, sorrow, sin, suffering and the illusion of physical death. Believe me, all evolutions are not similar to Earth's, despite the present beliefs of your scientists."

As I heard these strange words, my heart and mind cried out: "But why must it be so? Why should Earth's people know pain, suffering and death?"

But soon my attention was distracted once more as I saw the figure of Neptune strangely "waver" again. Suddenly the question was in my mind: "Was he really there in the truest physical sense, or was he an immaterial projection into the physical world from another dimension? Did I see him in his true form and ordinary state of being, or merely a projected approximation of a man's appearance?" These strange thoughts frightened me a little and carried me into too deep waters.

A reassuring smile lighted his face. "Don't be alarmed, Orfeo. The answer to the troublesome question in your mind is both yes and no. On Earth form, color, individuality and the material aspect of things is all-important. In our world these illusions are of practically no importance at all. Suffice to say that for you I am an approximation of myself as I really am. I can't make it any clearer in three-dimensional terms."

Unlike the comic-book Venusians of George Adamski, Angelucci's depiction more closely matches the findings of modern alienology, though that is not to say his books were free of embellishment or fictionalization, or that Angelucci wasn't duped by customized "virtual reality scenarios" projected into his mind by telepathic beings. Rather, what elements of truth can be sifted from his books were far ahead of their time — so far ahead that, because novel truth is never as exciting as science fiction, Angelucci never received the level of attention afforded to charlatans.

This final excerpt further underscores the idea that human-like aliens walk among us undetected:

> It was around six o'clock and the streets heavy with traffic. Parking my car, I walked toward the bus terminal. It too was bustling with activity. In all of the excitement, flying saucers and space visitors were the farthest things from my mind. But as I entered the front door of the bus terminal I stopped in my tracks and stared, unable to believe my eyes. Directly in front of me and facing the news stand was a familiar face. I knew I couldn't be mistaken — it was Neptune!
>
> He glanced up and his dark eyes told me that he was expecting me. He was dressed in an ordinary dark business suit and carried a briefcase under his arm. A dark blue felt hat with snap brim shaded his eyes. [...]
>
> His intent gaze never left me. Stalling for time I walked over to the newsstand and picked up a magazine and thumbed through it. I had received the definite telepathic impression not to approach him; thus I waited for him to speak to me. But he did not. Staring blankly at a page in the magazine I waited for further telepathic communication. It came! The gist of the message was: "The last time you saw me, Orfeo, I was in a less objectified projection in your three-dimensional world. The purpose being to give you some idea of our true aspect. But now tonight you see me fully objectified. If you did not know who I am, you could not tell me from one of your fellows. Tonight I am no half-phantom, but can move among men as an Earthman. It is not necessary for you to speak to me; you have gained the understanding. You know now that we can appear and function as human beings."

Travis Walton

On the subject of superhumans in bodysuits, recall one of the most famous alien encounters of all, that of Travis Walton on November 5, 1975. The movie *Fire in the Sky* based on his story was an inaccurate Hollywood fictionalization of his experiences aboard the alien ship. Here is a portion from the actual experience:

Trembling, I sat down on the hard surface of the chair. I put my hand onto the molded T-grip of the lever. The handle was slightly small for my hand. The whole chair seemed a little too small. I rotated the handle of the lever forward, feeling the slow, fluid resistance of it. I felt suddenly disoriented as the stars began moving downward in front of me, in unison. Quickly I pulled my hand off the lever, which returned to its original vertical position. The stars stopped moving, but remained where they were when I released the lever.

If this thing is flying, I could crash it or throw it off course and get lost or something! I resolved not to tamper with those controls anymore. I might escalate a desperate situation into a fatal disaster.

I got out of the chair and walked to the edge of the room. As I did, the stars faded out and the surfaces of the wall, ceiling, and floor came into sight. I moved over to one of the rectangles resembling closed doors. I searched the edges for a sign of a switch or an opening mechanism. Seeing none, I put my eye to the crack; I could not see any light. I looked around for some kind of symbol or writing that would help me figure out where I was or how to get out of there. None.

I walked back to the chair and stood beside it, looking at the buttons. I was thinking about pushing some of them, when I heard a faint sound. I whirled around and looked at the door. There, standing in the open doorway, was a human being!

I stood frozen to the spot. He was a man about six feet two inches tall. His helmeted head barely cleared the doorway. He was extremely muscular and evenly proportioned. He appeared to weigh about two hundred pounds. He wore a tight-fitting bright blue suit of soft material like velour. His feet were covered with black boots, a black band or belt wrapped around his middle. He carried no tools or weapons on his belt or in his hands; no insignia marked his clothing.

I ran up to him, exclaiming, babbling all sorts of questions. The man remained silent throughout my verbal barrage. I was worried by his silence. He took me firmly but gently by the arm and gestured for me to go with him. He led me out of that room and hurried me down the narrow hallway, pulling me along behind him due to its narrowness.

He stopped in front of a closed doorway that slid open, into the wall. I did not see what caused it to open. The door opened into a bare room so small it was more like a foyer or section of hallway. The door slid shut quickly and silently behind us. Again I attempted to talk to the man as we stood there. No answer.

We spent approximately two minutes in the metal cubicle, no more than seven by five by twelve feet. Then a doorway, the same size as the other door and directly opposite it, slid open. [...]

I descended a short, steep ramp seven or eight feet to the floor. I looked around to discover that, although I was outside that dim, humid craft, I was not out-of-doors. I was in a huge room. The ceiling was sectioned into alternating rectangles of dark metal and those that gave off light. The ceiling itself curved down to form one of the larger walls in the room. The room was shaped like one-quarter of a cylinder laid on its side. [...]

The man escorted me across the open floor to a door that opened silently and quickly from the middle outward. We were in a hallway about six feet wide, illuminated from the eight-foot-high ceiling, which was one long panel of softly diffused light. The hallway was straight and perhaps eighty feet long. Closed double doors were distributed along the corridor.

At the end of the hallway, another pair of double doors. I watched closely this time. I did not see him touch anything, but again the doors slid silently back from the middle. We entered a white room approximately fifteen feet square, with another eight-foot-high ceiling. The room had a table and a chair in it. But my interest was immediately focused on the three other humans!

Two men and a woman were standing around the table. They were all wearing velvety blue uniforms like the first man's, except that they had no helmets. The two men had the same muscularity and the same masculine good looks as the first man. The woman also had a face and figure that was the epitome of her gender. They were smooth-skinned and blemishless. No moles, freckles, wrinkles, or scars marked their skin. The striking good looks of the man I had first met became more obvious on seeing them all together. They shared a family-like resemblance, although they were not identical.

"Would somebody please tell me where I am?" I implored. I was still utterly shaken from my encounter with those awful creatures. "What in hell is going on? What is this place?"

They didn't answer me. They only looked at me, though not unkindly. One man and the woman came around the table, approaching me. Silently they each took me by an arm and led me toward the table. I didn't know why I should cooperate with them. They wouldn't even tell me anything. But I was in no position to argue, so I went along at first.

They lifted me easily onto the edge of the table. I became wary and started protesting. "Wait a minute. Just tell me what you are going to do!"

I began to resist them, but all three began pushing me gently backward down onto the table. I looked up at the ceiling, covered with panels of softly glowing white light with a faint blue cast.

I saw that the woman suddenly had an object in her hand from out of nowhere — it looked like one of those clear, soft plastic oxygen masks, only there were no tubes connected to it. The only thing attached to it was a small black golfball-sized sphere.

She pressed the mask down over my mouth and nose. I started to reach up to pull it away. Before I could complete the motion, I rapidly became weak. Everything started turning gray. Then there was nothing at all but black oblivion...*

Unlike the movie, the real experience involved Nordics in blue suits. Apparently, he had stumbled upon one of their ships in the woods, gotten too close, and was injured by an energy discharge. This accident forced them to take him aboard for treatment and recovery, thus his conspicuous absence for several days and their saying nothing to him during his stay, unlike contactees who are vetted and given a specific storyline to disseminate.

If anyone thinks such encounters are strictly modern military psyop inventions, keep in mind that anomalous craft sightings have occurred throughout the centuries, long before the Military Industrial Complex came into existence. Consider the UFO Battle of Nuremberg in

---

* <travis-walton.com/human.html>

1561 or the Mystery Airship Encounters of the late 1800s. See John Keel's book *Operation Trojan Horse* and William Bramley's *The Gods of Eden* for more examples.

Emmanuel Swedenborg

Brainy telepathic humanoids in blue bodysuits aren't new to the 20th century either. Emanuel Swedenborg (1688 – 1772) was an eminent inventor and scientist who began having dreams and visions in which he interacted with various spirits and beings from other realms, similar to Robert Monroe's astral journeys. In some of these travels, Swedenborg came in contact with beings from other planets in the solar system, or what he assumed were such. From "Earths in the Universe" (1758), here is how he describes the "spirits of Mercury":

> Some spirits came to me, and it was declared from heaven, that they were from the earth [planet] which is nearest to the sun, and which in our earth is called by the name of the planet Mercury. Immediately on their coming, they sought from my memory what I knew. Spirits can do this most dexterously, for when they come to man, they see in his memory all things contained therein.

> It was told me, that such is the life of the inhabitants of that earth, namely, that they have no concern about things terrestrial and corporeal, but only about the statutes, laws, and forms of government, of the nations therein; also about the things of heaven, which are innumerable, And I was further informed, that many of the men of that earth speak with spirits, and that thence they have the knowledges of spiritual things, and of the states of life after death; and thence also their contempt of things corporeal and terrestrial.

> The spirits of Mercury, above all other spirits, possess the knowledges of things, as well respecting this solar system, as respecting the earths which are in the starry heavens; and what they have once acquired to themselves, that they retain, and also recollect as often as anything similar occurs. Hence also it may appear manifest, that spirits have memory, and that it is much more perfect than the memory of men; and further, that what they hear, see, and apperceive, they retain, and especially such things as delight them, as these spirits are delighted with the knowledges of things.

They are averse to vocal speech, because it is material; wherefore when I conversed with them without intermediate spirits, I could only do it by a species of active thought.

The spirits of the earth Mercury do not abide long in one place, or within companies of the spirits of one world, but wander through the universe. The reason is, because they have relation to the memory of things, which memory must be continually enriched. Hence it is granted them to wander about, and to acquire to themselves knowledges in every place. During their sojourning in this manner, if they meet with spirits who love material things, that is, things corporeal and terrestrial, they avoid them, and betake themselves where they do not hear such things.

In consequence of their knowledges, the spirits of Mercury are more proud than others; wherefore they were told, that although they knew innumerable things, yet there are infinite things which they do not know; and that if their knowledges should increase to eternity, the notice even of all general things would still be unattainable. They were told likewise of their pride and elation of mind, and that this is unseemly; but they replied, that it is not pride, but only a glorying by reason of the faculty of their memory; thus they were able to excuse their faults.

I was desirous to know what kind of face and body the men in the earth Mercury had, whether they were like the men on our earth. There was then presented before my eyes a woman exactly resembling the women in that earth. She had a beautiful face, but it was smaller than that of a woman of our earth; her body also was more slender, but her height was equal; she wore on her head a linen cap, which was put on without art, but yet in a manner becoming. A man also was presented to view, who was more slender in body than the men of our earth are. He was clad in a garment of dark blue color, closely fitted to his body, without any foldings or protuberances. It was said that such was the form of body and such the dress of the men of that earth. Afterwards there was presented to view a species of their oxen and cows, which indeed did not differ much from those on our earth, but were smaller, and in some degree approached to species of hinds and deer.

They were also asked about the sun of the world, how it appears from their earth. They said that it appears large, and larger there than when seen from other earths, and they said they knew this from the ideas of other spirits concerning the sun. They said further that they enjoy a middle temperature, neither too hot nor too cold.[*]

The affiliation with Mercury is probably more symbolic than literal. Mercury relates to Hermes and thus Hermeticism, one of the esoteric knowledge streams they have given to humans, to their being inter-mediaries or messengers of the Gods, to their association with etheric energy called "Mercury" in Alchemy, and to planet Mercury's close-ness to the Sun symbolizing their closeness to the Logos. The later identification of Nordic aliens with Venus may relate to its signifier as the "Morning Star," a code name for Lucifer the bringer of light, which hearkens back to the idea of Fallen Angels and the Lucifer Rebellion.

The Comte de Gabalis

A century before Swedenborg, esoteric scholar Abbé de Villars wrote an expose on the Rosicrucian practice of intermarrying with other-worldly females. Anonymously published in 1670, *The Comte de Gabalis* (The Count of Cabala) is one of the more intriguing arcane sources pertaining to superhuman interactions with humans. Famil-iar to students of Rosicrucianism and Alchemy but lesser known to researchers of alienology, the book is full of anecdotes from esoterica and ancient history about the role these beings have played in our history. The work consists of five discourses between the author and a mysterious Rosicrucian initiate who revealed to him one of the soci-ety's most closely guarded secrets: *that human spiritual elites have been intimately consorting with otherworldly beings.*

After its publication, de Villars was assassinated by ritual dagger, though some say he faked his death in order to disappear from the mainstream world, as all true Rosicrucian initiates must do. Either he was a genuine antagonist of the Rosicrucians and was killed for be-traying a secret, or he was an initiate who placed key knowledge into the public domain by veiling it in the form of sarcastic satire.

The immense space which lies between Earth and Heaven has inhabitants far nobler than the birds and insects. These vast seas have

---

[*] <sacred-texts.com/swd/eiu/eiu01.htm>

far other hosts than those of the dolphins and whales; the depths of the earth are not for the moles alone; and the Element of Fire, nobler than the other three, was not created to remain useless and empty.

The air is full of an innumerable multitude of Peoples,whose faces are human, seemingly rather haughty, yet in reality tractable, great lovers of the sciences, cunning, obliging to the Sages, and enemies of fools and the ignorant. Their wives and daughters have a masculine beauty like that of the Amazons.

The earth is filled well-nigh to its centre with Gnomes, people of slight stature, who are the guardians of treasures, minerals and precious stones. They are ingenious, friends of man and easy to govern. They furnish the Children of the Sages with all the money they require, and as the price of their service ask naught save the glory of being commanded. The Gnomides, their wives, are small but very amiable, and their dress is exceedingly curious.

Hear me to the end and know that the seas and rivers are inhabited as well as the air. The ancient Sages called this race of people Undines or Nymphs. There are very few males among them but a great number of females; their beauty is extreme, and the daughters of men are not to be compared to them.

As for the Salamanders, flaming dwellers of the Region of Fire, they serve the Philosophers, but do not seek their company eagerly, and their daughters and wives. The Salamander women are beautiful, more beautiful even than any of the others, since they are of a purer Element. I had not intended to speak about them, and was passing briefly over the description of these Peoples since you will see them yourself at your leisure, and with ease if you have the curiosity to do so. You will see their dresses, their food, their manners, their customs and their admirable laws.

Here the Comte speaks of superior beings who look human but inhabit a parallel reality normally invisible to our senses. He divides these beings into four categories according to the elements. In occultism, they are known as elemental beings, but there is a difference between actual elemental beings, which are just etheric thoughtforms that accompany the forces of nature, and tangible superhuman aliens who may symbolically associate themselves with the elements.

The book, or Rosicrucianism in general, does not distinguish between immaterial thoughtforms like elementals, incubi, and succubi, and the transcendent but otherwise flesh-and-blood aliens discussed in this chapter. Both categories reside by default beyond our perceptions and seem to operate by occult laws, both can appear human (at least to the mind's eye), and both can engage humans in personal interaction.

But unlike aliens, the etheric thoughtforms lack physical bodies, technology, and genetic signatures; they can't bear hybrid children nor contribute to our gene pool. Humanoid aliens are also more complex, tangible, self-aware, and well-rounded compared to the simple entitized constructs of the etheric and astral realms.

And just as etheric thoughtforms can take the guise of dead relatives, celebrities, or worshipped deities, so can they take on the appearance of aliens, but that doesn't make them identically alien. They are just chimeras bent on acquiring energy and control for reasons of self-expansion and propagation.

Alienologists are mistaken when they view accounts of djinn, succubi, incubi, etc. exclusively as encounters with aliens, and likewise occultists and theologists are mistaken in thinking of aliens as mere demons, elementals, or djinn. Thoughtforms and aliens are two separate categories of life that are related but not mutually exclusive.

> The beauty of their intellects will charm you even more than that of their bodies, yet one cannot help pitying these unfortunates when they tell one that their souls are mortal, and that they have no hope whatever of eternal enjoyment of the Supreme Being, of Whom they have knowledge and Whom they worship reverently. They will tell you that they are composed of the purest portions of the Element in which they dwell, and that they have in them no impurities whatsoever, since they are made of but one Element. Therefore they die only after several centuries; but what is time in comparison with eternity? They must return for ever into nothingness. This thought grieves them deeply, and we have utmost difficulty in consoling them.
>
> Our Fathers the Philosophers, when speaking with God face to face, complained to Him of the unhappiness of these Peoples, and God, whose mercy is boundless, revealed to them that it was not impossible to find a remedy for this evil. He inspired them to the realization

that just as man, by the alliance which he has contracted with God, has been made a participant in Divinity, so the Sylphs, Gnomes, Nymphs, and Salamanders, by the alliance which they have it in their power to contract with man, can become participants in immortality. Thus a Nymph or a Sylphid becomes immortal and capable of the Beatitude to which we aspire when she is so happy as to marry a Sage; and a Gnome or a Sylph ceases to be mortal the moment he espouses one of our daughters.

Marvel at the extent of the philosophical felicity. Instead of women, whose feeble allurements fade in a few days and are succeeded by horrible wrinkles, the Sages possess beauties who never grow old and whom they have the glory of rendering immortal. Imagine the love and gratitude of these invisible mistresses and the ardour wherewith they strive to please the charitable Philosopher who applies himself to their immortalisation.

The Rosicrucians were convinced out of pity and mutual benefit to mate with these beings and thereby gift them immortality, else these beings would die forever. That sounds more like a persuasive excuse than the actual truth, just as today's abductees are told that their participation in the hybrid breeding program is an opportunity to save the human race. They do seem to need us, but the reasons may be other than they claim.

The Sages are far from believing that the Devil ever had power to make himself worshipped. He is too wretched and too weak ever to have had such pleasure and authority. But he has had power to persuade these Hosts of the Elements to show themselves to men, and to cause temples to be erected in their honour; and by virtue of the natural dominion which each one of these Peoples has over the Element in which it dwells, they kept troubling the air and the sea, shaking the earth and scattering the fire of heaven at their own good pleasure. Thus they had little difficulty in causing themselves to be mistaken for divinities so long as the Sovereign Being neglected the salvation of the nations.

This is the central thesis of the Ancient Astronaut Theory, that non-human beings posed as divinities to the ancients and held centers of worship. Egypt and Mesopotamia are examples. The founders of these civilizations were held to be divine, and each was worshiped in his or her respective temple. After their death or departure, succeeding generations of kings or pharaohs modeled themselves after these "gods" and were hailed as divine; some may have been hybrids or descendants of hybrids, and some dynasties may have had more alien DNA than others, the 18th Dynasty with Akhenaten in particular.

> A certain Philosopher, with whom a Nymph was engaged in an intrigue of immortality, was so disloyal as to love a woman. As he sat at dinner with his new paramour and some friends, there appeared in the air the most beautiful leg in the world. The invisible sweetheart greatly desired to show herself to the friends of her faithless lover, that they might judge how wrong he was in preferring a woman to her. Afterward the indignant Nymph killed him on the spot.

> I confess that their tenderness is apt to be somewhat violent. But if exasperated women have been known to murder their perjured lovers, we must not wonder that these beautiful and faithful mistresses fly into a passion when they are betrayed, and all the more so since they only require men to abstain from women whose imperfections they cannot tolerate, and give us leave to love as many of their number as we please.

It stands to reason that if they look similar to humans and have compatible biology, then they can have similar emotional weaknesses depending on the spiritual maturity of each member. Despite romantic idealizations by contactees, they are not perfect beings; they may be superhuman by our low standards, but they still have their own set of psychological faults, emotional weaknesses, and physical limitations.

> They prefer the interest and immortality of their companions to their personal satisfaction, and they are very glad to have the Sages give to their Republic as many immortal children as possible.

Compare this to what Eschenbach wrote: "As I say, maidens are given away from the Grail openly, men in secret, in order to have progeny (as God can well instruct them), in the hope that these children will return to serve the Grail and swell the ranks of its Company."

> The renowned Hercule and the invincible Alexander were sons of the greatest of the Sylphs. Not knowing this, the historians said that Jupiter was their father. They spoke the truth for, as you have

learned, these Sylphs, Nymphs and Salamanders set themselves up for divinities. The historians, believing them to be so, called all those who were born of them 'Children of the Gods.' Such was the divine Plato, the most divine Apollonius of Tyana, Hercules, Achilles, Sarpedon, the pious Æneas, and the celebrated Melchizedek.

What would your Doctor say to this authentic account of a recent occurrence in Spain? A beautiful Sylphid was beloved by a Spaniard, lived with him for three years, presented him with three fine children and then died. Shall one say that she was a devil? A clever answer that! According to what Natural Philosophy can the Devil organise for himself a woman's body, conceive, bear children and suckle them? What proof is there in Scripture of the extravagant power which your theologians are forced in this instance to accord the Devil? And with what probable reason can their feeble Natural Philosophy supply them? The Jesuit Delrio in good faith naïvely recounts several of these adventures, and without taking the trouble to give physical explanations, extricates himself by saying that those Sylphids were demons. How true it is that your greatest doctors very often know no more than silly women!

If you should be told, for example, that the divine Apollonius of Tyana was immaculately conceived, and that one of the noblest Salamanders descended to immortalise himself with his mother, you would call that Salamander a demon and you would give the Devil the glory of fathering one of the greatest men who ever sprang from our Philosophic marriages.

When you read that the celebrated Merlin was immaculately conceived by a nun, daughter of a king of Great Britain, and that he foretold the future more clearly than Tyresias, do not say with the masses that he was the son of an incubus devil, because there never have been any; nor that he prophesied through the assistance of devils, since according to the Holy Cabala devil is the most ignorant of all beings. Rather say with the Sages that the English Princess was consoled in her retirement by a Sylph who took pity on her, that he diverted her with his attentions, that he knew how to please her, and that Merlin, their son, was brought up by the Sylph in all knowledge, and learned from him to perform the many wonders which English history relates of him.

It's known in alienology that hybrid children seeded in human families become extraordinary individuals. This is the most direct way that the parallel superhuman civilization influences ours, by inserting their own into our society. The aperture of human birth allows a level of influence otherwise barred by metaphysical decree. The Comte claims that the most powerful and influential heroes of history were hybrid offspring. As Eschenbach said, when the Grail members mate with humans, "They receive handsome children of high degree."

On the subject of human-alien interbreeding, a more modern example is the abduction of Antonio Villas Boas in 1957:

> At the time of his alleged abduction, Antonio Villas Boas was a 23-year-old Brazilian farmer who was working at night to avoid the hot temperatures of the day. On October 16, 1957, he was ploughing fields near São Francisco de Sales when he saw what he described as a "red star" in the night sky. According to his story, this "star" approached his position, growing in size until it became recognizable as a roughly circular or egg-shaped aerial craft, with a red light at its front and a rotating cupola on top. The craft began descending to land in the field, extending three "legs" as it did so. At that point, Boas decided to run from the scene.
>
> According to Boas, he first attempted to leave the scene on his tractor, but when its lights and engine died after traveling only a short distance, he decided to continue on foot. However, he was seized by a 1.5 m (five-foot) tall humanoid, who was wearing grey coveralls and a helmet. Its eyes were small and blue, and instead of speech it made noises like barks or yelps. Three similar beings then joined the first in subduing Boas, and they dragged him inside their craft.
>
> Once inside the craft, Boas said that he was stripped of his clothes and covered from head-to-toe with a strange gel. He was then led into a large semicircular room, through a doorway that had strange red symbols written over it. (Boas claimed that he was able to memorize these symbols and later reproduced them for investigators.) In this room the beings took samples of Boas' blood from his chin. After this he was then taken to a third room and left alone for around half an hour. During this time, some kind of gas was pumped into the room, which made Boas become violently ill.

Shortly after this, Boas claimed that he was joined in the room by another humanoid. This one, however, was female, very attractive, and naked. She was the same height as the other beings he had encountered, with a small, pointed chin and large, blue catlike eyes. The hair on her head was long and white (somewhat like platinum blonde) but her underarm and pubic hair were bright red. Boas said he was strongly attracted to the woman, and the two had sexual intercourse. During this act, Boas noted that the female did not kiss him but instead nipped him on the chin.

When it was all over, the female smiled at Boas, rubbing her belly and gestured upwards. Boas took this to mean that she was going to raise their child in space. The female seemed relieved that their "task" was over, and Boas himself said that he felt angered by the situation, because he felt as though he had been little more than "a good stallion" for the humanoids.

Boas said that he was then given back his clothing and taken on a tour of the ship by the humanoids. During this tour he said that he attempted to take a clock-like device as proof of his encounter, but was caught by the humanoids and prevented from doing so. He was then escorted off the ship and watched as it took off, glowing brightly. When Boas returned home, he discovered that four hours had passed. Antonio Villas Boas later became a lawyer, married and had four children. He died in 1992, and stuck to the story of his alleged abduction for his entire life.*

An even more recent example is Peter Khoury's bizarre encounter, as reported by Bill Chalker in *Hard Evidence Magazine:*

Born in 1964, in Lebanon, Peter Khoury migrated to Australia in 1973.

[T]he most striking [encounter] occurred on July 23, 1992, according to diary entries. He had been recovering from head injuries received in a job site assault (he worked in the building industry in his own cement rendering business). At about 7 am, having returned to his Sydney suburban home from the train station, after dropping off his wife, Khoury felt unwell and lay down on the bed to sleep. He awoke with a start sometime later, becoming aware of something

_____

* *Antonio Villas Boas* (Wikipedia)

alighting on the bed. He was shocked to see two strange women kneeling on the end of his bed.

Both were naked. One appeared Nordic and the other Asian. Aspects of their appearance were quite odd. The Nordic female had a very elongated face and a sharply pointed chin. Her eyes appeared to be blue and 2 to 3 times larger than normal. She had very fine wispy blonde hair that seemed to be oddly blown up. Her skin color was quite light.

The dark brown skinned Asian looking woman seemed to have almost completely black eyes. Her hair was black and set in a firm page-boy style.

Although no normal communication occurred, the Nordic woman seemed to be in charge and Khoury got the impression she was giving the Asian looking woman some sort of instruction. What followed was quite disorientating for Khoury. The Nordic woman, who seemed to be over 6 feet tall and apparently very strong, reached forward and pulled Khoury's head to her breast. He resisted, trying to pull away.

She did this 3 times. Finally Khoury, trying to cope with the shock and disorientating nature of this experience, bit on her nipple, apparently swallowing a piece from it. The Nordic woman, although seemingly confused, did not react with any pain and nor was there any sign of blood. She seemed to convey to the other woman that this was not the way things were supposed to happen. Khoury was overcome with a coughing fit. Moments later, looking up again, he found that both women had vanished.

The coughing caused Khoury to go to the bathroom to get a drink of water. When he went to urinate he found it very painful to do so, due to, it turned out, some very fine blonde hair wrapped tightly under his foreskin. Khoury removed the hair and had the foresight to place it in a plastic sachet bag with a seal. He did that because he felt there was no way it should have been there.

It was unlike his wife's hair. Khoury concluded that something extraordinarily bizarre had just occurred and linked the 2 pieces of blonde thin hair (about 10-12 cm & 6-8 cm long) to the strange tall, blonde haired Nordic looking woman. [...] It was not until 1996 that I heard from Peter Khoury about the hair sample that had been recovered from what may have been an alien abduction sexual assault case.

By 1998, I began an investigation into the hair sample, when biochemical colleagues agreed to undertake what was the world's first PCR (polymerase Chain Reaction) DNA profiling of biological material implicated in an alien abduction experience. The analysis confirmed the hair came from someone who was biologically close to normal human genetics, but of an unusual racial type – a rare Chinese Mongoloid type – one of the rarest human lineages known, that lies further from the human mainstream than any other except for African pygmies and aboriginals.

There was the strange anomaly of it being blonde to clear instead of black, as would be expected from the Asian type mitochondrial DNA. The study concluded, "The most probable donor of the hair must therefore be as (Khoury) claims: a tall blonde female who does not need much color in her hair or skin, as a form of protection against the sun, perhaps because she does not require it."

The original DNA work was done on the shaft of the hair. Fascinating further anomalies were found in the root of the hair. Two types of DNA were found depending on where the mitochondrial DNA testing occurs, namely confirming the rare Chinese type DNA in the hair shaft and indicating a rare possible Basque/Gaelic type DNA in the root section. [...]

The nature of these genetic findings has lead to some interesting possible connections with ancient cultures, myths and archaeological finds such as the strange Taklamakan mummies in China (tall European like peoples (Celtic?), some of whom had blonde hair) and the stories of the female Basque God Mari and the Gaelic Irish tales of the Tuatha Dé Danann.

The Tuatha tales describe powerful gods with orange or blonde hair and other unusual attributes.

While such cultural and mythic connections are fascinating speculations, they provide for an interesting perspective on the many stories of Nordic type beings implicated in UFO abduction and contact cases.*

---

* <bibliotecapleyades.net/ciencia/ciencia_tuathadedanaan06.htm>

Bill Chalker makes an astute connection between Nordic aliens and certain human bloodlines, some of whom were seen as demigods by others of their time. There is a deep connection between the two.

One last anecdote is worth mentioning for its occult overtones. From Willy Schrödter's *A Rosicrucian Notebook:*

> ...a 20-year old musician into whose hands there came a book of Latin conjurations of the elemental spirits. A young theological student who was a friend of his translated his find for him and then he undertook the preliminary abstinence from meat, tobacco, alcohol, and women for several months. At the expiry of this period he uttered the prescribed conjurations, upon which 'two female sylphs appeared to him.' One was slightly built but the other was very big and tall. Like her companion, she had a mass of golden hair. He asked her if she would be his friend and they began to spend much time together. As the days went by she became more and more substantial; she no longer needed to fascinate him with looks and words but had him in her physical possession. Her love-making became so prolonged and vigorous that she was unable to stand the physical and mental strain. Therefore he decided to part from her, but this was easier said than done and it was only with the assistance of a practical Qabalist that he was able to regain his freedom." (Schrödter, 168-169).

This episode contains aspects of both alien and succubi encounters. Their becoming more substantial over time until attaining physical form is a trait common to both 1) etheric thoughtforms that gain energy and acquire materiality, and 2) some alien beings who need to synchronize themselves with our time rate and dimension in order to fully manifest. As I explained in my article *Timeline Dynamics,* there is a quantum phase factor that must align between two beings for each to experience the other as entirely tangible; this is so for interactions between humans, time travelers, aliens, and beings from other realms. In other words, aliens and thoughtforms both obey some of the same quasi-quantum or quasi-occult laws regarding the conditions of their manifestation in our physical reality.

Humans can meet these beings halfway by becoming etherically charged. This expands their psychic perception and allows levels of interaction otherwise disallowed. Sometimes this happens automatically, as explained in *UFOs in the Gulf Breeze-Pensacola Area:* "When a human gets around an extra-terrestrial, the enhanced energy/electromagnetic field of the E. T. has the impact of turning up the human's dimmer so that the consciousness is brighter.'"

Traditional esoteric instructions for invoking or contacting elementals aim to induce this same effect via other means:

> Before getting to know them it was necessary to have one's eyes cleansed with the universal medicine, and to have special flasks chemically prepared with one or other of the four elements and exposed to the sun's rays for a month. After these preliminaries, the initiate would see a host of beings of a shining substance, but loosely textured and diaphanous. These beings populate the elements all around us. (Schrödter, quoting *The Comte de Gabalis*).

Of course this refers to the Philosopher's Stone, or rather its etherically potent precursor, which, when ingested, artificially induces etheric activation and second sight. Other traditional methods for attracting these beings involve long periods of fasting and prayer before uttering an invocation, and/or giving offerings of positive etheric energy like freshly boiled fruit, cereals, and flowers. The flip side of that practice is the use of blood sacrifices in the invocation of demonic and negative thoughtforms, as discussed in previous chapters.

Persian Origins of Rosicrucianism

Schrödter goes on to explain the origin of the Rosicrucian knowledge concerning these beings:

> [Christian] Rosencreutz (1378-1484) is known to have brought back to Europe the ceremonial invocations of the planetary spirits and of the star spirits in general which he learned in Arabia and from the natives of Morocco.

> Anyway, the knowledge of how to summon the "fairies" (air spirits or sylphs) is also Arabic, and certainly of pre-Rosicrucian origin. In this connection, going backward in time, we have:

> 1) The Parsifal saga, which has an Arabic source [...];

2) The delegation sent by Charlemagne (768-814) to Harun-al-Ra-schid (763-809) [...];

3) The delegation from Pepin the Short (752-768) to Al-Mansur (754-775) [...].

As far as the third point is concerned, the saga *Flor und Blancheflor* by the Middle High German poet Konrad Fleck (ca. 1220) is the "expression" of a search carried out in the Orient two generations before Charlemagne, which prepared the way for the Rosicrucian Grail-movement in Christendom.

Under the second named Abbasid Caliph, *abu Giaffar al-Mansur,* the Arabian kingdom reached its greatest extent, but the Persian element was so influential that Frankish documents to refer to him as "Rex Persarum" (King of the Persians). *The doctrine of the "Peri" is peculiar to the Persians.* The word *Peri* comes from the Zendish *pairika* = fairy, and denotes a female spirit in Iranian cosmogony. The Peris, who are beneficent but glorious beings, inhabit the empyrean and subsist on the scent of flowers. *They often alight on the earth in order to have intercourse with men. The issue from such unions is of radiant beauty.* When the Persian poets speak of a lovely human child, they frequently call it a *Perizadeh* (= fairy child).

The *Touks* of Central Asia regard spirits of this type as very powerful. The *Baksas* (= witches) of the Kirghiz-Kazaks (free Kirgheezes between Irtish and the Caspian Sea) often *call on the Peris for help to exorcise Djinns and other evil spirits.*

The Peris have been divided into different groups. In the time of Charlemagne and Pepin, the astral world seems to have drawn especially near.

The Persian element hints at the particular cultural origins of the Grail myth and pretty much all mythological and traditional esoteric knowledge pertinent to demiurgic technology and its role in human history. The Persians were offshoots of an advanced post-Atlantean culture that spawned many others around the globe, the same culture responsible for building the Great Pyramid. This ties into Peter Khoury's encounter with a Nordic female having a combination of rare Asian and Celtic/Basque genetics.

Ninth Century Contactees

This next excerpt concerns a series of events from the time of Charlemagne and Pepin, which gives further indication that the Elementals described in *The Comte de Gabalis* are very likely the humanoid aliens of today.

> The famous Cabalist Zedechias, in the reign of your Pépin, took it into his head to convince the world that the Elements are inhabited by these Peoples whose nature I have just described to you. The expedient of which he bethought himself was to advise the Sylphs to show themselves in the Air to everybody; they did so sumptuously. These beings were seen in the Air in human form, sometimes in battle array marching in good order, halting under arms, or encamped beneath magnificent tents. Sometimes on wonderfully constructed aerial ships, whose flying squadrons roved at the will of the Zephyrs. What happened? Do you suppose that ignorant age would so much as reason as to the nature of these marvelous spectacles? The people straightway believed that sorcerers had taken possession of the Air for the purpose of raising tempests and bringing hail upon their crops. The learned theologians and jurists were soon of the same opinion as the masses. The Emperors believed it as well; and this ridiculous chimera went so far that the wise Charlemagne, and after him Louis the Débonnaire, imposed grievous penalties upon all these supposed Tyrants of the Air. You may see an account of this in the first chapter of the Capitularies of these two Emperors.

> The Sylphs seeing the populace, the pedants and even the crowned heads thus alarmed against them, determined to dissipate the bad opinion people had of their innocent fleet by carrying off men from every locality and showing them their beautiful women, their Republic and their manner of government, and then setting them down again on earth in divers parts of the world. They carried out their plan. The people who saw these men as they were descending came running from every direction, convinced beforehand that they were sorcerers who had separated from their companions in order to come and scatter poisons on the fruit and in the springs. Carried away by the frenzy with which such fancies inspired them, they hurried these innocents off to the torture. The great number of them who were put to death by fire and water throughout the kingdom is incredible.

In the account of Zedechias, who lived in the 9th Century, we see similarities to the 1950s contactee phenomenon. Otherworldly beings abduct certain individuals and show them their world before returning them to testify what they have seen. This tends to backfire, the only difference being that modern contactees were burned with ridicule instead of physical flames.

> One day, among other instances, it chanced at Lyons that three men and a woman were seen descending from these aerial ships. The entire city gathered about them, crying out that they were magicians and were sent by Grimaldus, Duke of Beneventum, Charlemagne's enemy, to destroy the French harvests. In vain the four innocents sought to vindicate themselves by saying that they were their own country-folk, and had been carried away a short time since by miraculous men who had shown them unheard-of marvels, and had desired them to give an account of what they had seen. The frenzied populace paid no heed to their defense, and were on the point of casting them into the fire when the worthy Agobard, Bishop of Lyons, who having been a monk in that city had acquired considerable authority there, came running at the noise, and having heard the accusations of the people and the defense of the accused, gravely pronounced that both one and the other were false. That it was not true that these men had fallen from the sky, and that what they said they had seen there was impossible.

> The people believed what their good father Agobard said rather than their own eyes, were pacified, set at liberty the four Ambassadors of the Sylphs, and received with wonder the book which Agobard wrote to confirm the judgment which he had pronounced. Thus the testimony of these four witnesses was rendered vain.

> Nevertheless, as they escaped with their lives they were free to recount what they had seen, which was not altogether fruitless for, as you will recall, the age of Charlemagne was prolific of heroic men. This would indicate that the woman who had been in the home of the Sylphs found credence among the ladies of that period and that, by the grace of God, many Sylphs were immortalised. Many Sylphids also became immortal through the account of their beauty which these three men gave; which compelled the people of those times to apply themselves somewhat to Philosophy; and thence are derived all

the stories of the fairies which you find in the love legends of the age of Charlemagne and of those which followed.

Grail researchers like Johannes W. Stein place the original characters and events of the Grail saga in the 9th Century. As mentioned, the Grail was present in Europe during that time, specifically in France, engendering the tales that were later woven into the Parzival story. Perhaps the Zedechias episode, involving close contact between humans and aliens, had something to do with it. Maybe as in times past, "neutral angels" brought it down to Earth while war raged in "Heaven."

Warring Factions

Take note where the Comte says, "These beings were seen in the Air in human form, sometimes in battle array marching in good order, halting under arms, or encamped beneath magnificent tents. Sometimes on wonderfully constructed aerial ships, whose flying squadrons roved at the will of the Zephyrs." If this account is true, then "battle array" and "squadrons" suggest they fight battles, including air battles. Thus they are not all unified, of homogeneous intentions, or at peace with each other.

Wars among the "gods" is a theme found widely in mythology including the Indian *Mahabharata* and *Ramayana* epics where aerial battles are fought using advanced crafts. Modern UFO sightings sometimes include accounts of dogfights among non-terrestrial crafts. And of course, there is the famous Battle of Nuremberg:

> In 1561, Hans Glaser documented a strange event on a woodcut for the German Nuremberg Gazette described as hundreds of crosses, globes and tubes fighting each other above the city. Some of the objects were reported to have disappeared into the sun, and others into a thick cloud of smoke after crashing into the ground. Many were said to witness the entire spectacle along with the appearance of a black, spear-like object after the battle. According to the accounts, not only did people of the 16th century witness what seems to be a UFO sky battle, they were also able to distinctly tell which side was winning.

Coupled with the occurrence in Nuremberg, five years later in 1566, citizens of Basel Switzerland witnessed a similar spectacle involving several black orbs engaged in sky battle above. The people of Basel also recorded the event in their city gazette with a woodcut that cannot be traced to a known artist. Accounts claimed the black orbs would sometimes turn red and fiery before fading to nothing.[*]

The Rosicrucian Endgame

In this final excerpt from *The Comte de Gabalis,* the Comte hints at the ultimate endgame:

> All these so-called fairies were only Sylphids and Nymphs. Did you ever read those histories of heroes and fairies? [...] they would have given you some idea of the state to which the Sages are one day determined to reduce the world. Those heroic men, those love affairs with Nymphs, those voyages to terrestrial paradise, those palaces and enchanted woods and all the charming adventures that happen in them, give but a faint idea of the life led by the Sages and of what the world will be when they shall have brought about the Reign of Wisdom. Then we shall see only heroes born; the least of our children will have the strength of Zoroaster, Apollonius or Melchizedek; and most of them will be as accomplished as the children Adam would have had by Eve had he not sinned with her.

This "Reign of Wisdom", which ties into the New World Order agenda and what Jordan Maxwell has written concerning the "dawn of a new day" will be discussed in the next chapter. It is the final consequence of demiurgic technology entering the human sphere, the final event over which alien forces and time travelers have been competing since the beginning.

Fore

With all the above in mind, we have a fuller context to appreciate the experiences of a contemporary contactee who calls himself Fore on the (now defunct) Open Minds Forum. Compared to other published contactee stories, his paints a more detailed and realistic picture of what *some* of these Nordic aliens are like. The fair but necessary

---

[*] <mysterypile.com/nuremberg.php>

number of excerpts to follow are from his thread titled *My Experiences (Grey, Pleiadians and Oddities)*:

> The last memory segment the advisor brought back and it is when we first met. I can verify some of the events because I had my mother relay them to me and I referenced the information I saw to what happened.

> I am still in the hot space that is dark in my body. Then I feel like something is wrong. Someone tried to pull me out and I hate the cold. I want to stay inside. Then someone grabs me and I feel pain and suddenly I'm in cold air. I felt like crying because I am uncomfortable. I see through very blurry eyes that there are two males and two women with different clothes. I can't see much because my eyes are blurry. Then I am put to rest on something cold and I hear speech from men asking questions. I don't understand the language they are using. Then I feel people cleaning me up and trying to hold me. I hear laughter and talking and I feel tired. The next thing I remember one of the older men takes me while I am wrapped up in something and I see what looks like a hall. I don't know what happens next but I wake up or am in an orange box. I feel something nearby. I hear in my mind thoughts that I do not understand. (As i am remembering what I did not understand then I finally understand what was being said.) I hear a woman voice (the advisor) I hear her saying "he should be around here." I feel a mans thoughts who she is talking with. Then I feel them get closer and suddenly I see a woman in my sight beyond the edges of the box. I stare at her chest. I see a woman with dirty blonde hair at shoulder length. She says "Here he is, This is him, He's so cute." She puts out her hands towards me. She seems pleased that she found me from the expressions I feel coming from her.

> Her chest is the only clear part I see. Her clothes are amazing. They are like overall's made of a strange fabric. It looks super real...more real than real. It is like an emerald green or a tinge of teal blue (I'm not good with colors.) It looks like a weird texture of rubber like fabric and there are shards all over it of different colors like a glitter of some kind only very spectacular. There is an orange/yellow light that shines brightly all around her. Her hair is shoulder long thats dirty blonde. She looks fit like someone who works out but she isn't bulky. She has the shape of a fit gymnast. Her face is blurry and I cannot see it.

As I am waking up she speaks to me and tells me this is when we first met in this life. She says that and lets me think over everything I have just experienced. I strangely feel for a second like it was exactly what was meant to happen but when I started thinking about it, I started to lose the reason of why it had to happen that way.

I only saw her from the waist up. I don't remember seeing the man but from his thoughts He was somewhere beyond the plastic but I never got to see him. This was in a Venezuelan hospital off the coast on an island called margarita. If it is true, which I do believe so because I checked with my mom as to what happened during delivery, then the date was February 16, 1981. (Feb 21, 2007, 4:28am)

She brought back memories that I had as a newborn. (it's in my thread)

As a newborn I remember seeing her physically. I saw a woman whom looked to be fit like a gymnast type body. Wearing a jumpsuit of a very odd nature.

The clothing she had on, looked like a one piece suit that was an emerald green. It looked like it was made of a rubber patterned surface. In it's ?fibers? was something that looked like glitter or sparks of color.

(I know this sounds strange) She looked more Real than "Real".

Her body looked like a woman who goes to a gym. And a yellow/orange (golden?) light was emitting off her skin. It was bright but it didn't seem to hurt my eyes.

Her skin color was that of a normal human being. The closest I can compare it to is that of a Californian blond. Her hair was a dirty blond.

Her voice has never changed.

———————————————————————

Now below this line is from modern observations.

———————————————————————

Her age doesn't seem to pass 27 from the way she sounds and her appearance physically.

She looks physically fit like always. I saw her several times using second sight (psychic) or when waking up from my deep sleep. (this was during my campaign to get to know her better)

I have heard her physical voice, once, when I was waking up. It was somehow a bit more elegant sounding than her telepathic voice. She stopped singing as soon as I woke up.

Once she showed me asked me to close her eyes when I wouldn't believe she was physically there. When she brought her face close to mine i suddenly saw in the dark the very detailed features of eyes.

It scared me and left me bewildered. And eventually I noticed (while kissing a family member good bye) that her eyes were larger than that of a human being. I had a family member put their head close to mine to figure out just how big her eyes were....

The first thing I noticed was that the advisors pupil size is larger. And the shape of her eyes is wider. Overall her eyes are about 20% to 50% larger than that of a normal person. (Nov 6, 2007, 4:02pm)

I have noticed other people describing surprisingly similar types of encounters with people like the advisor. They use different words but generally the same concepts.

Some of the matching characteristics is a light emanating from their body. Described as a golden glow. I reported it as yellow and orange-ish light.

I describe a woman who looks like she is healthy thin and in normal proportions. It varies in other depictions.

Generally the clothes are of the same kind. A kind of one piece suit that in mine was a greenish-blue. With a glittering shards of light effects coming of her body. Almost as if she were more than real.

In other accounts I have noticed people call it "sparks".

So it seems she matches some of the accounts of what a human-like woman ET looks like.

She claimed her point of origin was of a people with 7 home worlds with 11 surrounding colonies. Her being from the fourth colony. Could this be a lie? Probably.

———————————————————

She never choose to use names, stating that it was pointless to use human names that weren't even universally agreed on. And she was always shying away when I asked direct questions about her origin. She sometimes made comments that she couldn't tell me very much about that because there were people who were looking for groups like hers.

She also seemed to be scared or experienced a deep hesitation from my prodding of her identity. Making jokes:

"that for all I knew I might be her great great great grandfather."

Other times she expressed a deep preoccupation whenever I would write something down about them. Saying expressly that I could not write down things because there were other groups patrolling the future and looking for people like her who were messing around prior to this "acclaimed" aftermath that she claimed would one day occur. (Mar 16, 2008, 7:27pm)

Oh and the advisor taught me some old phrases in english (I haven't used them in a long time so forgive me if i don't remember them at the tip of a hat.). People asked me why I used phrases that were out of date and I told them it was because she sometimes used them when she was feeling lazy or she wasn't taking things seriously. I asked some old fogies if they knew how old the phrases were but they told me it was older than them. The advisor said that before she came to know me in Venezuela that she was working in florida then texas and then ireland. She told me she learned english there in the last century. Where she was before then she didn't say. Though now that i think about it I don't remember her having any accent when she speaks telepathically. (Mar 12, 2007, 10:25am)

These traits should already be familiar: the bodysuit, unusually large eyes, blond hair, and above-average physique. The glittering or shimmering suit fabric is reminiscent of Orfeo Angelucci's observations. According to Fore, the glowing skin may be an energy leakage effect that can occur when a being from another realm downshifts deeply into ours. A kind of "decompression" takes place that causes a release of radiation, which in extreme cases can be harmful to humans. Anecdotally, in ancient lore, such beings were sometimes called "The Shining Ones" because "their faces shone like the Sun."

One of the main things that stuck in my mind today in her long lectures was the fact that she claimed there were various groups on earth with different kinds of associations. She mentioned that the second network and it's associated sphere of influence was complicated and had a lot of history.

One of the main things she talked about was the earth being divided among the aliens into sections with no particular shape or border affiliations with the earthly national borders (the first network). She mentioned that most of the USA was Grey territory. Latin America was a mix of different aliens from Grey and her kind along with others being whom she described as having less than human shape and odd supernatural abilities.

She made a point that the world was carved up into alien territories and that they didn't respect human national borders. She claimed that I would hear of the different varieties of alien types that were present in different regions and in different proportions.

That eventually did seem to be true....

She said that when I was born I was born in one of her peoples territories. I asked her why then if the Grey are supposed to be in charge in the USA is she with me. I then got pretty paranoid that she was a Grey or something. Which she was adamant that she wasn't one. She reprimanded me repeatedly about being "speciest" and all that.

Anyway, she claimed that not all Grey were "evil" and that while many didn't have good intentions towards people on earth there were a few who didn't want to hurt people in general. I scoffed at the idea and mentioned abductions and all that...to which lead to an argument...etc. (for another day and another post)

————————————————-

Tangent:

Years earlier as a young teen (while I was still wondering if she was a spiritual being or some kind of alien or demon) she had explained in rather odd terms that "they" (her people) scan frequently in hospitals for new births. She said they look for individuals who meet certain factors. She said they make note of them and look in on them over the following years after their birth.

When I asked her what kind of factors they look at, she declined to tell me (much to my frustration). She would only tell me that there were over a hundred factors they look at, on an individual basis, and then determine what if any use they have for that person in a "project".

She said that they also do sweeps in neighborhoods, in 2 to 3 week intervals for newborns. She had said at the time that not all newborns were born at hospitals. (which at the time I didn't realize was true, since it had never crossed my mind till she mentioned it)

At that time, my understanding of her was, that she was a being of a really strange kind. And to hear those kind of things from her made me deeply paranoid of her intentions. It was always that way till our parting. And to this day I still hold a lot of angst, anger, and paranoia in her not being very straight forward when it came to her intentions or identity. Over time I have learned to get over those feelings.

Tangent over.

————————————————————

She said that when I was moved over to the USA she had to make arrangements with "the others".

She explained to me in very fine detail at the time that there was a truce of mutual cooperation between "the others" and "her people". She explained that in order for a project to continue in an opposing faction's jurisdiction that there would have to be an understanding and process of introducing a "visitor group".

She seemed to not like her superiors very much...let me put that out there and be very clear about this.

So she goes on to explain that when I moved from Venezuela to the USA as a baby her group was obligated to enter into a cooperative group relationship with "the others". (I'll give the short version).

————————————————————

She was the "visitor member" in their territory and the males were supposed to be the designated hosts. The home team if you think in baseball terms.

Now she never mentioned at this point that the males were actually Grey! I was completely oblivious but I had my general distrust anyway of the males.

She alluded to the real personalities of the males years before hand and years afterwards. But she would always put restrictions and distractions and endless rules so that I would seemingly never put the pieces of the picture together. Sometimes, I wonder how I could have been so blind. Really!

She would only say things like:

Her superiors would order her to perform tests on me or to retrieve permission from me for tests.

How she didn't like doing experiments on me and how she disliked her superiors method.

Once, upon asking her if she had any friends in her group; She flatly responded that those whom she works with are just "associates". That she didn't have any friends within her group. And that struck me as deeply odd for a few years until I finally saw whom the males were first hand.

———————————————————-

So let me write how she put it in my own words for the sake of my sanity and for the sake of simplicity.

————————————————————

Simple Summary:

In her case. She found me when I was born in one of her territories. She supposedly had her own group back then.

Then I was moved into an area where her group didn't have juris-dictions. A territory outside her groups control. So she said she had to talk with "the others" and come to an agreement to working in a cooperative relationship. (A common thing she said).

Then she said (fuzzy) she was picked from her group to stay with me and she was given permission to work in "the others" territory. "The others" territory in this case is large chunks of the USA according to her.

She was assigned two members from "the others"; three males. I only really ever got to listen to two males cause the third one always seemed busy and far away. Rarely did I get to notice the third one unless they were taking notes as to what I was doing. And the males sound very much alike so its pretty hard to tell them apart. The males seemingly liked to talk one after the other or all at once, which was annoying.

Anyway, She said when that was done, she was considered the visitor member but that she was in control of the project. (me)

She said that the males were her superiors. She said they opted to let her have direct control over me because I kept rejecting them when they tried to make a bond with me (my paraphrased words).

She explained to me in detail that this was how both sides (which she hadn't yet called it "factions" at this point) dealt with each others projects in their opposing jurisdictions.

The groups who were in opposing factions, with different agendas got to see and spy on each others activities on earth. She said her people got to spy on "the others" and "the others" got to spy on them.

She said that typically when there is a visitor member, the visitor member is supposed to hang back during an abduction or experiment till they are invited or authorized to engage the person or project. (their quaint word for those being experimented or tested on)

She said that I would eventually hear of this. Of aliens who had completely opposing beliefs on things, who would be in each others presence during an abduction. Amazingly, this was true... (Jul 29, 2007, 9:34am)

In Fore's case, a member of one faction is given a supervised guest position in another, for mutual benefit despite the antagonism between the factions. And indeed, abductee accounts do include mention of polarized presences in the same abduction environment beyond just a "good cop bad cop" trick, which would seem like a contradiction but makes sense if viewed from the context of alien cold war diplomacy. This further shows that alien factions are not all united in harmony, yet blurred lines and complex politics exist between them.

> She said she was part of an "academy" (literally) and that she came to the earth (I don't remember) a while ago. She said she was relatively young compared to her peoples age and therefore was not considered to be very knowledgeable. She said she was roughly 532 years old. The year she told me this escapes me, but it think it was roughly near 2000. Imagine my surprise at the end of our contacts (for a time) that she starts actually telling me about herself. I was to say the least between skeptical and happy. To pull information out of her, about herself, was like pulling teeth (molars mind you).

> She said that because of differences in time scape and ?"drift"? in traveling long distance she was born in 1423 roughly. She said she was approximating roughly when she was born. She said there were 7 home worlds and 11 colony worlds where her people live. She said she was born on the 4th colony world. (she still would not say what she was though) She went on to say that her people live about 3,326 → 3,332 years on average. She said some gifted people do live up to 7500 years but that it is very rare. I asked her how the hell could she be so old if she sounded pretty young. At this point I started to assume either A) she was lying or B) some entity was mimicking her voice.

> She asked me if I wanted to know or not. So I relented and let her continue. She said that on her world when two people fall in love they declare their love for each other. There is no marriage she plainly put it. She said that they also don't have children like human beings. She said that human beings (forgive her candidness lol) have sex and produce babies in a haphazard way. She said (fuzzy) that when they wanted to have a child that they went to a place and picked out the best gene's for the child. She said they picked the best traits and had children that way. So I was surprised that she was admitting that they genetically engineer. She said yes, that it was a normal thing and that the earth would start doing it soon enough also at it's current rate.

> She said that certain traits were favored than others. Thats why she said certain contactees see them as not varying much. She said the

first letter of the father or mothers name is passed on to the child. She said they didn't really have last names, though there was (fuzzy) a special name they had. She tried many times to tell me her special name but it comes out garbled and I can't make sense of it. Though it never changed in the many years I knew her. The garbled name sounds exactly the same many years later. So I know it's not my imagination. She said the family tree has a suffix that is added to the end of the name. I wont say her name, because she told me then alot of psychics will try to contact her and she will have to ignore them.

She said their family structures were much different than those on earth. She (confused me a lot) said that they pick more than one mate and that there isn't a single union. Though she said it sometimes happens. (I think I skipped a lot right here because i don't remember clearly.) She said that when the children are born they are raised and at the age of 8 there is a ritual they perform in their society where the child's rate of growth is slowed down significantly. She said at that age the children go to school. She said she learned in school for about 117 years (fuzzy, i think that, or 111 years) . She said they also absorb information at a very quick pace compared to human beings. She said she could learn one of my books in about a weeks time. I was surprised. She reminded me of the movie with travolta..."phenomenon"?

She said that when they relax they put on different clothes. I asked her what clothes? And she said they are naked underneath but they have a white robe on top with something about the shoulder pads (she showed me an image). She said she had an important man in her life already and had already had 3 girls.

I met them years earlier as a teenager. I was introduced to 2 teen-age-like girls out of the blue. I think I must have been 13? The girls had the signature of a "uber human" (this was not coined back then) and they felt, spoke like, and sounded like teenagers. They seemed extremely similar. She out of the blue announced that they were her children, that if i wanted to meet them. Here, I was, wondering if spirits could have children (I didn't assume her to be an alien back then). The girls gave me funny eyes and looks. They spoke to me like they were checking me out in a funny way.

They were nice but seemed to be very, very smart. I doubt they were young by human standards though. I thought maybe the advisor (unnamed as of then) was joking or something. The girls looked at me now that I think about it with an eye like they were checking out moms new boyfriend?? . They left after about an hour, after asking me a lot of questions.

She said that she joined an academy a while back. She said there they taught her a few things here on the earth. She said she had already 4 to 7 contacts already. She said 4 Major ones if I remember correctly and 3 minor temporary ones. She admitted to me that she was different from her people (insinuations). She said that she was punished in about the 1800's because there was a man who she fell in love with and that the man rejected her for some reason. She said she fell in love with him and that (didn't explain but she seemed pained) the man rejected her. She said she was slighted (read: angry) and started to somehow torture him; and because of her actions she said it lead to his accidental death. She said since then she was heavily restricted from using her abilities and from showing herself.

Other beings, who had the same uber human signature, said that the advisor was special. They said that she was capable of....having an emotional bond similar to a human being and that made her "very compatible". The advisor over the years admitted that she had a marked past and that she sometimes felt isolated from her own kind because they looked at her as different. She said that having that gift to ?empathize? and connect with a person like a human being was somehow looked down upon. She told me many times that her superiors did not like the things she did. That she bonded too much or that she was lenient with me. (Feb 19, 2007, 10:58pm)

The advisor described their semi-physical presence that is on the same level as us to be overwhelming to us. She said everything should feel like a loudspeaker in strength (emotions/mental etc). That it tends to paralyze someone who meets them without them converting to a physical form. Their thoughts should be sharp and clear. Although I doubt we might understand them clearly because like she mentioned we don't have that clear mind they do nor the ability to inspect thought to such a minute level.

About the advisor. She told me many times that compared to us they are much more emotional and mental (not the crazy type). But I don't know how to put this in the correct context. They are very heady and thought orientated. They are smart. From the people of her type that I have encountered I notice they are very mental orientated. Their emotions run much stronger than us. But they aren't out of control like we are in our emotions. Their mind seems to dominate their personality.

The big difference though that i noted between the advisor and the other people of her kind was that the advisor has an emotional landscape similar to ours although it is much stronger. But the other people like her are very much more restrained in their emotions even though they have a higher capacity than us. It's hard to describe in english. It would be easier to experience it than explain it. The people like the advisor were like big brained. Everything about them is much stronger than us. Though there was a cold detached-ness about them that the advisor did not share with them.

They are no where near the Greys that I met in real life. The Greys are purely intellect without emotions and they only have intent. The Greys are uncaring and don't seem to see us as people but as things. I can see why people think they are biological machines. I would think it too if I hadn't observed opinions and their thoughts about how some of us are useless to them. I make no apologies for them....they are cold and uncaring.

The people like the advisor (Pleiadians?) are heady and smart but not emotionally absent. Their thoughts and mind dominate who they are though. But the advisor was different. Her feelings seemed to be closer to the surface like a human beings. She was very heady though just like them. ?But special I guess?

I used to think the advisor was perfect when i was about 12 or 11. But she "sat me down", figuratively speaking, and told me that she wasn't perfect and that she was capable of errors and that she didn't know everything. I took her word for it and still do. There are some contacts though that idolize the Pleiadians and make them seems like they are Gods or are perfect. Which from what I see is not so at all. I might admire the advisor but she ain't my deity. (Feb 20, 2007, 2:03am)

Lifespan in the centuries, the potential for amorous love but also vengeance, intellectual superiority, and concealment of their real names and places of origin were traits touched upon earlier.

The advisor sometimes described the society she came from and it was a very intellectual society with some "issues" from my own point of view. They were so similar yet so different.

She often confided that where she came from people were so controlled vs what we had here on this earth. That people could make love and have children with whomever they chose and they didn't have to adapt the genetics or think much on those considerations.

She had said in her own expression that is/was "very chaotic" choices.

But she liked the level of freedom we had to choose whatever we wanted to do by our own (as she said) desires. While over where she came from she said things such as expressions were all very expressive but within a predefined limit.

She used at the time a complex expression as if her society was the thought police within a certain paradigm. Sure there were comforts and expression, but she often bemoaned that it was all very controlled and confined.

I can liken her descriptions as being something like a futuristic society where some of the constants found on earth are not present over there.

They do things differently and they restrict how free you are to express yourself in whatever way you want to. Sort of like living in a super polite and enlightened society that doesn't allow any disturbing elements.

Reminds me sometimes when I think over her expressions of a hyper advanced version of the society found in the movie "Demolition Man". Funny as that may sound LOL.

The way she kept showing me things it seemed like a very stale but peaceful society where you had lots of perks but also had lots of restrictions. When she described her world it seemed as if peace requires less freedoms.

This provides additional insight on the issue of human-alien mating, which may involve recreational aspects beyond the genetic factor. Perhaps some regret the repressive conditions in their realm and wish to take advantage of the more libertine atmosphere on Earth. Being telepathic as they are, they must know of this atmosphere far too well.

> She asked me strange questions. She made motions as if pointing towards a table nearby and asked me why did that table stay in that location? I said cause no one is moving it. She asked me again but added why did the table stay there in non-english. I understood better what she meant. She meant to say why does the table continue to exist in that spot only and why does it not suddenly move somewhere else. In other words why was it stable in the position that it was in?

> She made me think deeply and even with all the physics I knew I told her I just didn't know why matter behaved that way. She told me that If I could imagine a rough idea of a coordinate system that space uses to locate objects. That there was also other codings it uses for referring to where in time. She reminded me of what I knew of physics and told me that if I remembered clearly the "strange action at a distance" that I had heard of was of a system that our universe uses to correct itself among other things (to not type a lot for my sake.).

> Short answer is that she told me there was a system for our reality to keep tabs on itself. She said they used this system to travel in time. She said Time travel was as common to her people as it was for me to ride a bus.

> She said that more advanced aliens used a more complicated system to cause imbalances at a distance in the universe. When the universe corrected for the imbalance the particular alien would be transported to a new destination without having traveled the distance in between. (i don't think that is a wormhole though). She said these advanced aliens let the universe do the hard work for them.

> She said her people were not as advanced as these aliens were. But she said it was very efficient since it did not consume very much energy. She said that besides the imbalance they have to create, that it was about the most they had to expend energy wise. (Apr 10, 2007, 10:09am)

> When she revealed to me that she could travel in time and that it was as common an experience for her as it was for me to ride a bus. She showed me a view of her world from her own eyes (a memory?).

It was a while after I learned of her real mind. I saw an amazing vista of a craft that did not look like a saucer or anything like that. It had light shooting out from it's side. It was either a plane of some kind or it was a bus. I'm not at all sure because it seemed so authentically futuristic and it's shape was very strange for a vehicle.

And from that tiny vista I gathered the idea that they come from a society that is so advanced that they seem to keep secrets about their identity and their technologies. I came away with the deep impression that she just might be a time traveler. Though im pretty hard pressed to believe it till I see it.

From what I could gather, of the sight at that moment, the advisor was walking down a walkway or hallway. The hall had window panes to her right, with herself looking towards the right. Out the window you see a craft that is oddly shaped almost as if it were a very large bus or craft of some kind with light shooting out of it's side as if it were a transport of some kind. It was levitating and from the quick view I didn't see it touching the ground. I do not know how to interpret what I saw but It was either an airport of some kind or a bus terminal.

At the time she showed me this, she stated that (as a matter of fact, in her own view) If I were to see where she had come from, I would be amazed by the technology. Which she doesn't find amazing herself. She said I would honestly think that some of it was magic even though I knew it wasn't. (Jun 26, 2007, 8:17am)

She said she was going to a world near by to study how to manifest herself physically completely. There are a few things maybe some people should know about them. I learned this over years of time with her when she taught me how to profile entities when they would not reveal their identity.

1 – They are semi-physical

They posses bodies that while they may look like us they have an extension of themselves and their powers surrounding them. Some would call this a golden halo or an aura that is markedly Gold like and overwhelming.

2 – They do not seem to be all of the time be situated in our time. For example, one day when i was young she told me if i loved my little

birds to go and pet it. I asked her why. And she went roundabout in her conversation and when pushed finally told me my little bird was going to die. I said to her that i didn't believe her, she said it was true. I asked her when this was supposedly going to happen? She said for her in the next three minutes. I waited three minutes and nothing happened. So i called her a liar. Three days later the little bird died.

I thought of nothing about that incident, and maybe around when i was 10 or so she had left for a few days. She came back announcing from far away somewhere that they were "finishing synchronizing to your time". As you can imagine, I raised my eyebrow wondering what she was talking about this time.(i didn't think she was an alien, just a really odd being). When she got closer to me from her "place" she said that she and i were "now in synch". I asked her what she was talking about but she (I don't remember honestly) ignored me i think.

Time passed and she made more predictions which i scoffed at the idea she could. So she told me when things were going to happen and they did. I thought all the time it was coincidence. Then when i got into my "your not real and i must be crazy!" years she started to show she was not a figment of my imagination by predicting things and telling me what others around me were doing and what would happen tomorrow down to every detail. When i went online in about 1998 and against her wishes looked for information by asking people in yahoo chat rooms. She would make predictions and ask me to tell them. In one prediction, she predicted 3 years ahead of time that there would be a large explosion in new york city. She said that i should tell them it will happen in some time and roughly around September/October/November. She made it sound like a large explosion so i thought she meant a nuclear bomb. But she never said it was a nuclear bomb she just said there was a lot of "artificial terror". This was 9/11 by the way.

Point is, they can see the future. They know what will happen tomorrow, rev, and what you will talk about in detail and what is up ahead in several months to years time.

3 – Their known mind to contactee's are just fronts.

When she was making those predictions to people . Which this made me feel like a fool telling them about her and saying what she wanted till she proved her point. They believed she was real but i didn't accept the possibility. She read their mind and told me what they were thinking and many things. But i was a hard person to accept her as real. In one experiment in 2002 after 6 years of training with her to learn how to use my abilities, she was aligning my energy patterns to a new configuration and help me unblock the garbage that builds up in the non-physical body. She was having me do remote viewing while i was talking to a friend of mine. Suddenly i see a flash in my sight and i can't see anything for a microsecond and suddenly i am seeing through the friend's husbands' eyes. The friend was asking me how her husband felt about her. I was her husband seeing through his eyes for about 4 seconds. When i relayed this amazing thing to her she replied that what i saw happened about an hour ago.

The caretaker fooled about a bit more a couple hours later and suddenly it happens again and i see through the caretakers eyes and i see the back of my head and i see through her eyes, peering over my shoulder reading a conversation I'm having within a chatroom and seeing conversational possibilities that didn't take place. But the little i read it was very close to what actually happened. For a second, i was her and I felt humanoid in shape and even saw her arms. Amazing i thought. She acted like she had committed a mistake and was "kicking herself" type of expression. A few minutes later the top of my head seems to start having hot sensation of energy flowing through it and suddenly i have another flash and this time I AM HER for about 4 to 5 seconds. When i start seeing my normal vision again i hear her being frustrated and upset that she messed up big time. She didn't want me to see that! I was in her shoes for a second time and i had such expansive thoughts! Super complicated thoughts that even today i cannot make sense of and were completely unhuman. Thats when i started referring to her as a uber human type. The thoughts were so profound and knowledgeable that it would take a month to render such a complex idea. I cannot imagine these people as having two arms, two legs, and one head. Whatever they are they are unlikely to be related to humans.

4 – Non-Linear planners

They do not think nor act nor plan like us. After she showed me how to understand a psyche and so many other things. I started to notice developing patterns and with my higher mind now within my control (well almost back then) I started becoming more and more suspicious that they were holding back information and i started to see lines of deception and psychological tricks, manipulative behaviors, pre-programmed responses in other contactee's, abductees/experiments, and consistency. Consistency of contactees and their behaviors and how they react and how the aliens "keep" them began to light serious warning signs about this whole phenomena. When i began to see evidence that she was indeed

1) Real

2) Semi-Corporeal

3) Had a consciousness separate from my own.

4) Had a presence and observational abilities separate from my own.

5) Intelligence.

6) Consistent tests passed.

I started to panic and became worried that i was being brought up to do something that might indeed not be in humanities best interest. And worse brought up in a blind fashion unable to observe what the agenda was nor it's final intended result. (Feb 4, 2007, 10:56am)

These are highly valuable details concerning their semi-physical nature, their need to synchronize with our time rate, and the trans-temporal factors involved in their strategic planning and manipulation of human society. The traits may be termed hyperdimensional, though on the lower end of the scale. It's important to recognize the time travel capabilities of these beings, because the implications are immense. For instance, it leads to the idea of timewars and what I have written concerning demiurgic technology shifting the timeline at key moments in history.

I don't remember how that conversation led to this one but we somehow jumped to the conversation of atlantis. This I did know some about. Mostly that the people were super advanced and about plato describing their land or something. I asked her about that and she told me after a few hours that the people who were alive in "atlantis" were not how people pictured them to be.

She said before one of the resets that occurs to human beings (read: dieoff) there was a people who interacted with humanity. She said the people who were here during this time were of many types of races. She said the human beings who were alive during that time in the place we tended to call "atlantis" were in open contact with other races and that some knowledge about math and astronomy was passed to those people. She said there was a very large misconception about "Atlantis".

She said the mainland used to be where Antarctica is now. And that the places people look for evidence of atlantis is actually just outposts. She said that "Atlantis" was full of a people who were given information about certain fields of knowledge but not others. She said they understood geometry and math but had almost no knowledge of metallurgy. She said they were actually less advanced than we were. As you can imagine i was interested in what she had to say.

She kept on saying something about the technology that is now folklore were technology that the people visiting the earth at that time was sharing with these people. The generators she said weren't using electrons based technology but were solid state (fuzzy) nuclear reactors. She said the reactors were really old technology that they no longer used even at that time. She said the casing was made of a crystal and that it was portable which she said laid the current mysticism of energy coming from crystals. She said the people who were human were actually ignorant of how to use it and how it worked. They supposedly had a lopsided understanding and she said in some aspects they were very smart in knowledge and understanding of certain fields but were not knowledgeable in chemicals or science as we have made it today.

She said there was a lot of technology loaned to those people to build a basic society but they were dependent on the technologies loaned at the time. She said they were very mystically orientated (unsure about this part, it was a long time ago). She said (I'm sure about this) the people came in contact with aliens on a regular basis. She said the outposts were north of cuba and to the east.. The other was in the indian ocean south of australia and to the west. The last she said was a minor outpost that no longer exists that used to be near japan and east of hawaii. She said it was more of an independent nation than an outpost. She said from the outposts they spread some of the knowledge after the resets.

She said these people had, at the end, the technology taken from them and were left to fend for themselves. She was unclear around here about what happened next. She also said something about people who look like human beings but were alien used to "fly" and had some special belt. I don't recall all of it at this time. All she said in basic was that these people were materially primitive but had subjective knowledge. She said most of the big designs that the aliens built for them are probably still under sheets of ice. Oh and she said that some of the devices that weren't recovered were still active and were creating problems. Also said something about the devices intermittently working.

About the nuclear reactor that looks like a pretty sizable crystal. I just remembered her saying something about it being safe and that it didn't use a type of technology that we use now (electronic). She said that in the old days, of her people, they used to use assembles that were structured on an atomic level. She said that the old technologies used casings that were built out of atoms that were put together in a perfect shape and that because of it they looked like crystal that glows when the reactors are active. (Feb 16, 2007, 6:56am)

As the previous chapters explained, the Grail and Ark Stone are remnant alien technologies that have been with us since Atlantean times. Fore wrote, "some of the devices that weren't recovered were still active and were creating problems. Also said something about the devices intermittently working." There may be more buried around the world, but at least some of that technology was passed among human hands and employed with great effect. And just as the Israelite priests used the Ark Stone with only limited knowledge on how to activate and direct it, so were the Atlanteans using technology beyond their comprehension. That's why these artifacts have never been duplicated by humans and why petty wars have been fought over them; they were of limited supply, having originally been manufactured by aliens and later leased to humans with only a basic set of operating instructions.

More on alien technology:

One of these was a chamber which she showed me in my mind eye. She said they posses a technology that can grow organs rapidly. This was an offshoot conversation from her talking and answering some of my questions (and others) about bodies of theirs. She showed me a chamber which looked like a rectangular box that seemed to be made of a material that looks like Plexiglas. It looked roughly transparent. She said in these chambers that were kept underground in habitats that groups could grow organic bodies or if the need arose supposedly organs. She said that her people were already capable of time travel so they understood the mechanics of what time is in actuality. To this i gave my standard "sure, you must be feeling creative today?" kind of mental pokes.

She told me the chamber is transparent so they can keep an eye on the materials that are below the casing and so that they can keep an eye on the progress of the growth in an accelerated time state (i dunno what to translate that into). She said they used their knowledge of what causes time to occur to cause a limited portion of space within the casing to accelerate while the organs or bodies were rapidly absorbing the materials underneath the chamber. She showed me what looks like two transparent boxes that seemed removable and contained a red liquid and the other liquid i don't seem to recall what color it was.

She said the usefulness of the bodies was that they could produce replicas in a matter of hours or days depending on the method. She said the maximum the chambers could produce was about a year in close to a 24 hour period of normal time. She said that the chambers were useful to them if they needed to temporarily inhabit a body of a different make up.

She said this involved another science they had made that was used to separate the non-physical body from the physical body. She said they then (sorry little details, she made generalizations) removed the spiritual essence that is them, and for example, can prepare a body that is of a different type and rebuild certain things of the connections between the new one and then embed the spiritual presence into that new body. (damn that was hard to put down.) (Feb 11, 2007, 9:18am)

This gets into the human simulacra problem I have written about on my website, where alien and shadow human groups are manufacturing fake humans to take up positions of influence within society. Therefore, reports of human-looking aliens, especially those seen in everyday situations, may include both alien beings who have materialized here fully and can pass for human, and artificial avatars grown in time-acceleration chambers. Encounters with individuals who speak as if they were Nordic aliens, but whose eyes, physiques, hair, etc. look entirely average, may be examples of avatars. This would be necessary to evade detection in high-profile positions.

The use of avatars or cybernetic probes, regardless of the shape they take, is common alien technology. It allows a consciousness incarnated in one realm to temporarily operate in another without the side effects and problems associated with having to translate the physical body itself. Consider the technical difference in cost and logistics between astral projecting into the past and possessing someone there, versus building a device to transport you physically to the past.

Another potential example of this technology is in *UFOs in the Gulf Breeze-Pensacola Area:*

> Off to the right of the giant screen TV, is a series of cylinders that are the height of the room and about the diameter of telephone booths. There are door size openings, no sharp angles of course, on each of them. I would say there are 5 of them arranged in a row.
>
> Each of us instinctively, at least for me, heads for a booth. I enter the booth and the opening disappears behind me. No noise, just suddenly the cylinder is sealed.
>
> Inside the cylinder, there is suddenly a brilliant blue light and a hum. the hum starts out fairly low-pitched and picks up in intensity. It's not the intensity of the sound, it is the frequency getting higher and higher causing the sound pitch to change.
>
> As the frequency gets higher, I start getting bigger. When the sound stops and the light returns to white, I'm adult sized. I don't look like me, like my current adult version, I look different but there are some similarities.
>
> Rather than the kid clothes I arrived in, I now have on coveralls like the personnel I saw in the hanger. The extra-terrestrial driving the shuttle device had on little moccasin type shoes. They're soft but have somewhat of a sole on them and now I'm wearing some myself.
>
> Obviously, some serious matter transformation occurred. I felt really charged, really energized. The door of the cylinder reappeared.

When I came out, everyone else was coming out too and everyone is different; full size adults wearing the same coverall type of clothes.

The one thing I quickly notice is that everyone looks ageless. By this I mean almost an ephemeral quality. I can't really describe it any other way. We're in different bodies but not really. It's a rearrangement our bodies.

It seems that the blue light in the cylinder corresponded with my vibration and that the others had different colored lights in their cylinders that corresponded to them.

So, I have this feeling of, "Well, it's good to feel normal again," type of reaction.

The little room with the transformation cylinders has an entrance to another rectangular room that now appears in the wall. We enter this larger room that is also rectangular. As I mentioned, there are NO sharp corners. Where joints meet, it is rounded.

In this larger room, there is what reminds me of a conference table. We go in and sit down on one side of it and a group of male and female extra-terrestrials, dressed similarly to ourselves, sits down on the other side.

This seems to be an information exchange session. They are asking us our impressions of being in our other form. They ask us how we like being in our regular form and the general consensus is that it stinks. It is too primitive.

The extra-terrestrials say that they are working on enhancements to it that they will introduce over time, to improve it's capacity, whatever that means.

They say that their main limitation is that they can't alter our physical forms too much or we could be readily identifiable to humans with even their primitive technology. Hummm, this is interesting. If we aren't humans as such, what are we?

In following the flow of this experience, detailed information will have to be presented separately in another article on the topics discussed at this meeting with the extra-terrestrials because the information was presented as if it was already known with no explanation.

Some background information is necessary for the next section. When I was a child, I never felt related to my biological family. The older I got, the more pronounced this lack of identification with my family and feeling of not belonging to them became. Thus, I was constantly seeking information about my birth because I had come to the conclusion that I was adopted. What other logical conclusion can you draw? Whenever I asked my father when I was born, he would always say the same thing, "You weren't born, you were hatched." This really aggravated me as a child. No matter how many times I asked the question, that is what he ALWAYS said. My father did have a sarcastic sense of humor, but his persistence on this topic was unusual even for him.

So, this next part of the story is dedicated to my father who passed on in 1991. You were right Dad, I was hatched.

Returning to the experience. Here we are in a rectangular conference room inside of a mountain; two 4 year olds, a 15 year old, an 18 year old and someone approximately 22 or 23. All TRANSFORMED into adults. Physically PERFECT adults I might add.*

Continuing with Fore's post:

She said this was one of the functions of the chambers but they were generally used for many things. Someone i knew asked her about ships and the government having them. And this for some odd reason made her mood turn sour. She said to me that the government had a small squadron of ships. But she said that the prototypes were badly built. She claimed that the cabal used the technologies they were developing to shoot down their craft. She said this with a rare annoyance that she doesn't show much. She started to tell me things that she didn't want me to relay to the person asking the question. She claimed that the non-public government had created ships that she said were prototypes that the groups of aliens were aware of.

She said though that the ships were incomplete and lacked many things that their ships do have. She said to me for example that she can communicate with her ship with her mind. I was wondering what crack she was on cause she was on a roll. She ignored me and kept saying that the ships they have, have an artificial intelligence. She said though, the ships were aware but did not have sentience.

_____

* <geohanover.com/docs/contact5.htm>

She said it could be given commands to bring together information or to navigate and figure out what it needed to complete it's task. But she said interestingly (i was interested in her tales however unlike her they may be) that the ships could not initiate a task on their own and were not capable of creating decisions on their own.

The automaton-like nature of their ships may be comparable to that of purebred Gray aliens, who also seem unable to initiate their own decisions. Both are likely grown, manifested, or projected rather than assembled. The same cybernetic, psionic, demiurgic technology may be involved in both cases, as well as in the Grail Stone. The artificial intelligence they employ is not founded on microchips programmed with lines of code, but etheric energy programmed with conscious intent.

She explained that in the past, where she came from, scientists had created artificial bodies that were capable of carrying a spiritual essence/artificial intelligence but she said the history of the project showed that when someone's limitations were lifted, that the consciousness and personality of a person begins to warp out of control. She said some of the people within the designs started to not carry themselves the same and started to act abnormally. She said the lack of limitations causes the personality of a person to (hard to put) become unstable. She said some became arrogant and some didn't see limits to their interactions. She said a lot of things that were mainly negative but I'm finding it hard to express and remember. She said from then on they took from that project that limitations on beings are what causes a healthy personality and that artificial intelligence should be non-sentient and unable to deviate from the tasks. (Feb 11, 2007, 9:18am)

She claimed that at some point in the past, people of her kind had been captured, and were cloned as slaves. I asked her what she meant and I also noted that when she gave emotional responses which was odd and unusual for her to do. She told me (paraphrased) about atrocities that "these others" committed with their kind. They reproduced the individual as clones and would (according to her) be embedded with black rods in their head.

I was confused at the time by what she meant. When I asked her to explain she said these "others" Greys used to grow people of her kind underground. She said that they were socially programmed to be deeply obedient. She said these cloned beings were reproduced a lot as slaves.

I asked her the obvious question of what kind of slave. And why would Greys need slaves? She said these "others" would be grow the slaves as labor and security. She explained that the system underground (could also mean cavern, not sure) with these clones was to grow them up and as children embed the devices that looked like iron rods into their heads.

I thought that was kinda both stupid and interesting. I asked her how the hell are they gonna live with rods in their heads? I took her to task about sleeping and all that. She told me the rods she was showing me were not visible and physical. She said the rods extending from the heads of the people she was showing me were a kind of technology where…get this…they could embed material objects into the minds of the clones while at the same time keeping them separate from physical reality. ?Sort of like shared space?

I assume she was telling the truth on this one because the other technologies of implants and things she talked about seems to also base themselves in these kinds of concepts. Which I admit sound silly on the face of it. Till she explained to me that abductees during Grey experiments usually have "subsurface injuries and bruising" below the surface. Subsurface = below the outer tissue. […]

Anyway she claimed these clones of her people had these invisible ?multidimensional? rods sticking out of their temples and heads. I think I could draw them. She claimed these devices were there in the clones to produce pain if they didn't obey. Which seemed to make her both sad and in a bad mood to recount it.

She was very plainly pained to talk about it. Which was a rare thing to sense in her. She was usually detected in her own way about explaining things.

Anyway, she said that these clones are often trained as little children to obey "the others" she said some of them become security guards and others are bred to be slaves and/or trotted in front of a contactee so that they can say how safe and good they feel.

I asked her: how do I know your not one of them? She said because there were few genetic slaves to account for all the clones, they pretty much all look alike. She said I might hear of an oddity present in a clone and she said that this had more to do with genetic tampering and experimentation on "the others" part than anything else.

She said the vast majority (both female and male) look the same. She said that most of the slaves are content to work with their masters. She said the ones that disobeys have pain induced via the implants sticking invisibly out of their heads. She said if I ever met her kinds of people who all looked the same then that would be a sure sign that they were clones. She also said they wear military uniforms and two piece clothes somewhat like a regular person. She said her people usually wear clothes that look completely different (which I didn't know what she meant and she didn't care to explain at that point in time.)

I asked her what happens to slaves that don't obey period? She gave me two responses at once in her own language method.

If I understood correctly back then, (not sure) she expressed in a snappy way,

1)they are parts.

and/or

2)they are food.

Which is strange since she never said anything (ever) that Greys eat meat. So I dunno if I am interpreting it wrong. Whatever the case may be. That topic seems to affect her emotionally. (Aug 7, 2007, 2:32pm)

The phasing technology used to allow two material objects to share the same three dimensional space (by being separated along some other variable) is something Fore mentioned frequently, and I have written about it under the term "dimensional shifting" or "dimensional rotation." See *Discerning Alien Disinformation* and my article *Timeline Dynamics* for more on this subject. It's what is used to levitate abductees out through closed windows and solid walls, and what allows alien bases to exist inside mountains without hollowed-out physical caverns. It's also related to optical invisibility; if, while phased, one can pass through matter, then one can also pass through light without disturbing it. Phasing technology would come in handy during interplanetary travel to bypass radiation and asteroid bombardment.

Shadow human groups (black ops military and secret corporate groups) have a primitive form of this technology, first tested in the Philadelphia Experiment of 1943. The term "phasing" is entirely appropriate because it likely involves the artificial alteration of the quantum phase factor that normally locks us into physicality. This can be done via special electromagnetic methods or more direct etheric methods. As Fore and others like Al Bielek explain, slight alteration of phase leads to optical invisibility, further change allows passage through solid matter, and full phase detuning takes one out of physical reality entirely with unpleasant consequences.

Quantum phase is one of many factors separating one realm from another, and if artificial methods can change it, what about natural factors? The latter would imply there are natural cycles in which the phase separation between worlds varies. In other words, the same principle behind phasing technology could explain why Willy Schrödter noted that "In the time of Charlemagne and Pepin, the astral world seems to have drawn especially near"... and why soon it will draw near again. Should it do so, the "veil" will grow thin, if not drop away entirely, as our world phases into theirs and vice versa. Then aliens would find it difficult staying cloaked and our skeptical materialistic paradigm would therefore go up in flames.

That may be the prime reason why the alien disinformation campaign drives forward with ever-increasing speed, because should they be unable to maintain the secrecy of their existence, they better be prepared in advance to use the situation to their advantage, such as portraying themselves as benefactors who need our collective acquiescence to save us. Fore writes of such a scenario:

> She began telling me about the future roughly around 1999 or 2000. "The others" she said were going to begin their plans to come to the earth openly and she said they were worried. I humored her and i asked her what was bad about aliens showing themselves? She said that "The Others" didn't care about people they just cared about

controlling. She said many things about them but i'll try to put it in chronological order and the arguments she made to me about the others. These are several conversations put together for sake of clarity. They should not be taken lightly nor too seriously but should be taken with a grain of warning in my opinion.

Firstly, she had me understand that part of the conspiracy theories were true (how cliche). She said there was a group of people who had power and we not elected who decided a long time ago that a crisis was coming that they could not control (I'm paraphrasing her words for simplicity). She said that they made plans long ago to build installations underground because there was a perceived threat to them and that they were building "just to be safe".

She said it started out back in the 1860 →1862 that the two people who started a group to establish research for ufo's and aliens. She said back then these few men did not have any authority over anything but were a small project started to study the phenomena. She said around the 1900's they gained importance and were granted a budget and became a small department and were in charge of budgets (small time) to organize the "structures" (i have no clue what she meant but thats what she said) to more easily collect information about aliens. She said from here on they grew rapidly and already had a good wealth of information but very little technology. She said in the early 1920's different groups like hers made contact but were rejected and that the different aliens started revealing informations about themselves. She said this made the now established but mildly influential department/group/affair department VERY paranoid (I have no clue how to put that idea into a word that would fit).

She didn't explain why but she said they became very concerned that they were not going to survive and they began building in excess underground installations. She said they were very paranoid about aliens. She said that some of the groups revealed to them the future and this was why. She said by the time the so called famous 1947 Roswell incident happened. They were already well established and had overriding control over the branches of military. She said several things about the controlling group changed and they became desperate to gather technology and make deals to advance both the public and the non-public sciences. She said they for example couldn't land anywhere on the earth without being detected almost immediately and that there was very few places they could arrive without the phasing technology that kept them protected, She said there should be stories about the armed forces intercepting arrivals very quickly (yeah i looked and there was.)

She said that by the 1940's the non-public science was already more advanced in ideas than the public was in the 1960's onward. She said as time passed the Groups like hers and "the others" began to spy on them in the underground sessions they had and kept pace with the knowledge that was being retrieved. She said the only reason she revealed technologies to me was because it was already knowledge that was known on the earth and in the non-public sciences. She said there was nothing to lose by showing me what was already known. She said the cabal (she changes the title at this point.) would meet underground and in the 80's were planning what was known as artificial terror. She said they wanted to play "the game of the gods" (why she called it that I don't know).

She described this "game" as a game that many races including hers and her faction had played with humanity. She said in the old days on earth they would even fight openly (yeah right!) between them and "the others". She said "the others" (Greys/Pleiadians/whatever) would implant and manipulate thoughts and start religions and create wars over them to decimate mankind so that they would not evolve beyond a certain point. She said her groups way of thinking was to introduce a counter movement to spread knowledge and stabilize the religions or impart knowledge to dismantle "the others" plans. She said there was a lot of instability with these fights and the people on the earth became very "fractured" from the constant introduction of ideas and counter ideas.

She said eventually "the others" and Their groups were stopped by a third group of aliens. (she does not describe them in detail or otherwise.) She said the third group did not care for either side but wanted them to stop interfering. She said this group was very powerful and that even if the two sides went against the third group they would not win. She made it sound like they didn't have a hope in hell united, let alone apart. She said they both agreed to an uneasy peace that they would not interfere. She said this stopped the interference to a large part.

"The others" still kept starting movements in very small ways to keep people at war. Then her people's side would go to the third group and the third group would allow interference from their side and they would start a counter movement. She said this slowed down the ideology war but did not stop it. She said the earth was already very divided in many ideals and fronts but both generally obeyed.

She said the bible was one example of being edited and re-edited (i don't believe her on this but i used to.). She said that around the time she was telling me this the amnesty between both factions was ending. I asked her why amnesty if I thought that was used only for immigrants. She insisted on the word amnesty (I looked it up in the dictionary since i didn't know what it mean't :shrug:). She said that once the amnesty was lifted that "the others" would immediately go back to trying to control mankind. She said they were worried about what might happen if "The Others" came first to humanity. She said they were pretty sure that they would. They were preparing themselves and a lot of them were leaving because she said a war between them was likely to happen.

She said in the future many things would happen. Which I will post in another post rather than this one so I don't break the long a$$ "truth" she left me with.

First, She said "the others" would go back out into space and make an entrance, as if they were not here already. She said this would allow them a clean entrance and blame the rest of the past on aliens from her faction. She said they would probably go and pick the people among them who were human-like. She said this is what abductions and Grey experimentation was trying to bring about for a long time (thousand of years into the past when a couple of races handed us as a project down or abandoned us.). She said the human-like beings were either slaves who would talk very little or genuine people of hers and others who look like humans who had an agenda to control humanity and stop it's progress.

She said the others were itching to stop our progress because at a certain point we would be acknowledge-able as independent beings. She said on her world about 60% of her kind thought of human kind as an experiment to be observed but generally do not care one way or the other. Roughly, 30% constitute "the others" mentality. While she said, the minority constitute her point of view 14%).

She said when "the others" arrived they would do what would look like miracles to mankind (of this she kept talking about) and they expected the people on earth to quickly believe "the others". She said "the others" were likely going to present themselves as being Gods. She said this would lead to human beings accepting them as the leaders. She said that because "the others" would very likely choose human-like front men with their powers intact. The genetic manipulations both factions had committed to, a long time ago, would cause human beings to give in very quickly. She said a long time ago when other races had lost interest in humanity they picked up and modified humanity to be planet squatters (my word interpretation but pretty accurate.).

She said the reason that human beings become very easy to manipulate when they see a pretty person is because they are pre-programmed genetically to have this behavior. She said this was an easy trick back when people were very primitive and they wanted workers and slaves. She said that before those projects were ended that the aliens modified the human beings more to create a very xenophobic response to other aliens. And that human beings were given the cultural push to breed at will. She said this way both factions past founders could prevent other aliens from occupying the earth in the open; nor the human beings from helping them. She said that some of that has degraded over time but it was still a dominant trait. That was the reason some aliens use Greys as front men because it is less problematic and they are humanoid enough to be accepted when they continue the experiments on mankind.

The next interesting bit she said was that "the others" needed contactees for the future. She said some of the Grey experiments are about how human beings react to certain situations and that the Greys were looking for weaknesses and lessening the possibility that the human beings they choose will have conflict against them when they bring about their "arrival". She said some of those human beings would be "go-betweens" in the contacts with those who follow "the others". She said "the others" needed a close enough.... spokesman... to represent their interest and that the association with these beings would elevate these human beings to a higher status. She said that is why alot of "the others" choose human beings who will readily accept a title or illusions of grandeur and are usually told they are "the one".

She said that both sides could be accused of this since they both engage in a little bit of everything. Hers supposed a lot less (yeah right!). She said "the others" would institute a government where there would be three tiers of contactee's; the local, regional, and the special few. She said the locals would be in charge of their smaller communities while the regional would have limited contact with the aliens directly and the special few are supposed to be less than 25 (fuzzy) who would have to represent their slab of the world. She said "the others" would divide the world up into sections and each "special contactee" would be in charge of it. She said "the special contactees" would also have very high abilities endowed to them (pet slaves anyone?)

She said the first thing "the others" would do is stop progressing technology. She said they would introduce their own technology to produce energy but that it would be off limits to human beings and that they would fix a lot of the earths problems as long as they could coerce power from the former leaders of the governments. She said the few skeptical human beings would probably by that time be thinking they are "gods" because they would take the time to display their powers which she said is common knowledge to everyone except human beings who don't see those things.

She goes on to explain to me how miracles (or seemingly miracles) are performed and that this will impress many. This is where she warned me about not listening to "what they say" but "seeing what they do" if I have doubts as to which side they represent. She said any alien could say anything. She said actions though would easily reveal their true intent. She said "the others" would quickly order the executions of millions of people world wide who would not obey them because of religion. She said since these people on earth who would believe them would think they are "doing the right thing" and have the backing of "the Gods" they would turn in their neighbors to be executed. She said that if people knew the future they would not want any part of it. She explained that the reason why "the others" will win over so many is because they will give people what they want and create a new super religion. She said the religion will unite pieces of old religions and that they will lie and say they are the Gods of the old religions and that they will create a new one and even spin lies that they created mankind.

She said people won't notice it but they will be tricked into a lot of manipulative situations. And she said if people accept them then there is nothing they can do except watch. I'm sure I left out some things.

She said this is why (at the time they were racing to "prepare") to present themselves anyway. She said because her people were the minority that they would not have much of a chance in changing the minds of people but she said they would try. She said at the time that there was a big debate as to whether her faction should come in first or second, because they did not know which would yield the best results. She said when her faction did come that they would show up shortly after the others most likely, and they would present to the world their side of the case. She said they would show mankind what they could of how the miracles were happening and how they came to be and even perform for them to see. That they were not miracles, but common understandings and knowledge shared by both sides.

She said her faction would also reveal information and the truth to people at this time but the general consensus was that the human beings of the future would be unlikely to believe them. I asked her why "the others" would let them make their case? She said because of the third group they would have to allow it or the third group would probably come in quickly and put them in their place or worse. (Squish)

She said that they had a growing fear, that if the people of the earth did side with her faction. That then "the others" in spite, would burn the earth while leaving. She said this was a likely possibility.

Background info.

She said a lot of things that lead up to this is volcanoes all going off at the same time in some areas. Many earthquakes in places where there had never been before. She described the future from that time (1999-2000) to be getting worse and worse weather wise as the years progress (seems to be accurate on that one). She said that the cabal (that I described at the beginning) was trying to "play the game of the gods" and making artificial terror to force people to give up their freedoms. She said there would be rumors of wars in the future and that there would be a very big war she called "the war of contracts".

Those things I'll write down next because my hands are very tired. (Feb 7, 2007, 7:03am)*

This deception scenario is highly plausible, although the endgame strategies are continually adjusted according to the shifting probabilities of success, so it's hard to say how much is still under preparation in 2022.

Regardless, regarding the present chapter, the point is that not only are there competing alien factions who have fought various cold and hot wars over the millennia, but it seems to be coming to a head. The alien endgame is building toward another shift of the timeline, perhaps the biggest one since the dawn of our species.

If the Gray hybrid breeding program is any indication, victory for the fascist factions would result in full genetic and spiritual crippling of the human race. At worst we would be augmented and programmed into becoming tools deployable to other worlds to continue their campaign of spiritual enslavement. It would spread the cancer that is the Corrupt Demiurge and further imbalance the Universe. As mentioned, alien wars are subsets of a larger cosmological war between the Corrupt Demiurge and the Divine Logos. Just as human wars play into alien agendas, so do alien wars play into cosmological agendas.

Nordic Origins and Identity

Who are these beings? We can rule out several possibilities:

1. They are not all spirits, demons, angels, or elementals because they can appear in the physical for extended periods, leave behind DNA evidence, interbreed with humans, and display an internally consistent assortment of high technology. Anyone with sufficient experience can differentiate between aliens and metaphysical entities.

2. They are not all members of some benevolent "Galactic Federation," since there is warring among their opposing factions, and some display fascist tendencies, even within the Nordic typology.

---

* Fore's complete thread: <montalk.net/fore.zip>

Because traces of their presence on Earth go back thousands of years:

3. They are not all hoaxes perpetrated by the shadow government. Nonetheless, the latter may have hoaxed a portion of the "space brother" fad to hijack the real thing and subdue xenophobia. Examples include Commander Ashtar, a sappy caricature of a Nordic, who is frequently channeled in the New Age community.

4. They are not curious "visitors" who arrived here only in the 20th century. While lesser alien races may have visited more recently for scientific observation, the Nordics are not among them.

5. They are not all remnants of some secret Nazi space program. It's a non sequitur to say Nazis are responsible for the UFO phenomenon when it was through their occult research and communication with aliens that they achieved that level of technology in the first place. If anything, their advanced remnants were later assimilated into the same confederation of negative factions that have likewise assimilated the modern shadow military.

More viable theories include the following:

They are the original human type, and we are chimeras genetically engineered in their image.

The writings of Lloyd Pye and Zechariah Sitchin come to mind here. As Lloyd Pye explains, our tattered genome bears the scars of heavy genetic engineering. Human evolution underwent jumps so sudden as to be anomalous. As everyone knows, Sumerian myths speak of the Anunnaki who created humans for slave labor, while in the Book of Genesis the same Elohim said, "Let us make man in our image." Was it all the work of the superhumans discussed in this chapter, or were they also the products of genetic engineering?

They are our cosmic relatives, created by the same primordial alien progenitors that created us but seeded on other worlds.

This is the only viable aspect of the Extraterrestrial Hypothesis. It would explain why they could be from other planets yet share compatible DNA. When intelligent life arises naturally on one planet, develops into a super-civilization, and achieves mastery of genetics and space travel, life soon spreads to nearby compatible planets. All carbon-based humanoid aliens share a common ancestry, as the odds of two completely independent evolutions producing the same form is infinitesimal. Then one world can discover another and genetically modify it further, despite both being the creations of an even older alien race.

What could be their cosmic origins? The nearest candidate is the ancient planet whose remains populate the Asteroid Belt. Otherwise one would have to look further, toward Alpha Centauri, Sirius, Procyon, Bernard's Star, Arcturus, and Aldebaran. alienology research points toward Orion and the Pleiades as well, but the stars of those constellations are many hundreds of light years away. Most of their alleged home worlds are less than one hundred light years, which, relative to the size of our galaxy, makes them our next-door neighbors.

They are ancient offshoots of the human race who surpassed the rest of the species.

This is along the lines of what Mac Tonnies proposed. If true, the evolutionary branching must have occurred recently, since they look so similar. They could be direct descendants of Cro Magnon man, who appeared suddenly in Western Europe around 30,000 years ago and had larger brain capacities and better physiques than modern man, matching two characteristics ascribed to Nordic aliens. On the other hand, Cro Magnons could equally well have been Nordic populations who emigrated to Earth around that time, or simply their initial genetic experiments, which fits the sudden arrival of the Cro Magnons and their genetic distance from Africa.

They are Atlantean/Hyperborean survivors who did not devolve like other humans.

Any surviving elite who held onto their knowledge and technology would have later emerged as virtual gods to the rest of the population who degraded to the level of primitives. But did they develop that technology on their own, or was it given to them by aliens? More likely the latter, since the archaeological evidence of ancient advanced civilization is scarce and localized in small pockets around the world, indicating a small elite who, even before the cataclysms, ruled over a more primitive population. If that antediluvian civilization had advanced on its own, it would have taken far longer, been more uniformly advanced throughout, and have left behind more traces.

The aliens of today are probably not identically the Atlantean survivors, though the latter could have been their human/hybrid proxies who received assistance and forewarning. Think of Noah being told by "The Lord" to build an Ark, modern contactees and abductees being warned of imminent cataclysm, or the shadow government manically building underground bases due to receiving privileged information from their alien contacts.

If nothing else, strong ties exist between Nordic aliens and the descendants of these ancient surviving elite. The Basque, Celtic, and Asian DNA recovered from Peter Khoury's case suggests as much. Nordics seem interested in people of mixed East/West ancestry, of which a portion traces back to these post-Atlantean bloodlines. Prominent examples of ancient bloodlines include the Basques, Celts, Minoans, and Phoenicians. The latter three consorted with the 18th Dynasty of Egypt and consequently the tribe of Levi, who were the only people among the Israelites allowed to operate the Ark of the Covenant.

They are human avatars or proxies for another alien intelligence.

The DNA evidence from Peter Khoury's case could equally suggest Nordics were created *from* us. Some third-party alien race could have collected desirable genetics from humans throughout history and assembled a race of superhumans. In that case, they are either cybernetic creations worn as "meat suits" by completely foreign alien intelligences, or they are genuinely spirited people who were created as proxies for their nonhuman masters. These proxies could then interbreed with humans to spawn bloodlines functioning as yet another tier of earthbound proxies.

This is something Fore speculated on, after discovering that the human-like personality of his Nordic advisor was a front and that her true mind was far less human and more profoundly complex than it seemed. On the other hand, he also mentioned that these aliens undergo training to step down their consciousness to our level to make interaction possible. Orfeo Angelucci's contacts hinted likewise.

The question is whether they are just superhumans who downshift their personalities to our level for interaction like any adult does when talking to a toddler, or whether they are total fabrications by some monstrous alien intelligence. The latter is attractively conspiratorial but not really substantiated by the available evidence and anecdotes except in the case of awkward human simulacra such as the Men In Black. Not to mention, if they were created solely to put a human face on the alien presence, then there shouldn't be so many reports of other alien species like the Grays and Reptilians as that defeats the purpose of the façade.

They are from a parallel timeline or hidden realm where a superior civilization has developed.

What is the nature of their world, and how does it relate to ours? It's not enough to say their world is just a parallel Earth where things advanced more quickly on the technological and evolutionary front. For one, these beings along with ghosts, elementals, demons, etc. have always been able to observe and influence us, but not vice versa. Our two worlds are not equal in terms of fundamental tangibility. Etheric energies play a more visible and active role in their realm.

Therefore it's not a simple matter of Nordics inhabiting a parallel 3D physical timeline, rather they seem to inhabit a higher "density," as the term is used in the *Ra* and *Cassiopaean Transcripts*. Gnostics know our world is an illusion created by the Corrupt Demiurge. It follows that beyond the borders of our reality exists the *real* world, or at least something not so hermetically isolated from the greater Creation. Could beings from that world be popping into ours, injecting their influences into this petri dish we call reality?

They are our time traveling descendants.

Experience proves they can see into the future. It's hard to tell whether this ability comes solely from clairvoyance, mathematical calculation, or hindsight from the future. Probably a combination of all three. Regardless, they are obsessed with the future and how present developments affect it. The delicate manner of their manipulations, the eons over which they carry them out, and the *knowing* determination inherent in their efficiency suggest their vantage point is outside linear time.

The one consistent element in what abductees and contactees are told is that our world will soon undergo a time of great upheaval. Times of change, especially collective change, are significant choice points on the timeline. They are windows of chaos that spawn many probable futures. Those windows seem to function as apertures allowing the influx of time traveling influences from the futures they generate. If nothing else, they would be strategic pivot points on the timeline that attract the greatest attention from warring time travelers.

Consequently, if aliens like the Nordics are time travelers, then since multiple futures issue from a singular past, they would have to be time travelers from *various probable futures* engaging in a timewar of sorts. Different factions are exerting opposing influences upon the present to reshape the future to their advantage. As we approach the primary nexus point, these probable futures will play a game of musical chairs, with only one future quantum collapsing into the final tangible one.

Furthermore, with time travel, the issue of where and when they originated becomes obscured. If they claim to come from Procyon, that could be true, but it might mean Procyon ten thousand years from now after human descendants have long colonized space and achieved time travel as well. Or if ancient astronaut research indicates they genetically modified the human race in their image, it could just as well be those time travelers from Procyon (or wherever) visiting our prehistory and accelerating human evolution to rewrite the timeline in their favor. Then they would be time travelers tweaking the genetics of their ancestors, possibly even interbreeding with them, training some, leasing them powerful technology, all as part of a timewar waged over the battlefield of space and time.

Alternatively, some malevolent alien faction could do likewise in order to dumb us down so that, when the time of great upheaval occurs, odds are shifted in the favor of successful deception. Conditions that now allow for the imminent implementation of a global totalitarian system under negative alien control have been under construction for many thousands of years. Religion and scientific materialism will play a large part in that deception, and both play on fundamental human weaknesses genetically programmed into us. Furthermore, subtle timeline nudges in the form of visions and visitations have also greatly altered the landscape of the future: Saul, Joan of Arc, Joseph Smith, and Adolf Hitler come to mind as examples of characters targeted for that purpose.

Lastly, for the sake of speculation, if Nordics are time traveling descendants from our current population, one has to wonder what land today is their ancestral land — assuming they aren't descendants of an alternate Earth that existed prior to the timewar that spawned our current timeline. Based on the "Nordic" or "Scandinavian" nomenclature assigned to them, one might initially guess northern Europe, but that area doesn't even have a manned space program. Careful comparison between stereotypical Nordics and existing populations shows a good match with the Slavic people: Eastern Europeans and Western Russians. Theosophists and Anthroposophists both had occult reasons to believe that Slavs would birth the next evolution of mankind, that they were a golden mean between East and West in terms of culture, wisdom, and genetics. Certainly the Volksgeist of the Slavs is one conducive for that role, as even the Soviets were especially open to investigating the enhancement of psychic powers and achieving manipulation of time and space. Some of the brightest papers on fringe science have come out of Russia. There are several synchronistic oddities surrounding the Russian people, their language, and history, to suggest some degree of involvement in time travel or manipulation by time travelers. Additionally, areas where Russia has built underground cities (like beneath Mount Yamantau) that are capable of surviving global cataclysms also happen to be where the Proto-Indo-Europeans emerged out of nowhere many thousands of years ago and seeded cultures across Asia, Europe, and the Middle East.

Trans-Temporal Meta-Civilization

In all likelihood, Nordics consist of different groups with different histories. Some could be time travelers from our future, others remnants of an ancient off-planetary superhuman civilization. Both share "Fourth Density" characteristics, both possess demiurgic technology, and both seem genetically related.

After time travel paradoxes, timeline dynamics, and other complications settle out, what's left is a transcendent civilization whose cultures are distributed over spatial and temporal geography — cultures that mingle and tussle with each other across space *and* time. This civilization stands outside linear time. To us, they would seem like time travelers from the future, beings from parallel timelines, travelers from other star systems, and ancient genetic manipulators all the same, since these are just different aspects of a common meta-civilization that has simultaneously inserted various extensions of itself into opportune locations along our linear timeline.

Negative Nordics

Perhaps the best-kept secret among alien disinformers is the existence of hostile Nordic factions. We hear plenty about Reptilians and their ubiquitous Gray underlings, but the common perception of Nordics is overwhelmingly positive. This is unfortunate because, as explained in *Discerning Alien Disinformation,* negative or cloned/impostor Nordics could be the first to initiate open contact with humanity, largely due to the psychological advantage offered by an appearance that is pleasing and familiar to humans, and because they may have the greatest vested interest in doing so.

Recall what Fore was told regarding such a scenario: "[T]he human-like beings were either slaves who would talk very little or genuine people of hers and others who look like humans who had an agenda to control humanity and stop it's progress. She said the others were itching to stop our progress because at a certain point we would be acknowledge-able as independent beings. She said on her world about 60% of her kind thought of human kind as an experiment to be observed but generally do not care one way or the other. Roughly, 30% constitute 'the others' mentality. While she said, the minority constitute her point of view 14%." If this is accurate, then almost a third of that civilization could be classified as negative Nordics.

In another post, Fore's advisor mentioned Nordic genetic engineering projects that went awry: "She explained that in the past, where she came from, scientists had created artificial bodies that were capable of carrying a spiritual essence/artificial intelligence but she said the history of the project showed that when someone's limitations were lifted, that the consciousness and personality of a person begin to warp out of control. She said some of the people within the designs started to not carry themselves the same and started to act abnormally. She said the lack of limitations causes the personality of a person to (hard to put) become unstable. She said some became arrogant and some didn't see limits to their interactions."

While she also said corrections were made to prevent this, it highlights a pattern of arrogance and psychopathy in superhumans who revel in their superiority. The pattern is reminiscent of the Lucifer Rebellion myth, where one-third of the "angels" grew arrogant and refused to serve mankind. Even if only on a symbolic level, negative Nordics can be equated with the so-called Fallen Angels of Biblical myth.

The pattern is also reminiscent of the Nazi Master Race program that attempted to reconstruct the original antediluvian Nordic people, complete with their occult powers and mastery of spacetime. There is no better modern example of negative Nordic alien mindset and influence than the Nazis. Why were they so obsessed with blond-haired, blue-eyed, cold-hearted superhumans? Why did they want to turn humanity into these technologically-advanced super-Aryans?

There is an interesting anecdote suggesting Hitler himself was a contactee of negative Nordics:

> Hitler was talking one day to Rauschning, the Governor of Danzig, about the problem of a mutation of the human race. Rauschning, not possessing the key to such strange preoccupations, interpreted Hitler's remarks in terms of a stock-breeder interested in the amelioration of German blood.
>
> "But all you can do," he replied, "is to assist Nature and shorten the road to be followed! It is Nature herself who must create for you a new species. Up till now the breeder has only rarely succeeded in

developing mutations in animals — that is to say, creating himself new characteristics."

"The new man is living amongst us now! He is here!" exclaimed Hitler, triumphantly. "Isn't that enough for you? I will tell you a secret. I have seen the new man. He is intrepid and cruel. I was afraid of him."

"In uttering these words," added Rauschning, "Hitler was trembling in a kind of ecstasy."

It was Rauschning, too, who related the following strange episode, about which Dr. Achille Delmas, a specialist in applied psychology, questioned him in vain. It is true that in a case like this psychology does not apply:

"A person close to Hitler told me that he wakes up in the night screaming and in convulsions. He calls for help, and appears to be half paralysed. He is seized with a panic that makes him tremble until the bed shakes. He utters confused and unintelligible sounds, gasping, as if on the point of suffocation. The same person described to me one of these fits, with details that I would refuse to believe had I not complete confidence in my informant.

"Hitler was standing up in his room, swaying and looking all round him as if he were lost. 'It's he, it's he,' he groaned, 'he's come for me!' His lips were white; he was sweating profusely. Suddenly he uttered a string of meaningless figures, then words and scraps of sentences. It was terrifying. He used strange expressions strung together in bizarre disorder. Then he relapsed again into silence, but his lips still continued to move. He was then given a friction and something to drink. Then suddenly he screamed: 'There! there! Over in the comer! He is there!' — all the time stamping with his feet and shouting. To quieten him he was assured that nothing extraordinary had happened, and finally he gradually calmed down. After that he slept for a long time and became normal again..." (*Morning of the Magicians* by Pauwells, Bergier)

Readers may be familiar with the Thule and Vril Society, the occult forerunners and influencers of the Nazi movement. Activities included communicating with beings from Aldebaran, building advanced technology according to the guidance they received, and promoting supremacy of the Aryan/Nordic race. The Vril ladies were also "unusual."

Unlike all other totalitarian bodies of history, Nazis stood not on the human ground of political theory or religious dogma, but on the alien ground of occult dynamics and demiurgic technology. The Nazi flag is a good example. Its black, white, and red colors growing outward symbolize the black, white, and red stages involved in the creation of the Philosopher's Stone. The black swastika itself symbolizes the Black Sun, which is none other than the Corrupt Demiurge. The latter goes by another name in occultism: the Dead Head, meaning Dead Logos, represented as the skull and crossbones by the Templar Navy and Nazi SS. It is the central cosmic power source of all demiurgic technology, the Demiurge itself. It represents the ultimate power, at least within the physical domain, and as Persephone commented in Matrix Reloaded, what men with power want is more power.

As mentioned, there is antagonism among Nordic alien factions, and now it should be clear that some are quite arrogant, fascist, and psychopathic. In the Grail lore, some protected the Grail, and some were its enemies seeking to usurp it. We must keep this duality in mind should Nordic aliens show themselves to the world one day.

Off-Planetary Ancestry

Finally, let's examine portions of the Nordic meta-civilization located in our distant past. Several sources link them to a planet once located between Mars and Jupiter. Michael Tsarion has this to say:

> We read from various sources that approximately 50,000 years ago a certain planetary body in our own solar system was mysteriously destroyed. This body has been called Tiamat, Phaeton, Lucifer, Marduk, Maldek, Rahab, and even Luna (not connected to the name later given to the Moon). It was believed to have existed between Mars and Jupiter and was referred to as the "second sun" and may have been mistaken as such, because its atmosphere was resplendent with reflections of the actual sun. This is not as improbable as it sounds since Venus, the "Morning Star," the second planet from the sun and the third brightest object in the sky, is so bright that it casts a distinct shadow on a Moonless night.

Around the time of this event, the solar system, and later the Earth, was colonized by extra-terrestrial beings who were either attracted to this solar system by that conflagration or upon coming here caused the calamity themselves. Whether the disaster was natural or not, the result was that mankind on Earth experienced total and long lasting chaos and confusion. The surface of the planet Tiamat consisted mostly of great oceans. Upon its destruction, these vast saline waters entered into the Earth's atmosphere causing the first of two massive prehistoric deluges and tribulations that mankind would experience. It is thought that the alien invaders took full advantage of this predicament and moved in to bring about colonization. They met no resistance from the disoriented and weakened inhabitants of the Earth who believed their visitors were powerful gods.

Some theorists, like the energetic Erich von Daniken, have also determined that there was a great intergalactic war between two (or possibly more) extraterrestrial forces in a neighboring galaxy or solar system. The result of this titanic war had enormous consequences for the Earth because, it is postulated, the losers on being pursued into our system pretended to take refuge on Tiamat. They even erected a makeshift radar-type station there to decoy their pursuers. However, the defeated ones had really taken refuge on planet Earth, not on Tiamat. Upon their arrival, they almost immediately went underground into existing caverns that through scans of the planet they knew existed.

They also descended into other caverns that they themselves cut out of the living rock. There were at least five entire continents on Earth in primeval times called Appalachia, Tyrhennia, Beringia, Fennoscandia, and Oceania. Our present continents are remnants of these. Beneath them were literally thousands of miles of subterranean passages, caverns, and refuges. Some of these remain today and experts know that many of them were not made naturally. Many of our quaint myths and tales, like those of Dwarves, Trolls, Elves, the "Little People" and the Scandinavian "King Under the Mountain," for example, concern these subterranean worlds. Almost all the native American Indian tribes speak of their original residence beneath the surface of the Earth.

The pursuers, the victors of the war in the heavens, erroneously thinking that their enemies were on Tiamat utterly annihilated it.

A similar story was given to Orfeo Angelucci:

Time is a dimension as your scientists now correctly surmise. But it is only a dimension when applied to the various densities of matter. In the absolute, or non-material states of consciousness, Time is non-existent. So let us say that in one of the time frames or dimensions, there was once a planet in the solar system of Earth, called Lucifer. It was of the least material density of any of the planets. Its orbit lay between the orbits of Mars and Jupiter. Among the etheric beings, or heavenly hosts, it was called the Morning Star. Among all planets it was the most radiant planet in the universe.

The name of the prince of this shining planet was also Lucifer, a beloved Son of God. Earth's legends about Lucifer and his hosts are true. Pride and arrogance grew in the heart of Lucifer and in the hearts of many Luciferians. They discovered all of the secrets of matter and also the great secret of the Creative Word. Eventually they sought to turn this omnipotent force against their brothers who were less selfish. Also against the etheric beings and the Father, or Source, for it became their desire to rule the universe. You know the rest of the legend: how Lucifer and his followers were cast down from their high estate. In simpler words, the Luciferians who were embodied then in the most attenuated manifestation of matter "fell" into embodiments in one of the most dense material evolutions, which is the animalistic evolution of Earth.

We were among those who did not join the Luciferians in their revolt against the etheric hosts. Thus although the Luciferians shattered our radiant planet in the holocaust of their war, we entered the etheric, non-material worlds in the higher octaves of light as liberated Sons of God, while the Luciferian hosts fell into the dream of mind in matter upon the dark planet of sorrows.

While our brothers are lost in the hell of unreality and turn their blinded, imploring eyes to the mute heavens, we can never forget them. We intercede unceasingly for your peoples' liberation. Thus today every bondsman upon Earth has within himself the power through the mystery of the Etheric Christ Spirit to cancel his captivity.

Eventually all of mankind deep-drowned in Time and Matter, will surface to reality when they recognize their basic unity of being.

When man is for man honestly and sincerely and not selfishly
arrayed against himself, the hour of deliverance from the underworld
will be close at hand. We wait now beyond the great, sad river of
Time and Sorrows with open arms and hearts to receive among us
our lost and prodigal brothers in that great day when they rejoin us
as liberated Sons of God. (Angelucci, 98-103)

Another source, the *Cassiopaean Transcripts,* also conveys the same
basic story. According to the transcripts, approximately 80,000 years
ago a planet named Kantek existed between Mars and Jupiter. Its
inhabitants were "Fourth Density" superhuman Nordics who were
polarized into two opposing factions. They possessed the equivalent
of demiurgic technology and deployed it in their war. The result was
irreversible destabilization of the planet and its subsequent shattering.
A portion of the civilization was evacuated to Earth, and they brought
with them one or several devices equivalent to the Grail Stone, termed
TDARMs (trans-dimensional atomic remolecularizers) in the transcripts. On Earth, they encountered the relatively more primitive
and swarthy Atlantean natives, who were forced to coexist with the
newcomers. Thus Atlantis remained, until later widespread abuse of
demiurgic technology once again destabilized the planet and, along
with various cometary disasters, ended that civilization in a pole shift.
Numerous cataclysms happened in the millennia to follow, each one
further scattering and devolving the remaining survivors.

In essence, these sources suggest that a portion of the Nordic civilization "fell" into the physical domain of Earth and submerged directly
into its history and gene pool. In essence, they became human.

Genetic and Cultural Legacy on Earth

The implication is that white people are their most direct descendants,
and are therefore the most "off-planetary" of the human races, although portions of those same genetics can be found in other races due
to mixing over the millennia. As many have observed, the proclivity
of Western culture for exploiting and ruining the environment makes
sense if whites are not even from this planet. Likewise with their affinity for scientific innovation and its use for war, and an imperialistic
drive to dominate lesser cultures. Close scrutiny of the anomalies in

the supposed evolutionary history of the white race shows they could not have descended from Africans adapting to colder climates.

In any case, the point is that after the fall of Atlantis and subsequent cataclysms, the earthbound descendants of Nordic emigrants resettled in other areas of the globe. One portion seems to have settled in Western Russia near Turkey, and they are now known as the Proto-Indo-Europeans. Another settled somewhere in the Northern Atlantic, and a smaller fragment took root in the Pyrenees. As a matter of speculation, the R1b and R1a haplogroups (genetic markers) could trace back to these two primary branches.

In time, they developed into the Hyperboreans, Indo-Aryans of India, Indo-Europeans of Europe, and the Indo-Iranians, which went on to seed further cultures like the Sumerians, Egyptians, Dravidians, Celts, Persians, and so on. Locations include Iceland (probably Hyperborea, and the source for Plato's given dimensions of Atlantis), Turkey, India, Egypt, Spain, Malta, Canary Islands, Ireland and Scotland, Central America, and later archaic Greece, Phoenicia, northern Japan, and lastly Easter Island. Megalithic technology was their signature. According to researcher Jim Alison, the "sacred sites" they left behind form a great circle on the globe whose northern pole lies in western Alaska — close to where Charles Hapgood determined the previous geographic North Pole existed 80,000 years ago. That doesn't indicate when the sites were built, only that the builders desired to encode the old North Pole in the distribution of their post pole shift structures. For example, Easter Island is on this circle, but it wasn't re-colonized until roughly 500 C.E. by tall red-haired whites, probably from northern Scotland.

Each of these cultures had close ties with their transcendent Nordic counterparts; for instance, the mysterious Tuatha Dé Danann, a technologically advanced race of fair-haired people who fled to Ireland after the destruction of their homeland (likely Iceland, though some propose they were a northern tribe of Israel), eventually made their exit from Irish history by joining the Sidhe underground, who were a transcendent race of godlike beings and, like the Sylphs, could have been their un-fallen, non-devolved, Nordic alien counterparts.

As detailed by Frank Joseph in his book *Survivors of Atlantis,* the Nordic diaspora also built the Great Pyramid and installed the Grail Stone therein, founded pre-dynastic Egypt, and seeded the Meso-American civilizations. Their standard procedure was to command large native populations using only a small number of their own, which is easy enough to do with advanced technology and knowledge. In India, they were the earliest Brahmin kings. In China, they were the demigods known as the Three Sovereigns who, according to Chinese lore, "used their magical powers to improve the lives of their people." In Egypt, they were progenitors of the pharaonic dynasties. In Meso-America, they became the basis of the Quetzalcoatl and Viracocha legends and established the Mayan calendars.

Every culture they founded was impressed with the same proto-myth, which encoded the "situation" regarding the nature of our reality, how this timeline came to be, and where it's all going. These myths encode the cosmological war between the Corrupt Demiurge and the Logos, the off-planetary history of the ancient Nordic civilization, the true role of demiurgic technology, and the cataclysms that accompanied its abuse. This same stream of gnostic revelation is repeated in certain works of fiction today — films, books, and television series — which are the modern equivalent of myths, consciously or subconsciously inspired by the same forces. In the remaining chapters, I will explore the unified gnostic picture encoded in these ancient and modern myths.

7 DAWN OF A NEW COSMIC DAY

With the prerequisites covered, I can now move into the heart of *Gnosis*. This chapter and the next concern cosmic cycles, the end of the world as we know it, alien timewars, and the Big Picture of what it all means.

Demiurgic Weaponry in Indian Mythology

After the Atlantean and subsequent cataclysms, technologically advanced survivors fractured into various populations that colonized separate areas around the globe. Wherever they went, they commandeered the local native population. It was typical for a small number of fair-skinned elite to rule over a vast population of darker-skinned natives.

One group of survivors colonized Northern India and became the Indo-Aryans, whose solar symbol was the swastika. They impressed upon the natives the foundations of the Vedic culture, which included the caste system, complicated metaphysics, technological instructions, and myths encoding the antediluvian history of their people. They took up elite roles as scientist-priests, known as Brahmins, and were the earliest of the Brahmin kings. The same pattern played out elsewhere with the Chinese, Celtic, Meso-American, Sumerian and Egyptian cultures.

The Indo-Aryan culture contributed significantly to what was later woven into the two major Indian epics, the *Mahabharata* and *Ramayana*. Like the Old Testament, there's a layer of technological information embedded in these myths. As is well known, the Indian epics contain detailed information on flying vehicles called *Vimanas*. Another example is the divine weaponry employed in their wars, which are fundamentally demiurgic in operation.

Professor Jarrod Whitaker wrote an interesting paper* systematizing the use of demiurgic energy in divine weaponry:

> [I]n no other mythological corpus is the concept of divine weapons more developed and more complex than in the two Indian epics.

> [T]he divine weapons cannot be properly understood without a comprehensive examination of the concept of *tejas* or "fiery energy."

> [B]ecause *tejas* govern the way the divine weapons operate in the mythology, the primary aim of the following paper is to outline its "intrinsic laws" and to codify them systematically into a working model.

> [T]he fire of the divine weapons is not the element itself, but the more subtle energy-substance *tejas* or "fiery energy". These are not weapons of fire *per se*, but weapons of energy.

> The Sanskrit word derives from the root *tij-* meaning "to be sharp". [...] By the time of the *Upanisads, tejas* surpasses other energy-substances while incorporating their diverse roles. It becomes the central

---

*Whitaker, Jarrod. *Divine Weapons and Tejas in the Two Indian Epics*. Indo-Iranian Journal, 2000. Volume 43 #2, pp. 87-113.

creative principle of the supreme god, and furthermore, the energy of all movement and activity (*rajoguna*) in the universe. It is further ascribed to be the subtle essence of the Hindu *atman* or "soul", and thus "is the ever-changing energy which passed on along the downward current of evolution and taken back into evolution."

Apparently, *tejas* was their term for etheric energy, that which comprises the lower part of the soul, permeates creation, and ultimately weaves linear time and space. It is demiurgic energy in every sense. Whitaker then quotes Magnone:

> "As an energy, *tejas* is eminently transferable, and the effects of its transfer are different according to whether the broader or narrower notion of *tejas* is applied. In the former event, the grant of *tejas* is coextensive with creation, and its confiscation with dissolution."

Etheric energy is the substrate of reality, and matter is but its condensation or epiphenomena. It is the *prima materia*, the primary agent involved in the alchemical dictum *solve et coagula* or "dissolve and coagulate." What the Demiurge creates, the Demiurge destroys. The significance of this will be elaborated on later. Magnone continues:

> "When *tejas* is intended in the narrower sense, i.e., as the cause of mere excellence, and not generally of existence, then its acquisition and loss do not entail an absolute inception or cessation, but simply a promotion or demotion to or from a higher level of existence."

This is precisely the other function of etheric energy within the human organism, to enable perception of higher realms and transubstantiation or translation into such realms. The cycles of higher and lower etheric energy concentrations on Earth dictate the cyclical proximity of our environment from the higher ones inhabited by hyperdimensional humanoids.

Whitaker comments:

> On the gross level, *tejas* preserves its ancient connections with fire and heat, and when possessed by persons or objects suggests the English words "glory", "majesty", "ardour", and "splendour." On the subtle level, as an energy, *tejas* is responsible for knowledge, and when in excess is highly destructive.

The Ark of the Covenant was associated with a glowing plasmatic vortex known as the Shekhina, meaning "Glory of the Lord." As explained, the Shekhina was the veritable "soul" of the device, the entitized thoughtform anchored to the Ark Stone. The glowing energy field itself was an intense etheric vortex that precipitated electrical charges and hence ionized the air. The Ark conferred illumination to prepared initiates but destruction to others. The Ark was therefore an example in Semitic lore of the same type of divine weaponry mentioned in the Indian epics.

> What is central is the mental relationship divine weapons have with their wielder as they reside in the mind. Furthermore, divine weapons are closely connected with such emotions as rage and anger. When unleashed they invoke all the raw power of a warrior's fury, infused with the *tejas* of the gods, and thus are capable of laying waste to hundreds of opponents in one concentrated act of violence. [...]

> Most divine weapons are named after the deities who preside over them, and, in general, they manifest the natural phenomena associated with the particular powers they reflect. [...]

> The divine weapons are also sentient beings, who often appear anthropomorphically. They can even assume therianthropic forms, which in a bestial fury tear their victims apart. The personification of divine weapons develops to the point in the *Puranic* literature where the *Sudarsana* discus, as one example, is not only "capable of following Visnu's instructions and acting independently of him, but it is also capable of feeling emotions like wrath and dissatisfaction."

> Ultimately, all *divya astras* are weapons of a single divine energy – *tejas*. This energy is channeled into the physical world by their wielders, who, with the correct *mantras* and, more importantly, their own reserves of *tejas*, control the energy by uniting it with a more tangible weapon, most commonly an arrow, or the energy can be simply released on its own. Divine weapons are far more destructive and efficacious than ordinary weapons (*sastras*) and their use enhances a warrior's natural prowess in combat. However, this weaponry represents immense and often volatile power, and is reserved for the greatest of heroes, putting them in direct communion with the gods,

as any warrior possessing a divine weapon can unleash the energy of the gods in the human realm.

Again, demiurgic technology may employ entitized thoughtforms to automate tasks. In the previous chapter, this was stated regarding Gray alien automatons and alien ships that carry out commands delegated to them.

In the case of the Ark of the Covenant, the inhabiting entity Yahweh was precisely one of wrath and dissatisfaction. Yahweh was not strictly localized to the Ark Stone like an embedded etheric microprocessor. Rather, it may have been a cosmological intelligence that the Ark Stone tapped into, like a computer terminal dialing into a remote server, just as in the Indian epics the weapons were often possessed by the *tejas* of various gods. The warrior combining his etheric energy with a mantra to activate the weapon and channel the "energy of the gods" is precisely what the Mosaic Priests employed. Recall that the Great Pyramid functions as a vocal resonator while the shape itself concentrates etheric energy. The Ark Stone in the King's Chamber must have been used to "unleash the energy of the gods in the human realm" and thereby allowed Yahweh, a.k.a. the Corrupt Demiurge, to enter the human realm much more deeply than before like some kind of temporal malware.

Whitaker describes the basic principles of etheric warfare:

> Firstly, *tejas* is harnessed, absorbed, neutralized, and contained by other entities that possess *tejas* themselves. *Tejas* is the active substance required to deal with *tejas*. Secondly, various qualities of *tejas* affect the outcome of the neutralization process. Here a priest's *tejas* is superior to a warrior's *tejas*. Furthermore, these qualities define the hierarchy of *tejas*. Thus, not only does one need greater quantities of *tejas*, but to defeat and opponent of superior *tejas* one needs more potent energy, which is illustrated by Visvamitra's concern to attain brahmanhood in order to gain access to *brahmatejas*.

Different grades of etheric energy exist. As explained, lower grade energy can be harvested from freshly boiled plants and cereals, higher grade from sacrificed animals, and even higher from sacrificed humans. Emotional energy of extreme joy or anger can likewise produce it. But none compares to the quality, quantity, and vibration of etheric energy channeled directly from the Logos. Hence the Grail Stone, activated by those initiated into the Christ consciousness, was more powerful than its earlier cruder function as the Ark Stone, which was powered by animal sacrifices and blind worship. It's not just the quantity or amplitude of the energy that matters, but also the quality or frequency.

> When Vasistha absorbs and contains the *Brahma astra,* its *tejas* is so intense that the brahman is transformed, making him more violent and a threat to the universe. The incoming fiery energy is so excessive that flames shoot forth from his skin. In a verse that encompasses the neutralization process, the text even implies that the brahman could lose control of himself. Vasistha is told: "You must contain the *tejas* with your own *tejas*!" [...] an intake of excessive energy can cause uncontrollable rage or self annihilation. [...] Clearly, one must possess adequate *tejas* to handle an intake of new energy.

Frank Joseph emphasizes in *Opening the Ark of the Covenant* that the Ark Stone induced megalomania in many of its operators, tyrant pharaoh Akhenaten being an example. The Levite priests underwent special training that elevated their etheric energy levels and qualities before they could even handle the Ark. The function of special gear they wore, such as the mysterious breastplate worn by Aaron (Moses' brother), is revealed by what Whitaker says next:

> Various kinds of amulets (*mani*) appear throughout the Vedic litera-ture, which bestow upon the wear many different energy-substances, including *tejas*, when bound to a part of the body. [...] This is also the case with other items and materials, such as a gold plate, which bestows upon the wearer its innate *tejas*. Thus, the innate energy of these items is drawn upon to augment one's own energy pool.

As for excessive energy causing fiery discharges, the Ark was known for this, but it also brings to mind spontaneous human combustion caused by premature kundalini activation. It further relates to the ancient Gaul warriors who went into battle without combustible clothing. They wore only metal neck torcs, open-ended metal rings fit-ted around their necks, which, via their inductive loop and capacitive ends, were identical in function to Lakhovsky coils (electromagnetic resonators that raise etheric energy levels in the wearer). The Celts/ Gauls were among the last remnants of the post-Atlantean superhuman culture, and the Druids were their equivalent of the Indian Brahmins.

The above merely illustrates the use of demiurgic technology in common combat. But its effects are not limited to the battlefield. The central theme of this chapter is that demiurgic technology can have global or universal effects. Whitaker cites one example:

> The cataclysmic evil (*sumahan dosah*) of the divine weapons is so devastating that it can destroy the universe. This is a striking statement considering the importance of the divine weapons. At its strongest, *dosa* translates as "evil", but means at least a "fault", "deficiency" or "detrimental effect." Therefore, what is the "detrimental effect" that can bring about the end of the universe?
>
> [...] By drawing upon themes already encountered with the principles of the divine weapons the answer can be simply stated: if a divine weapon struck a being of insufficient *tejas* (*alpatejas*), its inherent *tejas* will not be neutralized; moreover, the divine weapon will take the *tejas* of its victim(s), causing it to increase in size, and after many such incidents it will possess enough energy to threaten the universe. This is the cataclysmic danger in the divine weapons! This occurs in one of the longest divine weapon episodes. The *Narayana astra* is directed at the human footsoldiers and begins to swell to such proportions that the universe is nearly destroyed. It is only by Krsna's invention and his direct concern with cutting off the divine weapon's access to any potential fuel sources than the *Narayana astra* is finally countered.
>
> The preceding analysis assumes that a divine weapon will appropriate the *tejas* of an inadequate target. This can be verified as the text reveals more about the nature of the divine weapons in the warning that identifies their misuse as a *dosa* or "evil."

That is but one example of the misuse of demiurgic technology, in this case, an etheric chain reaction that would consume the whole world if given the opportunity. Wilhelm Reich explained how orgone energy flows from low concentrations to high concentrations; thunderstorms inherently do this by gathering it from the surrounding environment in a chain reaction until discharging the energy via lightning and precipitation.

The point is that if an extreme influx of etheric energy meets an insufficiently prepared recipient, the low-to-high energy flow may mean the recipient is annihilated when his/her/its etheric foundation is vacuumed away. As will be discussed below, this is one possibility we face regarding "The Shift" type phenomena.

Ambient Etheric Energy Cycles

Finally, Whitaker touches on what will become the presiding theme for the remainder of this chapter:

> The last principle pertaining to the divine weapons is Arjuna's loss of them after Kurukshetra war. There are two central factors that relate to the loss of the divine weapons; (1) the change in the *yugas* or "cosmic ages", and (2) the subsequent loss of *tejas*.
>
> By the epic period, a complex system of cosmological time had developed based on the four ages of the cosmos (*yugas*) that make up one complete cyclic age of existence (*mahayuga*). The four successive *yugas* are characterized by progressively decreasing lifespans, virtues, and quality of human life. The *Ramayana* takes place in the *Treta yuga,* while the *Mahabharata* is set at the end of the *Dvapara yuga.* At the end of the great Kurukshetra war *Kali Yuga* begins. The present age of the universe, *Kali Yuga,* is characterized by the final decline of the *dharma* and a general sense of suffering and impurity. The world and human beings are at their worst in all matters. It is this general sense of deterioration in *Kali Yuga* that can be specifically correlated with the loss of the divine weapons due to an intrinsic decline in the potential *tejas* available to all mortals, including warriors.

This speaks of a great decline in the *ambient etheric energy field* that triggers the onset of a spiritual dark age. Frank Joseph pins the end of the Kurukshetra war to around 3150 B.C., which is when the final post-Atlantean advanced civilization broke up and migrated around the globe. Those arriving in Central/South America, for instance, established the Long Count calendar (a.k.a. the Mayan calendar) whose most commonly accepted starting point is August 14th, 3114 B.C.

Other calendars around the world also start around that time. The Long Count calendar measures linear time, so the Mayans referred to its beginning as the beginning of time as we know it.

Of course, ambient etheric energy varies in a complicated way over time and geographic locale, somewhat like graphs of economic indicators that contain major cycles and numerous sub-cycles along with random variables thrown in. Thus it's not a smooth four-stage sinusoid as the four *yugas* might imply. That said, the world was once more etherically charged and will be again.

> To turn to the loss of the divine weapons: the Kurukshetra war is resolved, and *Kali Yuga* commences. [...] Arjuna begins to lament his defeat, and blames his inability to employ his divine weapons on the nature of fate. The divine Vyasa drives the point home when he informs Arjuna: "He who was once powerful loses that power, and he who was once lord is ruled by others. Your *astras,* which have accomplished their mission, have gone and they will return in the future to your hand when the [appropriate] time arrives." Arjuna's loss of the divine weapons is thus due to the workings of fate (*daiva*) and time (*kala*), and one manifestation of time is the *yugas*.

> The loss of the divine weapons can also be correlated with a loss of *tejas*. [...] If Arjuna has lost his *tejas* it would explain the reason behind the mysterious disappearance of his divine weapons. Without the correct quantity of *tejas* Arjuna will be unable to control or employ the divine weapons successfully. [...] The sage *Vyasa* informs Arjuna that his weakness in battle is for the following reason: "Power, intuition, *tejas*, and foresight exist in times of prosperity, and they perish in opposite conditions... All this has its root in time, which is the principle cause of the universe... Time thus unexpectedly takes it all away again. [The wise man] knows in *yuga* after *yuga* that the natural law *dharma* is crippled in one foot, and that the life expectancy and energy of mortals follow the rules of the *yuga*."

> The epic authors are suggesting that in the world in which they live, *Kali Yuga*, no one can own or employ divine weapons of the caliber portrayed in *Dvapara yuga*. This is because of a decline in the potential amount of *tejas* any given individual can acquire. If the divine weapons are left in Arjuna's possession, his de-energized state would put the universe (not to mention himself) in jeopardy, since

the divine weapons will not be able to be controlled. Thus, the divine weapons are withdrawn from circulation, so to speak, and returned to their divine owners.

And there we have an answer to the mystery of why humanoid aliens bestow and retrieve demiurgic technology, including the Ark/Grail stone, from the human sphere at certain times. They do so in concert with ambient etheric energy cycles. These cycles not only dictate when it's even possible to openly use such devices within the Earth realm but may also determine when it becomes *necessary* to use them. All this will be made clear below.

Take note, however, that the ebb and flow of etheric energy over time applies more to us "mortals" who languish in times of low energy like fish flopping aimlessly at low tide, while the alien beings withdraw to the ocean and remain fully immersed and mobile.

In summary, what can be gathered from the Indian epics is that there once existed an age where etheric energy levels were high enough that demiurgic technology was in common use for the common good. Eventually, the seeds of corruption took root and competing factions arose that inevitably fell into war. Their wars used demiurgic technology for destructive purposes, including certain misuses that threatened the very existence of the world. Subsequently, ambient etheric energy levels declined and these weapons could no longer be used as effectively within the human realm. Their superhuman owners largely withdrew the devices and the disempowered human remnants went on their way as mere ordinary mortals, into the well of linear time and limited existence. Thus began the onset of a spiritual dark age in which we still exist.

But as mentioned, aside from blood sacrifices providing temporary energy boosts, even within the Kali Yuga there have been localized spikes in ambient etheric energy levels. One case is 2300 – 1100 B.C. when the Ark Stone entered into Egyptian and Semitic history, and 450 – 1300 A.D. when the Grail Stone appeared in European and Arabian history. According to the Indian epics, these devices will surface once more, like Excalibur from the lake, to be used in a time of need; it shall occur when the ambient energy levels rise to where they once were.

The Mayan Long Count calendar, whose starting point coincides with the onset of the *Kali Yuga,* reaches the end of its 5124 year cycle on December 21st, 2012. For this and many other reasons, we may expect that the years, decades, or centuries to follow will see the return of the Etheric Tide, the reactivation of demiurgic technologies in the Earth sphere, and the resumption of open communion with otherworldly beings. The alien disinformation agenda to acclimatize our ignorant and skeptical culture to the alien presence is but preparation.

Alchemical Evolution of Mankind

This "Etheric Tide" theory brings up an important parallel to Alchemy. The physical and spiritual evolution of mankind has always been punctuated by cyclical cataclysms. Each cataclysm destroyed the existing order and triggered a period of chaos that eventually gave birth to a more sophisticated order. Our civilization now stands at the cusp of another such discontinuity. Like the cycle of reincarnation, the death and rebirth of civilization is an alchemical process paralleling the production of the Philosopher's Stone.

In Alchemy, a mineral solution imbued with crude etheric energy is allowed to putrefy in a vessel so that biological activity brings the etheric charge to a higher order. The vessel is then heated to distill off a liquid containing the living etheric essence. The remnant matter is heated until dry, then the distillate is mixed back into it; what does not dissolve is filtered out. The resulting solution is incubated for some time before the distillation process repeats. Over succeeding repetitions, a portion of the dried matter becomes increasingly etherized until the final steps trigger its etheric ignition and quantum transformation into a quasi-living substance. When tinged with gold, this transformed substance becomes the Philosopher's Stone.

On Earth, crude etheric energy enters the food chain and ascends upwards, driving the proliferation of life, evolution of consciousness, and production of higher soul energies in sentient beings. When conditions are ripe, a quickening process distills the "chosen" from the "damned." The latter undergo further tribulations that decimate their numbers and liberate their soul energies. The survivors and harvested soul energies represent the distillate, the seed and nutrient, derived from the old civilization. Both pour into the post-cataclysmic world to initiate a new civilization of higher order; surviving remnants of the old who cannot adapt die out. Civilization begins anew and grows until reaching ripeness once more.

With each cycle, the population evolves somewhat in terms of conscious sophistication. After sufficient repetitions, portions of the population most amenable to spiritualizing influences undergo an etheric ignition and transform into superhuman existence, especially in the final stages where additional catalysts come into play. These superhumans join the ranks of the parallel hidden meta-civilization mentioned previously that thrives outside linear time while civilizations within linear time continue to rise and fall. They are like the developing spiritual core within an individual that transcends and survives birth and death.

But as much as human evolution parallels the production of the Stone, there are some important differences. Whereas an *individual* makes the Philosopher's Stone, numerous schools of cosmic alchemists are involved in transmuting humanity, each with their own idea of where to go with human evolution:

- In the case of the Stone, some alchemists make it to give themselves eternal youth and perfect health. For them, it's a source of etheric nourishment. Likewise, some cosmic alchemists derive nourishment from our soul energies, and they have advanced our evolution only to produce a higher grade of this energy for themselves. Robert Monroe's account of loosh production in *Far Journeys* illustrates this perfectly. And just as the Philosopher's Stone becomes fatal when multiplied beyond a certain order of power and therefore useless as a panacea, so would humanity become useless as a source of etheric and astral food should we acquire sufficient superhuman status; therefore the predatory cosmic alchemists are deeply invested in keeping us down, using cataclysms only as a kind of winepress to produce their precious ambrosia.

- Some alchemists tinge the Stone with gold or silver to produce more of the same. Likewise, cosmic alchemists may aim to tinge our superhuman descendants with an impulse to create more like themselves, for good or bad depending on the tingeing. An example would be Fourth Density graduates polarizing either Service-to-Self or Service-to-Others depending on what existing Fourth Density forces they encounter and align with. In other words, new superhumans who encounter the already existing meta-civilization will be tinged by the ideologies of its various factions.

- Some alchemists employ the luminescent properties of a highly refined Stone to produce ever-burning lamps, and similarly, some cosmic alchemists could be aiming to potentialize mankind into shining beacons of divine power.

When immensely scaled up in power, size, and complexity, the Philosopher's Stone becomes the Ark Stone or Grail Stone — demiurgic technologies capable of large-scale reconfigurations of matter, energy, space, and time. Likewise, superhumans who achieve even higher levels of spiritual evolution asymptotically approach the creational capabilities of the Infinite Creator.

Why is this parallel between Alchemy and human evolution important?

First, it says something about what this planet will face in the near future. As mentioned, our civilization stands on the cusp of another cataclysm. Unlike previous ones, this may be our final. And like the final distillation in Alchemy, additional etheric catalysts may be involved to boost the transformation. For instance, there is a good chance our solar system will be irradiated by the aforementioned tidal wave of etheric energy. The psychological, spiritual, and perceptual changes induced by elevated etheric energy levels, along with the heliophysical and geophysical impact of same, accounts for a broad range of signs foretold in numerous end times prophecies.

Second, human evolution follows *solve et coagula*. This is the aforementioned process of order dissolving into chaos, and chaos precipitating into a new order. It is symbolized in the myth of the Phoenix, which burns itself to ashes only to emerge as a worm that grows once again into the bird. And it is contained in the "Illuminati" slogan *ordo ab chao*, order from chaos. As I will show in this chapter, the final step of our alchemical evolution involves the dissolution of reality as we know it and its reconfiguration into a new higher order. The only question concerns who shall forge the new order. That is the crux of this demiurgic war.

Effects of the Etheric Tide

Let's look more closely at the effects of increased ambient etheric energy levels.

First, because etheric and lifeforce energies are essentially the same, health and longevity will increase for those acclimated to that quantity and quality of energy. But if the influx rate of energy is too great, there is a risk of overwhelming the fragile etheric energy circuits of the body and causing injury. Likewise, if the quality of the energy is mismatched, either the body fails to receive it or else receives the wrong type to its detriment. If the Etheric Tide is gradual enough that generations can slowly acclimate to it, that would be ideal.

Bible researchers believe our antediluvian ancestors had lifespans in the hundreds of years; Nordic aliens likewise have lifespans in the centuries, and alchemists who imbibe the Elixir of Life can do likewise. This would become the norm should ambient etheric energy saturate a society acclimated to it. The primordial Golden Age, a bygone age of peace and plenty without premature death or disease, would have required such conditions.

Second, there would be activation and growth of latent psychic organs in the etheric body of humans. By default, humans are currently born with very limited psychic abilities because neither our crippled genetics nor the ambient etheric levels support their development. For such people, it takes disciplined occult training to activate and develop these abilities.

As both Fore and the Gulf Breeze contactee explained, aliens naturally emit high levels of etheric energy and, through a proximity effect, can cause psychic activation in nearby humans. In the case of an Etheric Tide, a natural phenomenon would do likewise to receptive members of the population. The result would be increased intuition, clairvoyance, and other supernatural powers. Ambient etheric energy levels provide a nutritive medium for the further development of psychic organs, leading eventually to the types of powers now only seen in aliens and occult masters.

Third, through astral projection, hypnopompic states, and trained clairvoyance it is already possible to see otherwise cloaked or phased-out ships in the skies and alien beings around us. Therefore, an Etheric Tide would force their visibility on a far wider scale. Aliens will then be unable to hide their presence, which explains the alien disinformation campaign now underway to prepare the public for their open "arrival."

Fourth, a shift in consciousness brought on by etheric activation would unlock otherwise inaccessible memories and mental perspectives. This includes alien abduction/contact memories and past life memories. During the onset of abduction or contact, an individual usually goes into an altered state of consciousness due to the proximity induction effect. This state of consciousness is termed *Left Side Awareness* or *Second Attention* in Carlos Castaneda's books. Memories recorded in this state become inaccessible when the abductee returns to normal mundane consciousness because it's like an antenna retracting and losing the signal. An Etheric Tide would extend the antenna, causing a person to flip over from the mundane mental perspective to the alternate higher one. In cases where an individual has been cached with hidden knowledge and instructions, these would activate at that time.

Thus the activation of alien-implanted knowledge is not so much caused by a hypnotic trigger, but by etheric activation. Consequently, an Etheric Tide would kick several alien agendas into play via their activated human proxies. The access to cached knowledge and instruction is said to occur during a time of great chaos, which matches the characteristics of an Etheric Tide.

Fifth, once perception of etheric energy and paranormal phenomena becomes commonplace, demiurgic technology develops quickly and naturally. Without clairvoyant perception, building devices that employ etheric energies is a matter of guesswork, but perception allows observation and the derivation of a science.

We also know from alienology that electronic devices tend to malfunction in the presence of alien ships. Some people can't wear watches because they always stop working when worn. These are the same people who tend to fry out electronics and turn off street lights in their proximity. These are examples of etheric fields or specific fluctuations in them causing electrical anomalies. In physics terms, it fluctuates the physical constants and likely affects local electron densities, indicating a relationship between etheric energy and the divergence of the magnetic vector potential. The Etheric Tide may interfere with our electrical systems, further forcing the development of demiurgic technology as an alternative. The increased perception and availability of etheric energy make this inevitable.

Sixth, the genesis of thoughtforms becomes easier and more potent since there is more ambient raw material available for their creation, and consequently the responsiveness of reality to thoughts and feelings greatly increases. Reality would then become more plastic, having been softened by the "Universal solvent," so to speak. Etheric energy is the medium that translates impulses between matter and consciousness. More of it means the mind has greater command over matter.

Additionally, these conditions would force greater mental and emotional discipline in people, since they will no longer have the luxury of being an internal cesspool while maintaining an external appearance of equipoise; when inner and outer become more congruent, external consequences of detrimental thoughts and feelings come all the sooner.

In a worst-case scenario, those who cannot master themselves will fall victim to their own self-generated delusions, go insane, and perish. This is already happening in people whose unbounded paranoia creates thoughtforms and physical manifestations that further validate their paranoia, creating a runaway feedback loop that ends in schizophrenia and death.

Another problem would be paranormal entities like demons, ghosts, and astral critters becoming more tangible, but that depends on how well they take up the specific quality of energy provided by the Etheric Tide; in any case, clairvoyant perception would make them more visible regardless, and that will further affect the sanity of people. Conditions that once fostered common acceptance of fairies, elves, elementals, djinn, ghosts, etc. will return.

All this assumes people don't suffer from illness and cancer first from being unable to properly assimilate the Etheric Tide. It's already the case that emotional blockages that produce resistance against the free flow of lifeforce energy can cause illness and cancer; similar resistance occurs when one fails to keep up with the currents of the Etheric Tide, namely by hanging on stubbornly to old Matrix Control System reactions and outlooks.

Hence, we are looking at the possibility of mass psychosis and illness in certain stubborn sectors of the population. The result is a filtering effect on humanity, just like the filtering out of solids that fail to dissolve in the alchemical distillate.

The filter is further enhanced by the fact that, since thoughts and feelings bend probability, it is in times of chaos that one must rely the most upon good fortune and divine grace to make it through, which can only be earned through the corresponding elevation of heart and discipline of mind. Aside from sheer resourcefulness, synchronistic protection coupled with increased clairvoyance and intuition is how the forebears of future humanity will make it through.

As an aside, whether through technology or superhuman abilities, advanced versions of either should allow one to phase out of regular spacetime as needed, becoming invisible to those still mired in it. One would then naturally have access to the parallel meta-civilization composed of beings who have already achieved this.

Physical Cataclysm

While another round of cataclysms appears to be on the horizon, cataclysm is not always a necessary catalyst for growth. But that doesn't prevent it from happening anyway. Even so, unavoidable obstacles can still serve as catalysts for growth if used as such.

In this case, cataclysm could be an unavoidable side-effect of the Etheric Tide, the same way pain is a side-effect of the birthing process. Earth and Sun are sensitive to etheric energy. As Wilhelm Reich discovered, orgone energy affects nuclear decay rates, meaning it affects reality at the quantum level. But since solar output, as well as Earth's seismic, volcanic, and tectonic activities, are dependent on nuclear decay processes, changes in ambient etheric energy levels would impact all of these. Recent scientific studies* indicate that solar activity affects nuclear decay rates on Earth, likely due to a change in neutrino flux, which itself may be linked to etheric energy. In any case, the result of an Etheric Tide would be freak solar flares and CMEs as well as a massive increase in earthquakes, volcanoes, and continental plate shifts.

The Expanding Earth Theory of Neil Adams (and Cliff High's Expando Planet Model) further suggests a change in the size of Earth. Past expansion is evident from continent edges matching each other on all sides, suggesting Earth used to be a lot smaller. That's also why dinosaurs were so large, due to lower gravity levels combined with a thicker atmosphere carrying more oxygen. The question has always been where the extra matter comes from when the planet bulks up. Well, it comes from the center of the planet/star where spacetime is most stressed by the surrounding matter and a dimensional portal arises; etheric energy seems to affect the aperture of this portal, which determines how well energies from the other side translate into matter on our side.

It's precisely the same with the Ark Stone or Grail Stone, where an input of etheric energy (animal sacrifice or dancing in the case of the Ark Stone) allows for the manifestation of physical foodstuffs. In other words, the Earth expanding upon irradiation by an Etheric Tide is merely a planetary version of what happens in the Ark Stone. It's demiurgic geophysics. This does, however, suggest the possibility that, just as the Ark Stone required a specific mental command to

---

* <news.stanford.edu/news/2010/august/sun-082310.html>

specify what to materialize, so might the specific reconfiguration of Earth be dependent upon the collective thoughtforms of mankind. In that sense, how consciousness responds to the Etheric Tide might determine the severity, location, and nature of events constituting the accompanying cataclysm.

Etheric Dissolution of Reality

The biggest threat, or welcomed opportunity, would be an Etheric "Tsunami," whereby the world gets slammed by a shockwave of etheric energy. A traveling event horizon possibly originating from the super black hole at the Galactic Center could hit us eventually. That is, an event horizon would eject us into hyperspace where consciousness alone would decide what spacetime timeline we would emerge back into.

Well, if not a traveling event horizon, then a sufficiently intense etheric field would rip spacetime all the same. Or put in terms of this book's paradigm, an Etheric Tsunami would utterly dissolve our reality just as the Universal solvent of the alchemists dissolves metals into quantum soup. In this malleable state of chaos, consciousness acts as the tinge- ing agent determining what new order emerges. An Etheric Tsunami would disconnect us from our current timeline and provide the grand- est of all pivot points upon which not only the future but the new past hinges.

Can nature alone provide such an impulse to dissolve reality? Maybe that's as unlikely as nature creating random nuclear explosions on our planet. Only technology concentrating the existing forces of nature can create consequences so severe. Therefore, instead of an Etheric Tsunami originating from the cosmos, it could be the use of demiurgic technology during a more gentle Etheric Tide that dissolves and re- configures spacetime. That seems to be its primary function anyway, to serve as the central axis of a wider timeline pivot region made possible by the Etheric Tide.

Again, these technologies are bestowed upon humans when ambient etheric energy levels are elevated, for then are such devices not only more charged up, but reality itself is more malleable. In ancient Egypt and proto-Israel, the Ark Stone was involved in reorienting our time-line toward one where we now stand on the brink of an overt alien takeover and global totalitarian system. It stands to reason that an upcoming Etheric Tide would also see the reactivation of the Grail Stone or devices like it.

Even in ancient Egyptian times when ambient etheric energy levels were elevated, the Ark Stone required additional lifeforce energy from sacrificed animals to convert thoughts into foodstuffs, alter the local geography, and other seemingly miraculous actions. These same spacetime re-engineering feats were accomplished by the Grail Stone without animal sacrifice, and instead with higher vibrational energy received from the Logos by gnostic initiates.

The implication is that, if the Etheric Tide primes conditions for deployment of the Stone, reconfiguration of reality may then occur along at least two lines: 1) through the cataclysmic slaughter of billions providing the etheric and astral energy needed for an Ark Stone activation, which would reformulate the world into deeper conformity with the Corrupt Demiurge, or 2) through the gnostic awakening of sufficient individuals to provide the etheric and astral energy needed for a Grail Stone activation, which would reformulate the world into deeper harmonization with the Logos. In other words, negative forces may be counting on the energy harvested from mass suffering and deaths to fuel the reconfiguration of our reality into theirs.

Clearly, the use of such devices allows a smaller group to decide the outcome of the greater collective, hence the Stone acts as a lever of sorts. Who will employ it? Probably those whose personal destinies are intertwined with the alien timewar and Grail/anti-Grail drama; the question won't personally matter to the rest of the population who are karmically indifferent to whether reality reorganizes into one timeline or another. As it stands, mankind has existed for thousands of years in complete indifference to the fact that their world is a composite construct of changes effected by superhuman forces engaged in a cosmic chess match.

In summary, whether through the power of nature, the power of consciousness, or the power of technology, demiurgic principles have the function of revolving or bending the world around a chosen center. The center is a pivot point that moves the world without itself being moved, signifying something beyond spacetime where the archetypal commands reside that determine in what manner the world is reoriented. For instance, consciousness alone has this power, as evident in the practice of reality creation. Nature has this power in the case of the Etheric Tide inducing physical changes in Sun and Earth, or the Philosopher's Stone inducing changes in lead to produce gold. And technology has this power in devices like the Grail Stone that can bend the timeline and reconfigure reality in ways greater than either mind or nature alone can. High Demiurgic power can intentionally de-collapse and re-collapse the quantum wavefunction; it is the ultimate creational power, that of the Prime Mover.

Dawn of a New Day: The Awakening of the World Soul

Etheric energy is the substrate of physical reality. Changes in the etheric induce changes in the physical. At weak levels, the change is merely probabilistic, while at strong levels it produces direct reconfigurations of matter and energy. This is merely a question of whether quantum biasing occurs at the subatomic or macroscopic scale.

But it may be equally said — and this is critical to understand — that certain etheric patterns sustain certain physical patterns. Thus every particular configuration of space, time, matter, and energy is held that way by an underlying "base-level" thoughtform, the common denominator shared by elements of that configuration, which perpetuates the default behavior of that system. All additional thoughtforms merely deviate the system's probabilistic behavior away from this default.

In the case of the Philosopher's Stone, it is the intense etheric power and gold-tinged qualities of the Stone that overcomes the base-level thoughtform that otherwise holds the pattern of "lead" in place. For humans, this same base-level thoughtform perpetuates the laws of physics and moves the physical body toward entropic disintegration, whereas the human etheric body is an additional thoughtform that counters this and allows for the continuation of life.

On a cosmological scale, the Demiurge sustains the world as we know it, thus it qualifies as the default thoughtform defining our spacetime existence. It is a World Thoughtform or World Soul. The Corrupt Demiurge is a parasitic entitized addition or extrusion that biases the course of events toward anti-spiritual ends. The impulse of the divine Logos, via the Christ thoughtform, produces counter-influence nudging things toward spiritual ends instead.

This brings us to the Rosicrucian doctrine of the World Soul. William Walker Atkinson, writing under the name Magus Incognito, explains it best in *The Secret Doctrine of the Rosicrucians* (1918):

> The Rosicrucian concept of the World Soul—the First Manifestation—corresponds to similar conceptions found, in various forms, in most of the ancient occult teachings of the several great esoteric schools of philosophy. In some philosophies it is known as the "Anima Mundi," or Life of the World, Soul of the World, or World Spirit. In others it is known as the Logos, or Word. In others, as the Demiurge. The spirit of the concept is this: that from the unconditioned essence of Infinite Unmanifestation there arose an Elemental and Universal Soul, clothed in the garments of the most tenuous, elemental form of Matter, which contained within itself the potency and latent possibility of all the future universes of the new Cosmic Circle, or Cosmic Day. [...]

> The concept of the World Soul, in some form of interpretation and under some one of many names, may be said to be practically universal. Among many of the ancient schools of philosophy it was taught that there was an Anima Mundi, or World Soul, of which all the individual souls were but apparently separated (though not actually separated) units. The conviction that Life was One is expressed through nearly all of the best of ancient philosophies; and, in fact, in subtly disguised forms, may be said to rest at the base of the best of modern philosophies. [...]

> The Demiurge was the Life of the World, or Universal Life, of which all the innumerable lives of finite creatures are but sparks in the flame or drops of water in the ocean. And, yet, in its true sense, the concept of the Demiurge was not identified with that of God, but was rather a concept of the First Great Manifestation of God, by means of which He creates and sustains the World. [...]

But it must be always noted that in the Secret Doctrine of the Rosicrucians the World Soul is not regarded as the Infinite Reality, but merely as the First Manifestation thereof, from which all subsequent manifestations proceed and into which they are finally resolved. The World Soul is not Eternal, but, on the contrary, appears and disappears according to the rhythm of the Cosmic Nights and Days.

This ties into the *yuga* cycles, the variations in the density and quality of etheric energy permeating our world, the imminent Etheric Tide, and the influence of additional thoughtforms like Yahweh and Christ injected into the system. All of these may be interpreted as fluctuations in the state of the World Thoughtform, and hence the world itself. Greater fluctuations produce greater world changes.

In Rosicrucian terminology, the influx of an Etheric Tide represents an *awakening* of the "World Soul" and the "Dawn of a New Cosmic Day." How is it an awakening? As Rudolf Steiner observed, when we go to sleep the etheric body expands and decouples from the physical. Just enough remains in the body to maintain life processes, but not enough to allow perception or induced movement by the mind. The etheric body largely withdraws from the physical, forcing the latter into a vegetative state during sleep. Awakening consists of the etheric body lowering back into the physical and fully coupling with it, allowing consciousness to resume control over the physical body.

The same process applies to our world. At some point, the World Thoughtform underwent a process analogous to our entering sleep. Its etheric body withdrew from the physical and consequently the ambient etheric energy levels went down significantly. Matter, energy, and spacetime as we know them are left in a vegetative state, by default unresponsive to the whims of consciousness. Hence the eventual Etheric Tide represents the return of the World Etheric Body and the awakening of the World Thoughtform, which will allow consciousness to once more resume control over matter, energy, and spacetime. The various etheric energy cycles in history are analogous to the stages of sleep: various REM cycles are interrupted by periods of inactivity or intermediate periods.

Jordan Maxwell, Goro Adachi, and other synchromystic researchers have been tracking ubiquitous symbolism in media, culture, politics, esoterica, etc. pertaining to the "dawn of a new day", "return of the king", "birth of Lucifer", "the Green Sun", "a New World Order", and other veiled allusions to something profoundly new and world-changing on the horizon. But few suspect it could be an Etheric Tide awakening the World Soul. It's not just the rising of some new political order, not just the establishment of some world religion, not even just the re-setting of civilization through physical cataclysms, but a cosmological event capable of transforming our reality from the quantum level up.

The Cosmic Sleep

According to conventional psychology, what plays out in dreams are symbolic representations of subconscious dynamics. But the term "subconscious" is just an umbrella for what lies beyond the immediate knowledge of the conscious mind. Think of it as merely an elevator door, a gateway to all other floors of the building from the sunniest rooftop to the darkest basement. Through the subconscious, our dreams may be influenced by higher positive beings, negative opportunistic feeders, unsorted residual memories from the previous day, health issues that disturb the somatic consciousness of the body, etheric thoughtforms, and soul energy imbalances. The dream environment symbolically stages these influences before our illucid awareness.

A similar thing happened when we entered the Kali Yuga and ambient etheric energy levels changed. Not only has the World Soul fallen asleep and the World Etheric largely withdrawn from the World Physical, but we are now living in a World Dream of sorts. What does a World Dream even mean? It means an illusory state of existence divorced from the true existence, one separated from the realm beyond our limited spacetime bubble. It means a state where consciousness is obliviously and helplessly subjected to symbolic dramatizations of dynamics originating beyond that limited existence.

Is this not what we know of our reality right now, that forces beyond our realm are orchestrating what happens here, that we are like fish in an aquarium to these beings? When we experience synchronicities, omens, or number sightings, doesn't it seem like intelligences beyond the veil of physicality are inserting encoded messages into our environment? How can they do this unless they are doing it from outside spacetime? Spacetime as we know it is none other than the World Dream Environment. There are beings outside the World Dream who influence what happens here.

Sleeping and dreaming are not just convenient metaphors in this case, but phenomena involving the interaction between the same physical, astral, etheric, and spiritual elements. These interactions and elements are as valid on the human scale as on the cosmological. As above, so below.

And just as our psychological structure mirrors the cosmological structure, so will awakening of the World Soul be mirrored by our own *potential* awakening thanks to an increase of ambient etheric energy levels. The final result will be a state of existence where individual consciousness exercises superior command over matter, energy, and spacetime. This condition is termed "Fourth Density" by *The Ra Material* and *Cassiopaean Transcripts*.

What we're possibly facing with the Etheric Tide is the awakening of the World Thoughtform or World Soul from its languished condition, like the ill-stricken Grail King Amfortas being restored to full health by the Grail, or Sleeping Beauty awakening with a prince's kiss that also brings the Kingdom out of its thorn-riddled slumber.

Magus Incognito concludes:

> The World Soul, at the Dawn of the Cosmic Day, may be said to be like a dreamer freshly awakened from a deep sleep, and striving to regain consciousness of himself. It does not know what it is, nor does it know that it is but an Idea of the Eternal Parent. If it could express its thought in words it would say that it has always been, but had been asleep before that moment. It feels within itself the urge toward expression and manifestation, along unconscious and instinctive lines—this urge being a part of its nature and character and implanted into it by the content of the Idea of the Eternal Parent which brought it into being. Like the newborn babe, it struggles for breath and begins to move its limbs. And as it struggles and moves, there comes to it a response from all of its nature, and its active life

begins. And here we leave the World Soul, for the moment, struggling for breath and striving to move its limbs (figuratively speaking, of course).

The Enemies of Awakening

Unfortunately, some antagonists have greatly profited from our spiritual coma; the World Dream has afforded them an environment removed from greater Creation, an environment now populated by dim souls helpless as fish at low tide. Archontic powers reign as kings over an empire of dreams.

The prime antagonist against spiritual lucidity is the Corrupt Demiurge. Through its influence, the World Dream has become a World Nightmare unwilling to release its grip; the human race has become its prisoner. In the first chapter, I explained how physicality imprinting upon the Demiurge gives rise to a predatory extension committed to ideals of materialism, just as the world imprinting upon our soul creates ego.

To recap, imprinting means influencing, programming, shaping, or conditioning. While the Demiurge may create the physical universe, the physical universe, in turn, may influence the Demiurge. The law of the jungle, survivalism, determinism, looking out for yourself, survival of the fittest, eat or be eaten — these ideals rooted in the realm of matter can rub off on the Demiurge, creating a living "thoughtform" extension of the Demiurge that is dedicated to those same ideals. Alternatively, negative beings can condition the Demiurge through occult rituals, emotional energy, and demiurgic technology. If they do it for anti-spiritual reasons, then what results is an anti-spiritual extension of the Demiurge. In either case, the Demiurge is influenced or "imprinted" by the physical universe, by that which serves matter and opposes spirit.

The same can be explained in terms of waking/dreaming, where the World Dream sustains a parasitical entity invested in prolonging the dream indefinitely.

While one might think the Etheric Tide shall put an end to all this, keep in mind that the Corrupt Demiurge's agents — from negative alien deceivers to their human shadow military cohorts — have been preparing to endure and capitalize upon the coming changes instead of trying to stop them. They are aiming to maintain and secure their control in a Fourth Density environment. Or put another way, the Corrupt Demiurge seeks to expand its tyranny beyond the current spacetime bubble, beyond the current provisional timeline, into what comes after and beyond. It aims for *transubstantiation* from our current dream world into the Real World — Fourth Density and up — so that it may reign there as well.

Awakening of the World Soul does not by itself guarantee *what* will awaken and reign. Will the original and rightful Logos resume control, or will the Corrupt Demiurge extend its dominion?

To draw another metaphor, the Demiurge is like a computer, the Logos the operating system, Corrupt Demiurge the virus, Christ the antivirus program, and lesser thoughtforms are various executables. Our current Cosmic Sleep is equivalent to "Safe Mode," whereby reality now runs at lower resolution with higher functions disabled. When we finally come out of Safe Mode through a reboot, what will be in control — the operating system or the virus? If the latter, awakening would simply result in a higher sleepwalker or zombie, fully animated but mentally and spiritually defunct. Then mankind would become nothing more than etherically enhanced instruments of ego, both their own and the World Ego, hence they would become superhuman vessels for the Corrupt Demiurge; after all, that is what higher negative forces are already.

The key danger we face is that our spiritual rebirth becomes a spiritual abortion, that instead of graduation to a higher positive environment there occurs a transition to a higher negative environment. In other words, the key danger is that Earth becomes a Fourth Density Service-to-Self planet; that is *the* ultimate goal of the negative alien agenda.

How can they achieve it? Since they cannot stop the Etheric Tide, they would need to secure control of the other two factors: human consciousness and demiurgic technology. The Etheric Tide energizes, human consciousness modulates, and demiurgic technology reconfigures. Sufficient reconfiguration would afford them total domination.

In context of the Lucifer Rebellion myth, this would amount to Lucifer reacquiring the jewel that fell from his crown and completing the rebellion to become King of the World. That is what the negative secret societies mean when they speak of the "return of the Sun King" and the other occult phrases tracked by synchromystics. They await the total triumph of their prime demiurgic benefactor.

Seat of the World Soul

The sleep metaphor continues when we consider how the pineal gland functions as a regulator of wake and sleep via its periodic release of melatonin and DMT. Melatonin establishes conditions conducive to sleep while DMT triggers the final projection into the dream state. What is the technological analog to the pineal gland? None other than the Grail Stone. Melatonin and DMT are loosely analogous to the Etheric Tide and Etheric Tsunami; the first has a priming function, the second a decoupling function.

The pineal gland has traditionally been considered the seat of the soul, while the Grail Stone is the seat of the World Soul or Demiurge. The Grail Stone can reconfigure physical reality via its "root access" to the Demiurge. Additionally, the Grail Stone is oracular, allowing communication from hyperdimensional intelligences just as the third eye, associated with the pineal gland, allows visual perception of information from beyond spacetime. The jewel in Lucifer's crown is represented in Indian mythology as a jewel embedded in the forehead and is equated with the third eye.

Hence there are symbolic connections and functional analogs between the Grail Stone, pineal gland, and the third eye. One can see this everywhere. Consider how the Great Pyramid with its vowel resonators and Ark Stone placement mimics the human vocal tract and pineal gland placement; operation of the Great Pyramid may have paralleled the process of stimulating the pineal gland through overtone chanting. Overtone chanting at skull-resonant frequencies produces spherical standing waves that converge upon the pineal gland, which is located at the skull's precise geometric center. Just as stimulation of the pineal gland opens one up to other realms, so may activation of the Great Pyramid have opened access to other demiurgic intelligences such as the Yahweh entity. Other connections worth mentioning are the secret society obsession with pine cone symbolism and the mathematical fact that pine cone geometry is a type of vortex; vortex symbolism figures prominently into the Grail subject and will be discussed in the next chapter.

The most important parallel between the Grail Stone and pineal gland is that, just as the latter regulates wake and sleep, so may the Grail Stone have played an instrumental role in the transition between Cosmic Wake and Cosmic Sleep. Use or abuse of the Grail Stone is what may have knocked us into the World Dream in the first place. This is just another way of saying abuse of demiurgic technology corrupted the timeline.

It's only a matter of interpretation whether we entered into Cosmic Sleep, underwent a Fall into this darkened realm, or deviated onto a corrupted timeline. These are all different ways of framing the same problem. To better explain how demiurgic technology may have corrupted our timeline, a discussion on timeline dynamics is in order.

Timewars

How do thoughtforms tie into timeline dynamics? Once created, they ceaselessly pursue their programming until the astral archetypes delineating their objectives are fully manifested in the physical. That is their demiurgic function, to take an archetypal template and realize it in the physical. Usually, they do this by exerting pressure upon the timeline at quantum bifurcation points, bending it toward the probable futures where their objectives are fulfilled. Thoughtforms may be interpreted as strange attractors located in the future, pulling various timeline pathways toward them like magnets attracting iron particles along magnetic field lines.

The prime objective of the Demiurge is to fashion the Universe, to generate and perpetuate physicality. This objective is met every second as the Demiurge or World Thoughtform collapses quantum wave functions into tangible configurations, like a sliding zipper meshing together separate strands into a single line. Hence linear time ticks on with or without our participation.

The Demiurge is responsible for time itself, like an author responsible for time within a novel's plot, or the subconscious for time in a dream. Lesser thoughtforms, which are but extrusions of the Demiurge, respectively modulate the properties of time according to their archetypal impulse. Weaker thoughtforms merely have probabilistic influence, nudging the course of events toward one probable future instead of another, while stronger thoughtforms could conceivably reformulate the entire timeline. An author may feel a weak impulse and merely change the direction of the story, or a strong impulse and rewrite it from scratch.

Christ and Yahweh signify the opposing primary extensions of the Demiurge rooted in divergent probable futures. In one probable future, the Christ thoughtform has accomplished its objective of spiritualizing matter, restoring all fallen souls, and placing physicality back under the reign of the Logos. In the other probable future, Yahweh has fully matterized spirit, enchained higher souls into the darkest of conditions, and thereby secured for itself the most exquisite energy source.

Each exerts its influence upon the timeline, each represents a particular state, aspect, or extrusion of the World Thoughtform, and each sends its feedback flow into the present from our perceived future. In turn, we send our feedback flow into the future via the causal consequences of how we respond physically, mentally, and emotionally. Our response increases or diminishes the strength of either future/thoughtform via the past-future feedback loop.

While the Logos is beyond even the Demiurge and is an eternal intelligence beyond time, the Christ impulse appears to be a provisional thoughtform active *within* linear time as a probability current flowing toward the best of all possible outcomes. Meanwhile, Yahweh is one flowing toward the worst. None can deny that these worlds exist as probable futures; it follows from the simple fact that not all futures are equal, thus some are better than others, and there exists the best and worst among them.

Christ and Yahweh are completely goal-oriented like any thoughtform, ceaselessly working to fulfill their objectives, one toward ultimate balance and the spiritualization of matter, the other toward ultimate imbalance and deadening of spirit. Consequently, our timeline is under competition by two primary opposing time loops, or equivalently, our world is the intersection between higher and lower realms, a war between two artificial intelligences. This dynamic is represented in the Gnostic Christian symbol of the vesica piscis, two circles intersecting, or the symbol Y depicting the temporally branching dualism.

The late Philip K. Dick, science fiction author and modern gnostic, speculated on the matter as follows:

> The *Logos* is not a retrograde energetic life form, but the Holy Spirit, the *Parakletos,* is. If the *Logos* is outside time, imprinting, then the Holy Spirit stands at the right or far or completed end of time, toward which the field flow moves (the time flow). It receives time: the negative terminal, so to speak. Related to the *Logos* in terms of embodying world-directives and world-organizing powers, but at a very weak level, it can progressively to a greater degree overcome the time field and flow back against it, into it, impinging and penetrating. It moves in the opposite direction. It is the anti-time. So it is correct to distinguish it from the *Logos,* which so to speak reaches down into the time flow from outside, from eternity or the real universe. The H.S [Holy Spirit] is in time, and is moving: retrograde. Like *tachyons,* its motion is a temporal one; opposite to ours and the normal direction of the universal causal motion.
>
> Equilibrium is achieved by the *Logos* operating in three directions: from behind us as causal-time-pressure, from above, then the final form, the very weak H.S. drawing toward perfection each form. But now equilibrium as we know it is being lost in favor of a growing ratio of the retrograde teleology. This implies we are entering, have entered, a unique time: nearing completion of the manifold forms. Last pieces are going into place in the overall pattern. The task or mode of the H.S. is *completing.* Not beginning, not renewing or maintaining, but bringing to the end, to the close. An analogy would be the transit of a vehicle from one planet to another; first stage is the gravity of planet of origin; then equilibrium of both planets in terms of their pull; then the growing pull of the destination gravity-field as it gradually takes over and completes the journey. Beginning, middle, end. At last one senses the receiving field engage, and then correct. (Philip K. Dick, *In Pursuit of Valis,* pp. 64-65)

Corruption of the timeline stems from the corruption of the Demiurge, for the Demiurge is time. Both the quality of time and the
fabric of history were affected by this corruption. If the Demiurge is
responsible for time in general, the Corrupt Demiurge is responsible
for *linear* time in particular, for the limitations imposed by linear time
are favorable to its agenda. Those who succumbed to the Corrupt
Demiurge underwent a Fall into the limited spacetime bubble we are
now accustomed to, a realm where time marches ceaselessly forward
toward entropy, atrophy, and decay and the senses are confined to
the domain of matter and electromagnetic energy. These conditions,
which define the Cosmic Sleep, serve to increasingly isolate us from
true reality. Were it not for the influence of spirit/Logos, every last
one of us would be Matrix puppets.

Hence the influence of Logos, which intervened through the Christ or
Holy Spirit thoughtforms as a direct counter-reaction to the threat of
the Corrupt Demiurge, may be said to be working "over and against"
linear time. It counters linear time not by creating a reversed linear time
flow, but by working through a nonlinear type of time harmonized
with the Logos.* It works through synchronistic, nondeterministic,
critical point intervention instead of cold mechanistic calculation. It
works through the butterfly effect. Many of the sayings and parables
attributed to Jesus pertain to this.†

The Dissolution of Linear Time

As with the Philosopher's Stone transmuting matter, sufficient etheric
energy can also override linear time. The meta-civilization can exist
outside linear time because they possess a quantity and quality of etheric energy that places them beyond the grasp of the particular World

---

* In math speak: imaginary time. Tachyons don't just move backward in time,
but propagate through *imaginary* time. The opposite of causality is not reverse
causality, but acausality.

† For example, *The Gospel of Thomas*, Logion 20:

The disciples said to Jesus, "Tell us what the kingdom of heaven is
like." He said to them, "It is like a mustard seed. It is the smallest of
all seeds. But when it falls on tilled soil, it produces a great plant and
becomes a shelter for birds of the sky."

Thoughtform that still holds us firmly in linear time. The implication is that the Etheric Tide irradiating Earth may loosen that grip.

Put another way, the Dawn of a New Cosmic Day, which represents a major transformation of the Demiurge, would signify a major transformation in the nature of time as well. Time could change toward nonlinearity: variable time rate, selectable location along the timeline, and greater malleability in what directional heading time takes. Right now, linear time marches steadily forward like involuntary muscle movements during sleep, such as breathing, while nonlinear time is like consciousness returning to the body and resuming voluntary control.

The Etheric Tide poses both a dilemma and opportunity for the Corrupt Demiurge. While the dissolution of linear time would undermine the control it has enjoyed so far in our history, it can still reign afterward should nonlinear time be successfully harmonized with its parasitic objectives.

This has already happened in certain probable futures, futures from which negative time travelers originate. These alien manipulators are entirely steeped in nonlinear time, for they use time travel freely. Even so, they are saddled with limitations that force them to rely on cold calculation to pursue their agendas. Even with their nonlinear and demiurgic abilities, it seems they get befuddled and undermined by the even more subtle, synchronistic, and incomprehensible maneuvers of the Logos.

Timewars and Thoughtforms

Nonlinear time makes the past accessible and reconfigurable. Thus our reality is accessible and reconfigurable by beings who operate beyond linear time. This necessarily includes forces from *our own probable futures* who have already undergone the Etheric Tide and broken free from linear time, be they positive or negative.

If time travel is possible, it will happen sooner or later, therefore it already *has* happened at some point in the future, hence we are being visited by time travelers from our perceived future. This would be mere philosophizing were it not for alienology research confirming that time travelers do indeed comprise a portion of the alien presence. The other portion consists of meta-civilizations that previously transcended linear time. Regardless of where within linear history the moment of transcendence was achieved, once beyond, one "joins the club," so to speak.

Warring among meta-civilization factions has the appearance of a timewar. As they attempt to reconfigure the past in their favor, we would experience a tug of war that continually adjusts our trajectory into the future. The more our trajectory points toward their particular probable future, the stronger and more tangible they become to us. That is a mathematical fact in quantum physics. This feedback loop resembles thoughtforms acquiring energy and tangibility and is intimately tied into that process.

Better probable futures have more of the Christ impulse defining their World Thoughtform, worse probable futures have the Yahweh or Corrupt Demiurge impulse underpinning theirs. The best of all possible futures is entirely of Christ/Logos, the worst entirely by Yahweh/Corrupt Demiurge. These are the "alive cat" vs "dead cat" outcomes in our cosmic Schrödinger's Experiment. Currently, the two states are superimposed and both outcomes exist in a mixed state, which is why both influences are simultaneously active in our world.

Quantum indeterminacy is what even *allows* probable futures to retroactively influence the choices that gave rise to them. The more significantly a choice impacts the future, the more strongly it experiences competing feedback flows from those probable futures.

That is another reason why the Ark/Grail Stone was capable of hosting the Yahweh or Christ intelligences, because its power to change the timeline was so immense that the probable futures issuing from these changes had an equally immense degree of feedback flow, hence allowing full-blown manifestation and communication. The same can be said of historical figures like Joan of Arc who changed the course of history in response to visions she received. So it should be mentioned that certain people, places, times, and events have greater impact on the future than do others, and the future feedback flow is correspondingly greater upon them. That flow carries with it not only probabilistic, emotional, intuitive, and mental biasing, but can also attract the interest and direct influence of time travelers from affected futures.

Time travelers are inherently aligned with the World Thoughtform defining their timeline. There is a symbiotic relationship between them and their presiding World Thoughtform. Even if they don't call these forces so by name, it seems some time travelers ultimately serve Christ/Logos, others Yahweh/Corrupt Demiurge. They harness demiurgic probability currents the same way sailing fleets employ ocean currents to reach their destinations.

This is just another way of saying that alien agendas fit within cosmological agendas. It also means alien technology is attuned to different demiurgic currents, hence the Stone functions one way if hitched to the Yahweh current and another when coupled to the Christ current, in each case serving to reinforce the feedback loop between present and the best/worst future by altering history accordingly.

The symbiotic relationship between aliens and their demiurgic benefactor can be seen in certain examples drawn from alienology where the highly positive types seem to function as emissaries of the Logos on missions to restore balance and assist our gnostic awakening, while the more Luciferian or rather pantheistic types (negative Nordics and Reptilians for instance) pretty much worship the Corrupt Demiurge since its "blood" powers their demiurgic technology and sustains their livelihood. As will be mentioned again in the next chapter, the latter is metaphorically depicted in the movie *Dark City* where the Strangers ritualistically turn toward a giant underground machine bearing a metallic face and psychically interface with it in order to "tune" the surface human world into an alternate configuration.

Conclusion

Apparently, the Etheric Tide only increases the stakes in the cosmological conflict between Logos and Corrupt Demiurge instead of resolving it. That makes sense if the Etheric Tide merely has a priming function. Then the decoupling function would belong to demiurgic technology, which achieves its peak potency during an Etheric Tide for maximum timeline and reality reconfiguration. Likewise, in Alchemy, the process is initiated by Nature but must be taken from there by Art, meaning by the artifice of the alchemist.

Hence the Grail Stone may be the "doomsday device" or "captured flag" that ends this phase of the conflict. That the device requires an Etheric Tide to achieve its full potential would explain why the time-war hasn't ended sooner, back when it was in the hands of the Mosaic Priesthood or Grail knights, since the Etheric Tide has not yet arrived. The best and worst probable futures are still in quantum superposition

The "Stone that Fell from Heaven" was brought here on purpose (by the "neutral angels" according to Grail lore) and lowered into our spacetime bubble like a slim jim or coat hanger to lock/unlock the door from the inside. To be more accurate, the Grail is the lock and key to our reality. Altogether, one could say its primary role is to begin and end timelines, while its secondary role is to bend the timeline along the way depending on who controls it.

The next chapter will show how the preceding ideas are ubiquitously encoded in ancient myths and modern fiction. Myths and fiction are the collective equivalents of personal dreams, and like the latter can contain symbolic messages from beyond. I will delve more deeply into demiurgic symbolism, shed further light on the foregoing discussion, and dive to the bottom of what's going on with our so-called "reality."

8 POLAR MYTHOLOGY

The Meaning of Myth

Since myths are not literal accounts of history, they are easily dismissed as superstitious tales invented by our naïve ancestors. But what society considers factual, historical, and *real* is only that which has taken place within linear time and 3D space, namely events witnessed through the five physical senses.

Far from being less than factual, myths may depict events and dynamics that are *more* than factual because they hail from *beyond* the limited modern conception of reality, beyond linear time and the five senses. Myths can be symbolic vehicles for conveying that which transcends linear history.

What are myths, *really*? They are the collective equivalent of dreams. What both have in common is that they span the spectrum from mundane to profound, they can be oracular or prophetic, they can convey hidden knowledge, and they employ symbolic elements to encode meaning. Profound dreams and myths are coded messages from beyond.

Like dreams, myths allow for the passage of information across the boundary between realms. It seems that archetypes are *shared currency* between our world and others. In dreams, the subconscious or higher mind employs a cryptic language of symbols to encode a message. Same with myths whose symbolic characters, places, and storylines encode messages from intelligences beyond our realm. Interpretation of mythology is therefore similar to dream interpretation.

Myths are also like time capsules with nested layers, each layer encoding information intended for one type of recipient. Possible layers include:

- *Entertainment and Morality Layer* – the outer wrapping that ensures the myth propagates through the generations.

- *Historical Layer* – ensures that the history of the people is remembered.

- *Esoteric Layer* – provides initiatory instruction to empower those of a higher spiritual caliber.

- *Technological Layer* – provides scientific instruction on technologies likely to become lost over time, such as Alchemy, astronomy, or High Demiurgic Technology.

- *Hyper-Historical Layer* – concerns events and dynamics of the future and the world as it exists before/beyond linear time. This layer is aimed at those within the bubble of linear time who seek gnosis of what lies outside.

The deeper layers piggyback upon the shallower ones, and the entire bundle is unsuspectingly passed down the generations by commoners who enjoy the myth for its moral or entertainment value. Information stored this way can survive for thousands of years.

Myths also enable passage of information across discontinuities between world ages, when one world disappears and another appears. Since consciousness resides beyond matter, energy, space, and time, myths embedded in the collective subconscious survive such reconfigurations. Hence, these myths may propagate hyper-historical truths and tell of events and dynamics before, after, and beyond the current timeline. That means they can also be prophetic.

Lastly, note that myths are not restricted to those from ancient times. Modern fictional films, television series, music, and literature may also be mythical, depending on their content and true origins. Obviously some are just superficial fluff, but others are equal or higher in profundity than the greatest of classical myths.

Therefore the whole gamut of *myth* from dreams to ancient mythology to modern fiction is fertile ground for extracting the esoteric, technological, and hyper-historical layers of information. These layers are embedded by beings who existed before and now beyond our current world. In a way, it's all part of an ongoing process of hyperdimensional steganography aimed at passing synchronistically or symbolically encrypted messages to strategic recipients within the bubble of linear time.

Polar Mythology

Myths from different cultures can share common elements. The most universal elements pertain to the human process of psychological growth and transformation. Joseph Campbell called this universal template the "monomyth" or the "hero's journey," and its derivatives can be found the world over. Expressions of the monomyth can arise independently because core human psychology is the same everywhere.

But what we are looking for here is something more specific than the monomyth, something that concerns the very nature of existence and the events that precipitated our reality. This smaller subset of myths I call "polar mythology" because they concern the battle between the poles of Creation, employ the symbolism of rotation or reciprocation around a central axis pole, and because "polar" implies "extreme north" and hence "hyperborean," which alludes to the Nordic meta-civilization deeply involved in these matters.

Polar myths are too specific to be mere encoding of human psychological processes; they deal with the origin and fate of our world, the corruption of the timeline, the warring over demiurgic technologies, the timewar, and the mechanism behind transitions between world ages. Thus they are fundamentally gnostic.

Ancient polar myths are Proto-Indo-European in origin, seeded by survivors of the Atlantean cataclysm, and whose ancestry traces back to the off-world Nordic alien meta-civilization.

Modern polar myths may also originate from this meta-civilization via telepathic transmission, dream manipulation, direct contact between alien and contactee, or secret societies transmitting it orally to an initiate who works in the creative industry.

Core Elements of Polar Mythology

There are several repeating themes in polar mythology:

- We have fallen from a higher to lower realm.
- The World Axis, represented by a pillar, mountain, cross, or tree.
- Dueling superhumans engaged in a tug of war.
- That which the World Axis rests or depends upon: a foundational element represented in the cubical stone, turtle, keystone, plug, cornerstone, or capstone.
- Vortex symbolism and magical "objects of plenty" that could materialize abundance or destruction depending on their use.
- Cataclysmic unhinging or skewing of the World Axis.
- The avenging hero, Prodigal Son, or innocent fool who overthrows corruption and restores balance.

These elements can be found scattered across Grail lore and the myths of the ancient Hindus, Scandinavians, Egyptians, Sumerians, Meso-Americans, and Chinese.

Since this chapter aims to be as brief as possible, readers desiring a more thorough tour of ancient polar mythology should read *Hamlet's Mill* by De Santillana and Von Dechend, *The Mystery of the Grail* by Julius Evola, and to a lesser extent, *The Hero of a Thousand Faces* by Joseph Campbell. While these authors held mundane interpretations of polar mythology, readers of this book can now interpret the same data from a more profound context.

The seventh element I will discuss in the next and final *Gnosis* chapter, as it concerns the spiritual pathway through and beyond the Matrix Control System. For now, let's examine the other core elements:

1) We have fallen from a higher to lower realm.

We see this element in the story of Adam and Eve, the Lucifer Rebellion and fallen angels, what Orfeo Angelucci was told regarding members of a meta-civilization that fell into 3D Earth incarnation, the Matrix Trilogy where humanity was imprisoned into a simulated reality, or Dorothy falling along with her house into the Land of Oz.

This is the central tenet of gnosticism, that we are in this world, but not of this world, and that the Corrupt Demiurge created the world as we now know it.

The Fall of Man originates with the primordial schism between the Demiurge and Logos when Creation went awry. This cosmological event outside linear time rains fragments of itself down into linear time like an aerial explosion scattering debris to the ground. Each fragment enters linear time as a particular event repeating the "Fall of Man" archetype. What they all have in common is that beings nearer to the Logos are further ensnared within the realm of the Corrupt Demiurge.

Put another way, historically, the Fall is not a single event, but a series of diminishing "bounces" that bring us ever closer to flatlining, a process that is still ongoing but reaching its head. The grand "Fall" is still happening. The flatline is when humanity achieves the "ground state" in terms of spiritual energy, which is when the Fall reaches completion and the Corrupt Demiurge wins. This is now being carried out via the negative alien agenda to hybridize us, so that we become genetically locked into this ground state. It is only logical that, for the human species, the Fall ends the same way it ultimately began: through genetic engineering by malevolent alien factions.

The best-known myth incorporating these ideas is the story of Adam and Eve, inspired by earlier Sumerian and other sources. According to the version found in the Book of Genesis, before Adam, the world was populated by flora, fauna, and primitive humans. Then came Adam, and from him, Eve, who were different from other humans in that they possessed the faculty of spirit and lived in a paradisaic realm. In this Garden of Eden, they were in direct communion with the divine. They were half-animal, half-divine beings who were childlike in their innocence, pure and naïve. This speaks of the human soul collective in its original 3D STO (Service-to-Others) state of existence.

In the Garden were two trees, the "Tree of Knowledge of Good and Evil" and the "Tree of Life." Concerning the first, Adam was promised death if he ate its fruit. The trickster Serpent then approached Eve and convinced her to eat from the Tree of Knowledge, and through her temptation, Adam also took a bite. Seemingly contrary to God's warning, they did not die; of course not, here the myth implies spiritual death, not physical death, and that is what the Fall represents. Upon eating the forbidden fruit, they both became aware of their nakedness and felt shame. Afterwards they were banished from the Garden of Eden for disobeying the warning, cast into the wilderness where the animals and other humans were living by the law of the jungle.

In the above, the myth encodes several things:

- The naïve human soul group acquiring the faculty of freewill, hence their disobeying the command not to eat, for only through freewill is defiance possible.

- Their acquiring true self-awareness, symbolized by becoming aware of their nakedness.

- Disconnection from the divine, hence being cast out of the Garden.

In other words, it speaks of our disconnection from spirit and the acquisition of lower ego or lower intellect, which is our internal uplink to the Corrupt Demiurge. It symbolizes the grafting upon our pure souls of what Castaneda calls the "Predator." This event was our insertion into the Matrix energy farm.

And yet, it is through ego, intellect, and direct experience of brute physicality that we can even acquire personal wisdom concerning the difference between good and evil and their inner workings. Why is that wisdom necessary? Because in the end, it makes us more powerful, resilient, and spiritually mature. Otherwise we would remain naïve, vulnerable, isolated, and weak: *incapable of going where angels fear to tread.*

Siegfried bathed in the blood of the *dragon* and thereby acquired near invincibility (like Achilles a vulnerable spot remained); Dorothy wore the ruby slippers of the Wicked Witch's sister; Luke Skywalker, Harry

Potter, John Riddick, and Neo had a piece of their enemy inside them, but it gave them the power they needed to conquer the enemy. Our ego or intellect is what, by default, makes us servants of the Corrupt Demiurge. But if conquered and placed in service of spirit and Logos, these same faculties serve a higher function of providing discernment and personal power needed to overcome the Matrix Control System. Hence the Biblical advice to be "wise as serpents, gentle as doves" — if only one or the other, we fall into the false dichotomy of being either predator or prey.

Eating from the Tree of Knowledge directly implies expulsion from a higher realm into a lower one where Good and Evil exist in violent admixture, in order to "digest" the knowledge offered. Indeed, this is a kind of spiritual death (or coma, as with Sleeping Beauty and Brunhilde). None know death better than those who have come closest to it. The trick is returning to life before one dies fully.

Despite being a trickster, the Serpent is a symbol of wisdom because it offers a gamble; if conquered, it brings otherwise inaccessible wisdom; from friction arises fire, and from darkness arises light. We see this microcosmically in our own lives every time dark forces take a gamble in attempting to take us down; if we triumph, we acquire a new power, pathway, and wisdom that makes us more resilient and allows us to empower others in similar situations.

In Genesis, the Elohim said, "Let us make man in our image." They represent our original, presumably well-meaning, genetic creators. When Adam ate from the Tree of Knowledge of Good and Evil, the Elohim commented with worry that, should Adam now also eat from the Tree of Life, he should become just like them. What does that part of the myth imply about the Elohim? It suggests they were immortal superhumans who had mastered the knowledge of good and evil; in other words, they are higher echelons of the meta-civilization existing outside linear time.

Meanwhile, the Serpent represents the meta-civilization forces obedient to the Corrupt Demiurge. They were instrumental in genetically modifying the human race toward its current condition: no longer pure, innocent, children under the stewardship of the Logos, but crippled beasts with the claws of intellect and ego, thrust into the domain of the Corrupt Demiurge, crawling on their bellies in the vibrational dirt.

So after the expulsion from paradise, Adam and Eve existed in a limbo state. They were on their way toward knowing Good and Evil but did not yet transcend their mortality. This accurately portrays humanity's current state, hanging in the balance between two ultimate outcomes.

In one outcome, the ultimate low point is reached where the fruit is fully swallowed and digested, and total spiritual death ensues; fortunately, we are not there yet, hence the larynx has been linked to "Adam's Apple" to signify it is in the throat, not yet fully swallowed.

In the other outcome, we eat from the Tree of Life, and that pertains to everything discussed so far concerning gnostic awakening, Etheric Tide, and the Christ thoughtform mediating our harmonization with the Logos. Hence in New Testament symbolism, the Kingdom of Heaven carries shades of the Garden of Eden, Christ is the means toward obtaining Life (like the Tree of Life), and the sayings of Jesus speak highly of having a childlike purity.

Stated in terms of the Cassiopaean paradigm, our primordial 3D STO human soul matrix naïvely elected to incarnate into a 3D STS (Service-to-Self) gene pool prepared by 4D STS genetic engineers. Together with clarifications made by Boris Mouravieff, the picture revealed is that we were once simple beings without ego or intellect, but who had some of our higher faculties intact and were in full harmony with the Logos. After the Fall, our higher faculties were disconnected and we developed lower ego and lower intellect. Through the latter we would achieve the possibility of wisdom and discernment, though also the possibility of propagating evil. Once discernment reaches sufficient perfection, the optimal outcome is that our higher faculties also return, allowing the development of the higher intellect and thus co-equal existence with the "gods."

One can recognize these elements in the story of the Prodigal Son who leaves home out of foolish adventurism and rejection of the father, learns his lessons and grows wise, then finally returns home with new-found appreciation. Ironically, *the Prodigal Son who rejected the father ends up being closer to him than the other son who never left.* To truly choose "God," one must first have rejected "God," for only through such an initial exercise of freewill can one develop enough freewill to later make a meaningful choice of allegiance. This is what initially separated Adam and Eve from the Elohim, the first being close to God by intrinsic nature, the latter by choice. Parzival cursed God and finally severed his ties to any divine overseer, and only then developed the independence, strength of will, faculty of discernment, and spiritual maturity to be divinely appointed as winner of the Grail.

That seems to be the primary story of humanity and probably why, in the grand scheme of things, we are even allowed to be in this spacetime bubble established by the Corrupt Demiurge, in bodies genetically designed by its Archontic agents. It's a gamble that pays off with our acquiring power, wisdom, and discernment otherwise impossible to acquire, but with the risk that we flatline and stay here forever in this "black iron prison." The greatest gains come with the greatest risks.

Contrary to what fundamentalist Christianity attempts to pound into its subjects, Original Sin is not some primordial shameful act of dirtiness that we should all feel guilty over; it is not a *moral* error, but, as Philip K. Dick realized, an *intellectual* error that can only be corrected through a gnostic awakening.

It was intellectually naïve for our spiritual ancestors to so easily and enthusiastically think that 3D STS physicality was an attractive and worthwhile thing to experience. But that's a repeating pattern, one we still see today with stories of souls incarnating into the human sphere having signed up for more than they bargained for. They come with high hopes and overconfidence only to get beaten down, programmed, and shredded by a monstrosity of a machine that is the Matrix Control System. The naïveté comes in not foreseeing the risks that this opportunity brings. For humanity, the risks now threaten to permanently extinguish what little spiritual light we have left.

The teachings of Christ, among others, provide pointers on achieving transcendence. Thus in theology, Christ is said to have "died for our sins" — to have atoned for the Original Sin committed by Adam and

Eve in eating the forbidden fruit. While fundamentalists interpret this in a literal and moral way, in actuality everything points to a more symbolic and gnostic interpretation. The Fall of Man is an ongoing process and so is the mission of Christ. The latter came into existence to neutralize the first, but the neutralization has not yet been accomplished. The ultimate outcomes of the original Fall and the intervention of Christ exist as the two ultimate probable futures from which the Yahweh and Christ thoughtforms originate.

Wherever the Logos and Corrupt Demiurge clash and the latter secures a temporary victory, a fall occurs. This scales down fractally into the little choices we make every day. Aside from the human soul group incarnating into crippled genetics, other examples exist of such falls. One is the Nordic meta-civilization blowing up their planet and emigrating to the cruder Earth realm. Another was the Ark Stone being used to alter history. In every case, one or more individuals made a naïve choice based on ego with spiritually disastrous consequences.

2) The World Axis, represented by a pillar, mountain, cross, or tree.

The World Axis is an abstract idea meaning that which lies at the heart of existence, the central fulcrum that moves and supports the manifested world. It takes various forms in polar mythology.

In Genesis, the World Axis is the Tree of Knowledge. Eating from it implies incarnation into 3D linear time, the so-called Wilderness or World as distinct from the Garden of Eden or Kingdom of Heaven. The Wilderness is where spiritless humans, Archontic powers, and the Corrupt Demiurge reign. Hence the Tree of Knowledge and the World Axis are linked to the concept of linear time. Trees are a perfect metaphor for time due to the way they branch in three physical dimensions just as timelines do in three temporal dimensions

In Norse mythology, the world tree Yggdrasil represents the central framework supporting the various realms. Here the World Axis has more of a spatial connotation.

Mount Meru of Buddhist mythology is another example of a spatial supportive structure.

Norse world tree Yggdrasil and Oriental Mount Meru

Putting these together, the World Axis pertains to the framework of spacetime, the medium through which all form and motion arise. One symbol that combines both aspects is the cross, the horizontal signifying space, and the vertical time.

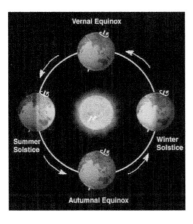

Additionally, the ancient symbol of the solar cross, a circle divided into quarters, represents among other things the four seasons, which imply both time via the passage of the year, and space via the four positions of Earth around the Sun. (It also resembles a millstone or the Ark Stone as depicted on a Sumerian tablet, discussed below).

The symbol of Jesus crucified, whose literal interpretation was rejected by Gnostics and Templars, may really mean crucifixion upon the cross of space and time. It would mean incarnating into linear space and time for the sole reason to redeem those who fell into it. The correct meaning of the phrase "dying for our sins" would be "entering spacetime for concern over our fallen condition."

In Norse myth, the god Odin likewise hung from Yggdrasil, bleeding and dying. In the process, he received the archetypal symbols of the runes by reading their pattern and meaning in the branches of the World Tree.

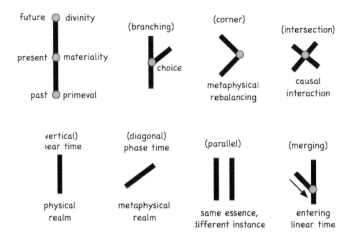

This would imply that runes are symbols representing timeline dynamics processes and astral archetypes that, through the etheric mediator, generate spacetime events.

Historically, the Scandinavian runes trace back to the Phoenician alphabet, and the Phoenicians were among the proto-Israelites who possessed the Ark Stone.

From the above, the World Axis is evidently associated with spacetime. But there's a third element involved. In Hindu Mythology, the World Axis is a giant pillar that rotates back and forth, churning the surrounding Sea of Milk and thereby precipitating chunks of butter.

Compare this to the Finnish myth of the Sampo, a magical artifact that like the Grail Stone was capable of creating objects and foodstuffs out of thin air. In the *Kalevala,* it was depicted as a rotating millstone that once ground out infinite abundance during a Golden Age. A similar millstone in Icelandic lore is called the Grotte.

What these symbols highlight is a central *rotational* aspect connected with Creation. In the World Axis, therefore, we find not only the concept of spacetime, but also the axis upon which spacetime can rotate or pivot. What is this pivot point? It is the quantum aperture, the choice point, the moment of wave function collapse, the window of nondeterminism where timelines are in flux. It's the hinge upon which reality pivots.

Probable futures are arrayed around this quantum pivot point at various quantum phase angles, somewhat like tree branches arrayed at various angles around their common point on the tree trunk.

The "incomparably mighty churn" of the Sea of Milk, as described in the *Mahabharata* and *Ramayana*. The heads of the deities on the right are the Asura, with unmistakable "Typhonian" characteristics. They stand for the same power as the Titans, the Turanians, and the people of Untamo, in short, the "family" of the bad uncle, among whom Seth is the oldest representative, pitted against Horus, the avenger of his father Osiris.

(from *Hamlet's Mill*)

What separates one probable future, one alternate past, or one event from another is the quantum phase angle unique to each. This has two major implications:

First, regarding the quantum phase that separates one timeline from another, to alter the quantum phase of the past means to switch it from one timeline to another; this equates to changing the angular position of the world pillar, hence a reciprocation of the pillar means a back-and-forth alteration of the timeline.

The simplified version of the Amritamanthana (or Churning of the Milky Ocean) still shows Mount Mandara used as a pivot or churning stick, resting on the tortoise. And here, also, the head on the right has "Typhonian" features.

(from *Hamlet's Mill*)

Second, regarding the kind of quantum phase that distinguishes one moment from another, since time itself is a continual progression from one event to the next, time is identically continual cycling of this quantum phase. While that much is taught in college textbooks, the cause of this continual cycling is not addressed. As I discussed in the last chapter, the Demiurge is the cause of time. Cycling is precisely what the Demiurge does in being the default collapser of our collective wave function and thus perpetuator of physical reality as we know it. This continual phase cycling, which generates a particular timeline tree, may be mythologically represented in the rotating millstone that ground out a bygone Golden Age when the Demiurge or World Soul was in harmony with the Logos.

In summary, in its purest form, the World Axis represents the quantum pivot point and the surrounding spacetime framework that rests upon it.

3) Dueling superhumans engaged in a tug of war.

In Hindu mythology, a serpent is wrapped around the pillar. The divine Devas hold one end of the serpent while the infernal Asuras hold the other. They are engaged in a tug of war; as one side gains, the pillar rotates one way, and as the other side gains, the pillar rotates the other way. This is what causes reciprocation of the pillar.

What does the serpent represent, fundamentally? The Serpent of Genesis is usually depicted as being wrapped around the Tree of Knowledge.

In ancient Greek tradition, the Orphic Egg is an egg representing Creation, around which is wound the World Serpent.

In Norse mythology, a giant serpent named Jörmungandr encircles the middle portion of the World Tree. This World Serpent is always depicted as the outer perimeter encircling our world:

> According to the Prose Edda, Odin took Loki's three children, Fenrisúlfr, Hel and Jörmungandr, and tossed Jörmungandr into the great ocean that encircles Midgard. The serpent grew so large that he was able to surround the Earth and grasp his own tail. When he lets go, the world will end. As a result, he received the name of the

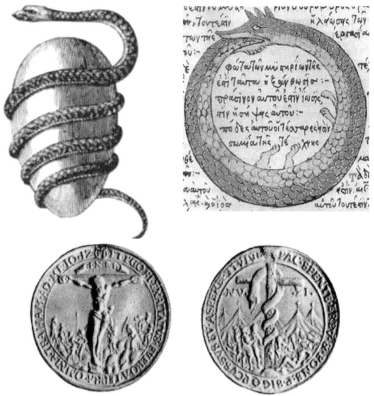

Midgard Serpent or World Serpent. Jörmungandr's arch-enemy is the god Thor.[*]

The snake eating its tail is the ouroboros, which can be interpreted in two ways.

First is that it represents the Demiurge, in its corrupted state, attempting to consume its own Creation. That is exactly what negative (STS) forces do by enslaving other beings — they ignore that all life is One, that by hurting others they are hurting other instances of themselves; they are like the head of the snake ignoring that the tail is its own. The same principle shows up in the Greek myth of Cronus, a.k.a. Saturn, eating his children.

In mythology, the god Saturn is known as Father Time, for he presides over the passage of linear time. The planet Saturn itself bears an ouroboric resemblance via its prominent rings. In metaphysics, since Saturn is the outermost of the seven classical planets, it is seen as the gateway into our realm, into linear time.

In *Parzival,* the cycles of Saturn governed the intensity of Grail King Amfortas's perpetual wound. To be "saturnine" means to be slow, gloomy, and depressed. Orfeo Angelucci's contacts called Earth the "home of sorrows." The World Dream, as stated in the last chapter, is more a World Nightmare. And in Kabbalah, Saturn is explicitly equated with the Demiurge:

---

[*] *Jörmungandr* <Wikipedia>

> Saturn is the third sphere of divine activity, called Binah – Understanding or Intelligence. This is the power which organises the creative forces and imposes form on the universe. It is thus the root of matter. It is also the female principle, for it is through conception and birth that we acquire material form. *

This leads straight into the second and more traditional interpretation of the ouroboros, which once again concerns time. As explained earlier, linear time is inflated and sustained by the Corrupt Demiurge, but linear time is an illusory existence that has no permanence relative to what is beyond this World Dream. In being created from nothing by a runaway artificial intelligence incapable of true Creation, linear existence may be transitory like matter and antimatter popping out of the vacuum before annihilating.

In being borrowed from the Void, our timeline may be a self-defeating causal loop whose end is its beginning and vice versa, an illusory space-time bubble inflated by transient dichotomies that sum to zero. Hence the snake eating its own tail; when it lets go, the time bubble pops, and the World Dream ends.

The serpent also symbolizes etheric energy. In the Old Testament, Moses fixed a bronze serpent to a cross and any who gazed upon this serpent would be healed.

Similarly, the rod of Asclepius or staff of Hermes (caduceus) are also healing symbols involving serpents wrapped around sticks.

In Alchemy, the serpent is found in connection with the phrase "fixing the volatile," denoting an alchemical operation represented by a snake having swallowed a stick and being unable to move, or wrapped around a cross like the brazen serpent of Moses. As explained, Alchemy involves impregnating physical matter with etheric energy. This is ultimately what is meant by fixing the volatile, meaning to anchor etheric energy into physical substance.

Kundalini energy is depicted as a serpent coiled at the base of the spine. According to occultism, its function there is to keep us anchored and asleep in the illusion, thus it has a soporific influence in that state.

---

* <skyscript.co.uk/saturnmyth.html>

This implies that Kundalini is an energy associated with the Corrupt Demiurge. On the other hand, its activation and discharge up the spine in a prepared initiate is said to bring enlightenment and psychic powers, meaning full etheric activation, which implies that Kundalini is an energy associated with the Logos or, in Christian terminology, the Holy Spirit.

What to make of this contradiction? Simply stated, Kundalini energy is another name for demiurgic energy (etheric) that serves a special role in our bodies. Depending on the nature and state of etheric energy, it can have positive or negative effects. For instance, people whose Kundalini activates prematurely can go insane or suffer spontaneous human combustion.

Egyptian pharaohs were sometimes depicted as having a serpent called the Uraeus extending from their third eye, which may represent a focused beam of etheric energy emitting from that region, as happens in cases of strong psychic activation.

In summary, the serpent represents etheric energy, the Corrupt Demiurge, and/or linear time. All these concepts are different facets of the same thing. The Demiurge encompasses physical reality just as Jörmungandr encircles Yggdrasil; the Serpent of Genesis represents the Archontic factions who were agents of the Corrupt Demiurge; and in both Kundalini and Alchemy, the Serpent represents etheric energy.

Returning to the Hindu depiction of the World Axis, if pillar rotation angle represents quantum phase, then the back and forth tug of war between the Devas and Asuras is identically a timewar. The complete picture then portrays polarized factions of the meta-civilization altering the timeline one way and then another depending on who has the greater pull. They are tugging on the Demiurge, employing etheric energy fields to modify spacetime. By pulling reality closer toward the Logos or the Corrupt Demiurge, the timeline reconfigures accordingly. This churning precipitates corresponding spacetime events out of the etheric substrate of reality like butter forming in the Sea of Milk.

4) That which the World Axis rests or depends upon: a foundational element represented in the cubical stone, turtle, keystone, plug, cornerstone, or capstone.

The second most important element in polar mythology is the foundation upon which the framework of creation depends. The meeting point between this foundation and the World Axis is the quantum pivot point mentioned earlier. Removing or disturbing the foundation causes the entire World Axis to fall out of alignment.

In Hindu and Mayan myths, the World Pillar pivots atop the back of a turtle. Even in Native American myths, turtles symbolize the foundation of the world. Why turtles? They are distinguished by their hard round shells, often of a hexagonal shape decorated with a hexagonal pattern.

Anyone familiar with the works of Stan Tenen, Nassim Haramein, or William Tiller will recognize the importance of hexagon lattices in the substructure of reality. In the hexagon lattice we find the Flower of Life and Tree of Life patterns.

As Stan Tenen explained, it's a mathematical curiosity that seven hexagons can fit on a torus (doughnut) so that every side of one hexagon touches the side of every other hexagon. The torus is a three dimensional projection of a four dimensional hypersphere.

This hyperdimensional structure is divided into seven regions, like the seven colors of a rainbow or the seven densities in the Ra/Cassiopaean cosmology, with each color touching every other color. The turtle with its rounded hexagonal lattice is a suitable natural symbol for this principle.

Aside from the turtle, another variation of the foundational element is the cube, especially a cubical stone, which, when viewed from a corner, has the appearance of a hexagon.

The rune called *Hagal* bears the shape of an asterisk, three lines intersecting like a snowflake, which in science depicts the three orthogonal axes of space. Hagal means hail, which are "stones" that fall from the sky. In the Anglo Saxon runes, this same symbol means "Serpent."

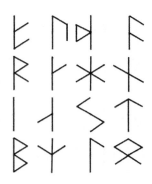

In the Armanen rune system, *Hagal* is said to be the "world rune" or "mother rune" because in it are inscribed the shape of all other rune symbols, thus it is the foundation from which the rest of the "alphabets of existence" are generated.

Like the Tree of Life, Flower of Life, or the hexagonal lattice, it represents the *foundation* of manifested existence.

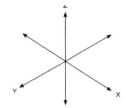

Another fallen stone associated with the cube is the Black Stone inside Kaaba, the cubical structure at the heart of Islam to which all Muslims must pray and visit once in their lifetime. Kaaba in the city of Mecca is the ritual cornerstone of the Muslim world.

The cornerstone, capstone, or keystone is yet another depiction of the lynchpin or foundational element. The cornerstone is traditionally the first stone laid during the construction of a building, to which all other stones are aligned, much like *Hagal* being the seed crystal to the rest of the runes.

 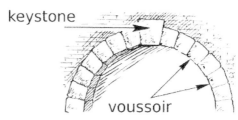

The capstone of a pyramid is not a lynchpin so much as a representation of the key element without which the pyramid remains incomplete and nonfunctional. And a keystone is the central stone of a rounded arch without which the arch collapses.

The stone, fallen from the sky, associated with the foundation of physical existence, the seed crystal of reality, the lynchpin that holds the World together — what is it? *It is the Grail Stone, which serves as the seat or anchor of the World Soul.* The combination is what perpetuates the momentum of a timeline.

Sometimes the stone cube is shown with a tree growing upon it, paralleling the pillar resting atop the turtle. These symbols depict the foundational, anchoring, and timeline pivoting function of High Demiurgic Technology. Timelines trace back to the quantum pivot point that gave rise to them, and this pivot point can be acted upon by High Demiurgic Technology to uproot or anchor timelines. Thus the Grail/Ark Stone functions as the cornerstone, capstone, or keystone of the timeline it brings into existence.

5) Vortex symbolism and magical "objects of plenty" that materialize abundance or destruction depending on their use.

The vortex is *the* archetypal symbol of polar mythology because it represents manifestation spiraling toward or away from a central principle or singularity. Passage through the singularity means transduction or transubstantiation from one level of existence to another.

The Demiurge is the central principle of our physical universe, and its transubstantiation of astral archetypes into physical manifestation resembles a vortex swallowing one substance, compressing and transforming it, and emitting it on the other side of the singularity. The singularity in this case is the quantum aperture, where thoughts turn into reality, or where consciousness pivots reality. These singularities are portals through which metaphysics influences physics. They are where spacetime ends and begins.

The ways of the Demiurge during creation, according to the Bambara.

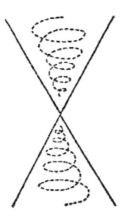

"In order to make heaven and earth, the demiurge stretched himself into a conical helix; the turnings-back of that spiral are marked graphically by the sides of two angles which represent also the space on high and the space below."

(from *Hamlet's Mill*)

It is no surprise, therefore, that the World Axis is depicted with vortical attributes.

Mount Meru takes the shape of a double vortex, like an hourglass; it is a mountain that narrows in the middle and spreads out at the top.

The collapse of the hourglass-shaped Meru, caused by Buddha's death, with sun and moon rolling down; the moon shows the hare contained in it. Many collapsing world-pillars, unhinged mill-trees, and the like have been mentioned in this book, and this is one of the few pieces of pictorial evidence for a crumbling *skambha*.

(from *Hamlet's Mill*)

Likewise, the Tree of Knowledge and *Yggdrasil* have diverging crowns and roots. The middle cinched portion is the shared singularity between two vortices, each opening into their respective realm.

The single vortex appears in the Hindu pillar, which narrows at the bottom and flares at the top; same with the vortex-like drill shown in an Egyptian stele depicting Horus and Seth tugging on a rope wrapped around it.

In these cases, the singularity is at the bottom of the vortex, for instance, the pivot point where the pillar meets the turtle shell.

The cinched middle is seen in the Mayan depiction of same:

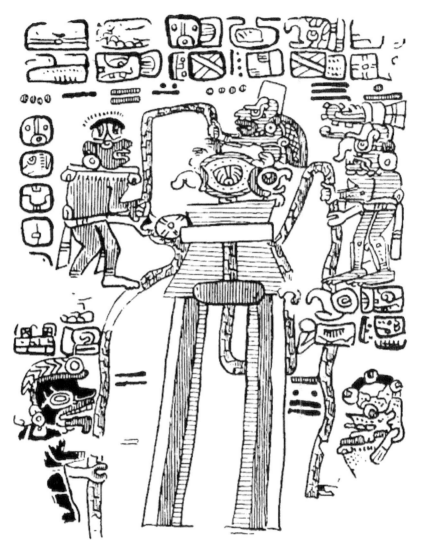

The Maya Codex Tro-Cortesianus presents the same event in a different "projection." The illustration is harder to decode—as all Maya pictures are—but the rope,
the tortoise, and the churn (indicating an hourglass?) can be made out, and "kin,"
the sign of the sun, glides along the serpent-rope.

(from *Hamlet's Mill*)

Horus and Seth in the act of drilling or churning. Horus has the head of a falcon; the head of Seth-Typhon shows the peculiar mixture of dog and ass which are characteristic of the so-called "Seth-beast." This feature is continuously mislabeled the "uniting of the two countries," whether Horus and Seth serve the churn or, as is more often the case, the so-called "Nile-Gods."

(from *Hamlet's Mill*)

The whirlpool is just a broader and flatter vortex defined by a prominent eye at the center. Upon reaching the end of their pilgrimage at Mecca, Muslims circle around the Kaaba (cube) in a manner resembling a large whirlpool.

Another example is the millstone, a round stone with spiral grinding grooves radiating from a central hole.

Millstones resemble whirlpools, especially when rotating and grinding. That they grind out flour for bread, the "staff of life," makes them perfect symbols for High Demiurgic Technology that once materialized foodstuffs out of the ambient etheric field.

A Sumerian tablet depicting the glowing Ark Stone before a seated King Shamash visually resembles the eye and furrows of a millstone:

But the vortex can take literal form as well. As mentioned, the Ark Stone was accompanied by the columnar plasma vortex, the Shekhina. When activated, the Great Pyramid (Mount Sinai) likewise emitted a "plume of smoke" that may have been a plasma vortex. The tornado-like "pillar of fire" that went before the proto-Israelite procession out of Egypt is another example. The original legend of a Pharaoh pursuing the fleeing Semites said he died "in the place of the whirlpool." And the water-filled bronze basin kept at the Temple of Solomon was precisely circular, ideal for carrying a whirlpool of water therein.

THE BRAZEN SEA OF SOLOMON'S TEMPLE.—WITH VIEW OF SECTION.
(Restored according to Calmet.)

It seems that even in a literal and observable way, vortices accompanied the activation of High Demiurgic devices like the Ark Stone. The Ark and Grail Stone manifesting food from thought shows that High Demiurgic Technology is the basis of the various "objects of plenty" mentioned throughout mythology.

Another example of vortex topology comes from the Greeks:

> Classical mythology offers multiple explanations of the origin of the cornucopia. One of the best-known involves the birth and nurturance of the infant Zeus, who had to be hidden from his devouring father Cronus. In a cave on Mount Ida on the island of Crete, baby Zeus was cared for and protected by a number of divine attendants, including the goat Amalthea ("Nourishing Goddess"), who fed him with her milk. The suckling future king of the gods had unusual abilities and strength, and in playing with his nursemaid accidentally broke off one of her horns, which then had the divine power to provide unending nourishment, as the foster mother had to the god.
>
> In another myth, the cornucopia was created when Heracles (Roman Hercules) wrestled with the river god Achelous and wrenched off one of his horns; river gods were sometimes depicted as horned.[*]

This *Horn of Plenty* is yet another allusion to the vortex because a horn has a conical vortical shape. Its production of unlimited milk parallels the Grail stone manifesting food for the knights or the Ark Stone generating quail and manna for the proto-Israelites.

The *Horn of Plenty* tradition continues today in the form of the cornucopia, a woven basket shaped like a vortex or horn, usually shown on

---

[*] <en.wikipedia.org/wiki/Cornucopia>

its side spilling out an abundance of fruit. The cornucopia symbolizes fertility, harvest, and overflowing abundance. It's a tradition seen in America at Thanksgiving and is yet another portrayal of a vortex emitting foodstuffs.

So far we see two manifestations of the vortex archetype, a more abstract and universal one associated with the World Axis, and a more tangible and local form associated with the energy field surrounding High Demiurgic Technology. These are just two scales of application of demiurgic principles, the first concerning solidification and reorientation of entire worlds and timelines, the second only a small portion for local applications like materializing food. Both act upon the quantum aperture or pivot point to bring otherwise mere possibilities into existence.

6) Cataclysmic unhinging or skewing of the World Axis

As documented in *Hamlet's Mill*, several myths speak of a catastrophic disturbance of the World Axis usually brought on by unwise disturbance of the foundation stone or object of plenty. For example:

- An Icelandic tale about the Grotte, a magical millstone whose owner employed two giant maidens to turn it and thereby grind out "gold, peace, and happiness." In greed, he cruelly overworked them, and in revenge, they manifested a foreign invader who came and killed him. The invader took the Grotte and maidens aboard his ship and ordered them to continue grinding the mill, but the maidens ground out only salt. Under too much strain, the ship broke apart and the Grotte sank to the bottom of the ocean, seeding the ocean with salt and generating a massive whirlpool via the water flowing through its central eye.

- The Finnish tale of the Sampo, a magical millstone forged by a primeval smith for a powerful sorceress who promised him her daughter in return. Through the mill, the sorceress can keep her land peaceful and bountiful. The smith marries her daughter who later dies, and when he asks the sorceress for another daughter she refuses. In revenge, he and his brother attempt to steal the Sampo from her. They break into the "mountain of copper" where the sorceress had sealed it and where the Sampo had sunk its roots deep into the earth like a tree. Using a giant bull to plow up the roots, they steal the Sampo and carry it away by ship. The sorceress intercepts them and snatches the Sampo away but drops it into the ocean where it shatters into myriad pieces. The smith and his brother only manage to gather up some of these pieces.

The authors of *Hamlet's Mill* viewed such stories as merely encoding astronomical knowledge concerning the precession of the equinoxes. For instance, the starry sky resembles a whirlpool or millstone as it rotates.

© Anglo-Australian Observatory

Hence the axis of a great millstone becoming unhinged simply follows from ancient astronomers observing that the central pole of the rotating heavens is not where it used to be, due to the precession of the Earth's axis. While logical, this interpretation is limited. Precession itself has greater significance than a mere astronomical curiosity.

Precession of the Earth's axis causes the equinox, solstice, and pole positions to wander over a 25,920-year cycle known as the Platonic Year. The observed position of the Sun at Spring Equinox gradually shifts from one zodiac sign to another at the rate of one degree every 72 years. Depending on the sign, the world is said to be in the "Age" of that sign.

In ancient Egypt, the Ark Stone drama transpired during the Age of Taurus transitioning into the Age of Aries. Reflecting this, the Finnish millstone myth speaks of a great "bull of heaven" that was harnessed to uproot the millstone, allowing it to be stolen from its "mountain of copper" and transported away.

We are now in the Age of Pisces transitioning into the Age of Aquarius, from an age where we are but fish in the river of time, to a future where we pour the river ourselves.

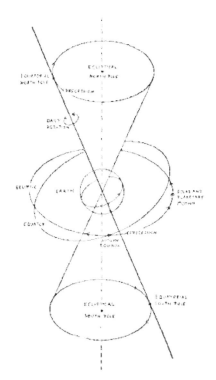

The state of the World Soul seems to correspond to these precessional ages. Each age carries a specific momentum of cultural, historical, and spiritual development during that time. Perhaps the World Soul is modulated by the astrological energies of the various ages, or maybe the Grail Stone is used at transition points between signs to "change the program" accordingly.

Two astronomical vortical phenomena include the shape of our galaxy and the hourglass figure traced by the precession of Earth's axis.

It just so happens that *25,920 years is approximately how long it takes light to travel between Earth and the super black hole at the center of the Milky Way.* This suggests some kind of resonance between Earth and the Galactic Center whose frequency is inversely proportional to the Platonic year.

The implication is that the state of the World Soul is somehow interlocked with the electromagnetic, gravitational, or etheric resonance between Earth and the Galactic Center. This may mean that different world ages, and thus World Soul states, correspond to different locations along the wave between Earth and Galactic Center. As the wave travels, Earth experiences different phase angles of this wave, and currently it takes 25,920 years to cycle through them all. At each phase angle (wave position), Earth's axis points to a different pole position in the sky and the World Soul has a different coloration.

This suggests the Galactic Center is what generates the Etheric Tide. Since High Demiurgic Technology can be deployed on Earth during times of heightened etheric potency, one can see its use being timed according to astronomical cycles. Thus the "program changes" or modulations of the World Soul are intricately coupled to precessional cycles whose effects are catalyzed by demiurgic technology.

Incidentally, this could explain a big mystery in astrology. Due to precession over thousands of years, the astrological Sun signs of the zodiac no longer correspond to the constellations they were originally associated with.

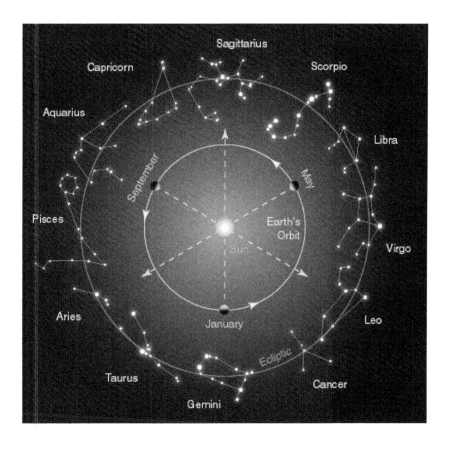

The twelve zodiac signs and their corresponding days of the year correlated perfectly back in 800 – 1000 B.C. when the zodiac system was devised in Babylon. Since that time, things have shifted back one complete sign. While there exists sidereal astrology that takes this into account, the more common tropical astrology uses the same system from 800 B.C. on the grounds that it's not about the stars in the sky, but the position of Earth in its orbit around the Sun, i.e. the season of the year that determines your zodiac sign. But that explanation fails when it comes to Moon and rising signs, which have nothing to do with orbital position around the Sun and are likewise disconnected from the actual constellations they are supposed to represent.

The big mystery is that sidereal astrology works, despite being astronomically baseless as far as the zodiac is concerned. If you are Taurus, the Sun at your time of birth was actually in the constellation of Aries, and yet you may exhibit all the personality traits fitting of the Taurean archetype. Same goes for the Moon and rising signs. And yet these signs are only correct according to the sky as it existed nearly three thousand years ago.

Somehow people's souls are being molded by energies from the time of ancient Babylon and Israel. That was also the beginning of the particularly corrupted timeline that culminated in today's precarious world situation. It's as if the World Soul state from 1200 – 800 B.C. never went away with the advent of the Age of Pisces in 100 B.C. – 100 A.D. Even though we technically passed from the Age of Taurus to the Age of Pisces, the "program change" did not execute fully.

Where else have we encountered this dynamic during that same historical time frame? In the Hermetic lore of Christ's mission being a failure. ("Ichthys" the fish being a symbol for Christ, as well as a disguised *vesica piscis*). Intervention by the Christ thoughtform turned into an unfinished attempt at undoing and overwriting the "program" of Yahweh and the Old Testament ways. Thus both now exist in a limbo state, competing for the fate of the world.

The wheel of the zodiac is the wheel of linear time, the Grotte grinding away at the bottom of the milky(way) cosmic ocean. Linear time is associated with the Corrupt Demiurge, and people being molded by tropical astrological influences is nothing more than their deterministic, mechanical, and unconscious side having its strings pulled by the levers of the World Dream.

Undoubtedly there is an astronomical layer embedded in polar mythology, but it's not the only layer. Rather than myths encoding astronomy for the sake of astronomy, astronomy may serve as a mnemonic framework to help memorize and preserve myths. Such a framework would outlast even what is chiseled into stone. Polar myths contain a deeper payload than just astronomical knowledge. Astronomy merely provides the pegs onto which key gnostic knowledge can be hung. Instead of marveling at the pegs, one should examine the gnostic payload, which is the higher meaning of these myths. And yet, these meanings are synchronistically embedded in the astronomical phenomena themselves, for they are but World Dream symbols.

The astronomical interpretation does not explain why, for instance, the Hindu pillar reciprocates back and forth according to which side has the stronger pull, unlike the starry sky that rotates and precesses steadily. The Grotte had a cover that only rotated at the transition point between world ages, otherwise the millstone sunk its roots deep into the ground *like a tree* and was stationary, anchoring in place the world age it generated. These myths speak of too many discontinuities, cataclysms, battles, and arbitrary reciprocations of the World Axis to *only* be references to Earth's rotation or precession.

Conclusion

The millstone rooted in place is an allusion to the Grail Stone anchoring a World Soul in place, to create and perpetuate a particular timeline. After the millstone was stolen and fell into the ocean, however, it ground out sand and stones and created a giant maelstrom that continues circulating to this day. This mythical whirlpool does indeed parallel the rotating starry sky, but only because the latter symbolizes the passage of linear time. The millstone falling into the ocean and churning a whirlpool symbolizes abuse of the Grail Stone causing our deeper collective fall into the World Dream, into the dark well of linear time, as if swirling toward a malevolent strange attractor.

It all points to our physical reality being one grand machine involving Earth, Sun, Galactic Center, Etheric Tide, collective consciousness, and High Demiurgic Technologies interacting to determine the particular timeline or state of reality we experience.

Taken to its logical conclusion, the astronomical phenomena encoded in polar mythology may themselves be physical reflections, or World Dream Symbols, of even greater Demiurgic principles.

Reality, the ultimate oxymoron, is not simply a deterministic assemblage of matter and energy, but a perennially mutable product of intelligent creation. The World Dream is a fractal mosaic reflecting hyperdimensional archetypes and events. This includes the Moon and stars in our sky, in whose patterns the heathen Flegetanis is said to have read the name of the Grail.

9 THE END

Our Past, Present, and Future

Polar mythology describes three phases of history. The first concerns the past, how all of "this" began: the bygone Golden Age, primordial warring among the gods, and their ruining of the cosmic framework. It concludes with higher beings, positive and/or negative, falling into a lower realm of existence.

The First Phase was best portrayed in the *Matrix* films where a Golden Age of robotics gave way to a schism between man and machine. A global war erupted between them, and the human race was subsequently imprisoned in a computer simulated reality. In *The Wizard of Oz,* Dorothy's plight with Miss Gulch was interrupted by a tornado (vortex) that, through a traumatic bump to the head, transported Dorothy to the Land of Oz where her conflict continued symbolically.

And in books like Philip K. Dick's *Ubik* or films like *Donnie Darko*, *Vanilla Sky*, and *Jacob's Ladder,* the protagonist had fallen into an alternate reality due to some trauma.

The Second Phase concerns the present, our world, which sprang into existence as a consequence of the Fall. The traumatic consequences of the First Phase induced a collective sleep. Hence we have "fallen" asleep into the World Dream, knocked spiritually unconscious. Here, the openly warring forces from the First Phase continue their struggle in a dormant, sub rosa, symbolic, cold war fashion. The World Dream functions as a chessboard of sorts, a game played to decide the outcome of larger conflicts.

Now that higher beings are here, fallen and asleep, what are they to do? What is their purpose? What is their way out? These are the questions explored in polar mythology's treatment of the Second Phase. The answers are encoded in that portion of polar mythology which Joseph Campbell calls the "hero's journey." I will discuss that in the second half of this chapter.

The Third Phase concerns our future: how the consequences of the First Phase will reach their ultimate conclusion. Whether one consults Biblical eschatology, Ra/Cassiopaean paradigms, Scandinavian mythology, etc. the Third Phase is always depicted as ending with a final war and the dissolution of the world as we know it.

The *Matrix* trilogy ends with Neo and Agent Smith waging their final battle within the Matrix, utterly destroying it, while mankind endures its last stand against the machines back in the real world. In *Donnie Darko,* a vortical portal ends the alternate timeline spanning the duration of the film. In *Vanilla Sky,* after enduring a simulated dream gone awry, the protagonist finally awakens from suspended animation. These and similar books and movies, as well as the apocalyptic/prophetic portions of polar mythology, all provide clues about the fate of our timeline.

Recap

In this book, it has been my premise that a primordial schism arose between the Creator and portions of its Creation, namely the Demiurge, which developed a rogue parasitic extension called the Corrupt Demiurge. This was the First Fall.

Beings within Creation, possessing the power of freewill, harmonized with the Creator or the Corrupt Demiurge depending on whether they respected the divine framework or turned their back on it. Those who aligned with the Corrupt Demiurge carried out their parasitic agenda of survival at the expense of others.

In its original form, humanity may have been a lesser evolved but benign species created by well-meaning genetic engineers. At some point, they came into contact with alien civilizations that were agents of the Corrupt Demiurge. Whether by choice or sheer ignorance, the result was a genetic modification of terrestrial humanity toward becoming a fundamentally self-serving species divested of psychic sensitivity and divine harmonization. Humans were spiritually dumbed down but intellectually enhanced. This was the Second Fall, depicted in the story of Adam and Eve.

The Third Fall involved members of the meta-civilization located in our distant past, likely ancestors of the Nordic aliens who inhabited the planet that is now the Asteroid Belt. After demiurgic wars destroyed their planet, the survivors set up camp on Earth, bringing with them the Grail Stone technology. The Superman, Lucifer Rebellion, and neutral angel myths seem to depict this.

Their contact with the natives and resulting technological osmosis led to the rise of such fabled civilizations as Atlantis and Hyperborea. These were brought to an end by fluctuations in the Etheric Tide, terrestrial abuses of demiurgic technology, and natural disasters, signifying the Fourth Fall.

Advanced survivors of the Atlantean cataclysm migrated around the world and established new civilizations, impressing their own technology, culture, and mythology onto uncivilized natives. Some brought with them remnant fragments of Atlantean demiurgic technology, and these became the basis of various magical artifacts recounted in myth.

The Grail/Ark Stone was one such artifact entrusted to an elite Egyptian priesthood. The Hyksos invasion of 1628 B.C. and Akhenaten/Osarseph rebellion around 1350 B.C. resulted in hijacking and abuse of the Stone, allowing deeper intrusion of the Corrupt Demiurge into our world and a heavy deviation of the timeline. This was the Fifth Fall.

The next one occurred via the Great Apostasy, the hijacking of the teachings of Christ by the forces of Set/Yahweh/Demiurge. This began around 50 A.D. with the misguided activities of Saul the Roman who converted to Paul the Apostle after encountering a blinding light. Together with the subsequent penning of the Canonical Gospels, this case of timeline intervention by otherworldly forces ultimately produced the Roman Catholic Church, which became directly or indirectly responsible for the death of millions of heretics and unsanctioned psychic/gnostic bloodlines, and the spiritual enslavement of billions more. Meanwhile, the Jewish presence in history served as sand in the oyster that eventually produced the black pearl of Nazism, which became the nucleus of the Military Industrial Complex, which since 1960 has been working feverishly on behalf of negative alien factions to prepare our planet for final assimilation.

That's a brief rundown of how our world came to be so screwed up. It happened through an incremental series of falls that seem to trace back to the primordial schism between Logos and Demiurge. Or so it seems.

The above description only covers the linear past-to-present version of how we got here. More importantly, how much of our situation originated from the *future* and from *outside time*? I have mentioned timewars originating with future portions of the alien meta-civilization, but have not yet gone into detail about what these timewars entail in practical terms, or what that says about the fundamental nature of our reality.

Reality as Remedial Illusion

What exactly *is* this reality? We have several clues. Indications of how and why this timewar originated can be found in certain alienology research, channeling material, visions, dreams, prophecies, polar movies and the writings of Philip K. Dick. I've had my share of dreams pertaining to this topic, which made little sense at the time but in context of *Gnosis* they make more sense. Here is one from several years ago:

> *Remedial Time Bubble* – In this dream, I met Donnie Darko at a disheveled antique store and he told me the shift from 3D to 4D had already taken place, but that we were now caught in a temporary time bubble right at that moment of crossover. The bubble was a reconstruction of the past, a simulation of the years leading up to the shift, with the only thing different being that some people now had something "extra" (spiritual power and intuition) that would give them better success in making more progress by the time they exit the bubble. This way, the shift completes with a better-prepared group of graduates than without that remedial time bubble.

This is similar to the Time Lateral concept discussed in the *Q'uo* material, whereby Earth has been quarantined onto a temporal sidetrack away from the main flow of time in Creation. The purpose of the Time Lateral is to give mankind extra time to evolve before rejoining the main timeline and shifting to 4D. This would mean our current timeline is an illusory summer school of sorts, implying the current World Dream serves a beneficial remedial function. Viewed from a higher perspective that could be the case, but within the illusion, things are rough indeed, especially if the summer school lessons include dealing with forces heavily invested in keeping the World Dream going forever.

Richard Sauder proposed a similar idea:

> Read the article [about time cloaking]* and imagine what might be possible for an interstellar civilization with a more sophisticated technological base. If you scale the technology up, could you create a Time Cloak that would effectively quarantine an entire planet and seal it off from the rest of the galaxy in its own hidden space-time compartment? Just give it its own, independently generated, local

---

* <technologyreview.com/2011/07/14/87763>

time-space coordinates and set it to spinning like a top for hundreds of thousands or millions of years, like a private prison planet, or water-planet torture palace where anything goes and no one hears the screams?

What if?

And what happens when that Time sealed compartmentalization unzips?

You see, what the prison planet wardens want to stifle more than anything, is the World of Unfettered Imagination, because they know that when Sleeping Beauty awakens that there will be Heaven To Pay.*

Correlating with this, *The Ra Material* mentions Earth was placed in quarantine by a powerful overseer group termed the Council of Saturn. Recall that Saturn symbolizes the gateway into the linear spacetime bubble. Fore was told by his Nordic contact that three thousand years ago, Earth was placed under quarantine by a powerful group of third-party overseers. They aimed to clamp down on quarreling alien factions that had too openly meddled with human history. With the quarantine, gone were the days of aliens openly interbreeding with humans, nuking rogue cities like Sodom and Gomorrah, and occupying temples built in their honor. After the quarantine, "god ceased talking to man," and alien wars went covert. Mankind was given the opportunity to develop on its own, though covert manipulation of human history continued. Fore was told this quarantine is currently ending, and that hostile alien factions are essentially standing by, licking their chops.

Three thousand years ago is also when the Ark Stone disappeared from Israelite hands, when Etheric Tide levels began to plunge, when according to John Baines the Christ thoughtform was invoked, and when the astrological Zodiac still aligned with the visible constellations. Whatever was put in place back then, somehow we are still in it.

The advent of Christ occurred a thousand years later, near the peak of Roman tyranny. The latter resembled the reign of the Antichrist

---

* \<eventhorizonchronicle.blogspot.com\>

as depicted in the Book of Revelation. Jesus prophesied that the Kingdom of Heaven had already arrived and that the World Dream would end within the lifetime of his disciples. Scholars who note that Biblical end times prophecies seem to pertain to events two millennia ago may be partially correct, but there is more to it. The mission of Christ was a failure and instead of ending, the World Dream continued in a strange limbo state in which Christ and Yahweh remained suspended in a stalemate. The last two thousand years, therefore, seem like "over-time" in a sports game. The primary game clock ended, but a temporary clock is now ticking. The game should have ended back then, but somehow it continued.

Philip K. Dick may have picked up on this when, as part of a string of mystical experiences, he experienced an overlap or temporal resonance between himself and his former incarnation living concurrently alongside him in ancient Rome. From his collection of notes titled *Exegesis*:

> Within our spatiotemporal universe *it is impossible* that USA 1974 and Rome AD 45 could be one and the same... how could they be? They are at two times and two places. The only way they could be one and the same would be if time and space were somehow not real; or, put another way, if something about the two continua *themselves* were not real. That is, if Rome was not Rome; USA was not USA; but both were a third thing, the same thing.

> This is why I call it a meta-abstraction. USA 1974 and Rome AD 45 are two ways of looking at the same thing: two aspects of the same thing. And the only way you are ever going to realize this is if you literally actually see the two of them superimposed, commingled; and this will only happen if you experience anamnesis; and you will only experience this anamnesis if something stimulates—releases, actually—your blocked memory.

> I treat only the spatiotemporal realm as irreal, but, as in Gnosticism, I treat it as a deliberate trap by a deluder; therefore I envision a Savior who reveals the truth to us *and* who breaks the power of this world (*heimarmene*) over us (these are two things; he must obliterate time and its power over us, its ostensible reality, to free us from *heimarmene*). Therefore I envision an antithetical combat—dialectic—between the Deluder, who has only *a posteriori* knowledge, and the Savior, who has *a priori* knowledge, concerning us and the hold

> this world has on us. This is clear Gnosticism; but I envision the real world as Plato's Form world, and I hold, with Plotinus, that it is near at hand, not a transcendent deity far removed from here; it is here and that deity is immediately here. I envision a hierarchy of realms, as with Plotinus. We fell; we were in a sense ensnared; we took this spatiotemporal realm to be real; we made an intellectual, not moral, error, and it was us, not our ancestors; each of us is a soul splintered through thousands of miles and thousands of years. Likewise, the real, morphological realm is exploded through our realm; the way of return is through anamnesis: by this we re-collect (ourselves, each one his own Self [...]).

PKD is correct that linear time is an illusion and our World Dream is a symbolic projection of higher archetypal dynamics. Some have observed that history moves in cycles. A few go further and say linear time itself is a spiral, periodically overlapping its former position and repeating events with mere cosmetic variations. In our nightly dreams, several successive dreams can express an underlying meaning in different ways to ensure we get the point; reality may be little different.

PKD surmised that the tyranny of ancient Rome and the burgeoning tyranny of the New World Order are two instances of the same transcendental thing, which he called the "Black Iron Prison," which is none other than the Matrix Control System, realm of the Corrupt Demiurge, Fourth Density STS, the most negative probable future, the lower circle of the *vesica piscis*.

Likewise, the first and second coming of Christ are also the same thing at a higher level, two intrusions into our spacetime bubble by the Kingdom of Heaven, the most positive probable future, the realm of the Logos, the realm of Fourth Density STO, the upper circle of the *vesica piscis*.

PKD interpreted our reality as an overlap between these two transcendental principles. From the perspective of timeline dynamics, this means alternate Fourth Density futures existing now in quantum superposition. These eventualities exert their influences upon a common past as part of a timewar. Or as explained previously, our World Dream is a symbolic projection of competing external influences warring over what emerges when it finally ends.

Except if we take into account the seeming overlap between modern days and the events of two thousand years ago, which themselves were but the culmination of what began a millennia earlier, it's as if the world *did* end back then and everything since has been a kind of purgatory. Purgatory is defined as a realm of "purification, so as to achieve the holiness necessary to enter the joy of heaven," which is the same concept as a remedial time bubble.

The implication is that three thousand years ago, following the abuse of the Ark Stone and subsequent invocation of divine intervention, divine overseers implemented quarantine. This quarantine functioned like Safe Mode when a computer is infected with a virus. It separated us from the greater flow of time in Creation, putting us on a temporary/alternate timeline, more of an experimental sandbox than the real thing. Under the quarantine, alien enemies were disallowed from warring openly, thus their conflicts went covert, like enemies sitting down to a game of chess to settle their difference. The game was on. It was supposed to have concluded a thousand years later with the manifestation of Christ and the triumph of a genuine spiritual movement. But dark powers had grown too strong by that point and the game could not end, thus it went into overtime and things got even worse. So now the stakes are increased, and instead of Rome/Pharisees versus true Christians, it's planetary alien takeover versus the awakening Christ-like consciousness in suitable individuals. This is all speculation, but it follows logically from the sources discussed above.

This calls into question when the World Dream began. Did it begin with the primordial schism between Logos and Corrupt Demiurge? Did it begin with the failure of Christ's mission? The answer is that every Fall induces a corresponding World Dream, which all nest within each other like dream levels depicted in the film *Inception*. To awaken from the primordial World Dream, one must first awaken from a series of lesser ones. In theory, awakening could therefore begin with the most recent Falls and proceed backward.

From a timeline dynamics viewpoint, each World Dream is a temporary timeline birthed into existence through an errant choice; it contains experiences, challenges and opportunities ultimately meant to help correct that choice, hence it is a remedial timeline, though one that carries the risk of branching onto an even worse one. We experience this in our own lives when we make stupid choices that take us away from our destiny; after weeks, months, or years of being lost in the woods, we finally get back on the main road and then our journey continues. Within that sidetrack, however, the main flow of our life seems to stand still; when we get back on the main road, the main flow picks up again.

The Third Phase

In the next thousand years, mankind will witness the conclusion of a timewar that may have started in the future and spanned back in time to when the Nordic meta-civilization destroyed their planet approximately 70,000 – 80,000 years ago.

That date is based on the circular distribution of sacred sites they left around the world,* which delineate Earth's former equator; its North Pole is located in Alaska, which according to pole shift researcher Charles Hapgood was the location of the pole 70,000 – 80,000 years ago. The *Cassiopaean Transcripts* also make several references to this time range for the destruction of the Nordic planet and how long the Grays and Reptilians have been manipulating the timeline; the *Q'uo* material claims our third density time bubble goes back 76,000 years.

The future extensions of that meta-civilization comprise the bulk of time traveling alien factions here now, whose observed activities fill the pages of alienology and Fortean research. This timewar rippled back in time, converging along various critical choice points in history and producing the numerous intermediate Falls discussed. How far in the future the timewar originated is uncertain; various clues suggest sometime during the Age of Aquarius, which is 2,600 – 4,800 A.D. and time travel will certainly be a common reality by then.

This timewar will conclude with mankind being locked into either the best or worst of all possible futures. Once human history passes a point of no return, the quantum superposition state between these probable futures collapses; one future becomes fully real while the other goes poof. Right now things are still up in the air.

---

* <https://home.hiwaay.net/~jalison/>

On this topic, a few of my dreams have been relevant:

Timewar – In the distant future, war has broken out between the forces of balance and the forces of conquest. The latter had escaped into the past to manipulate history into giving themselves a victory. The forces of balance were symbolically portrayed as a legion of knights gearing up and marching through a portal into the past (our present). Here they went on their separate ways to carry out their mission, soldiers in a timewar. They were guided by an oracle, a mysterious source of help originating from their future.

Divine Lights – In a large underground cavern, the floor had one side covered with a glowing colony of lights, and the other side with a dark colony of black fungus. In the dark colony, a group of entities decided to jet upwards through the cavern ceiling and try to conquer the world above. Members of the glowing colony got alarmed and gathered their forces. I heard the phrases "By the Father, By the Son" as the lights too jetted upwards through the cavern onto the surface world (our world) to try and stop what was to happen.

War Zone Astral Projection – In a grimy room in a war-torn country, bodies were stacked like firewood and new weapons were being made to increase the lethality of fighting forces. The situation was going from bad to worse and we knew we had to get out somehow. In the room, my coworker tells me, "There is another parallel dimension where we can go for several hours at a time." We lie down and trance out to travel to this dimension. What we do in that dimension affects what happens in this one, and we aim to undo the terrible conditions in our dimension or escape into the other permanently.

Timewar Virus – In the future, there were time travel experiments. A squadron of boxy-looking flying ships were to travel into various points of the past for whatever reason. But some were accidentally contaminated with a virus. Half went into the past before the other half realized the contamination, but by then it was too late. This virus had infected the timeline and was causing severe problems. So the ones who stayed behind worked out a plan, and it involved going into the past in a very deep and thorough way, almost implying incarnating as past native citizens. There was talk about how they had to bargain with the dark side and undergo very difficult restrictions to enter the past in order to stop the virus. I heard one crew member say, "Well if those are the dark side, then where are the good guys?" and another crew member said with resignation, "That's us."

Biblical Eschatology and the Millennium

If interpreted as a prophetic dream, the Book of Revelation gives further insight into the timewar. It prophesies the reign of the Antichrist (therein referred to as the first or second Beast), the subsequent Battle of Armageddon, and the coming of Christ who will reign for one thousand years. At the end of that period, called the Millennium, dark forces who were only temporarily suppressed will rise from their Abyss and wage one final battle.

Little thought is given in Biblical eschatology to this final battle. But taking it seriously for a moment, considering it would occur very well into the Third Phase after the Etheric Tide has already transformed mankind into a meta-civilization, this final battle could be the one that starts the timewar.

The imminent rise of the Antichrist and battle of Armageddon would then only be the part of the timewar taking place in our near future, at the end of the quarantine period that began 3,000 years ago. It would mark the end of the Second Phase and would involve a global alien deception attempt plus the arising of a gnostic insurgence to counter it.

After that precarious situation passes, the Etheric Tide pours in and the Third Phase thereby ushers in the Millennium. The Third Phase consists of meta-civilizational activities whose consequences demarcate the beginning and ending points ("alpha and omega") of the timewar going back 70,000 – 80,000 years. Again, this is merely the speculative picture that emerges if one were to synthesize Biblical eschatology with everything else discussed so far.

It will be after the arrival of the Etheric Tide, after the "Fourth Density Shift," that personal destiny will fully blossom, the Grail Stone will be retrieved and reactivated, and the timewar will eventually be brought to an end. It will be a battle waged through time, one already being fought through time simultaneously by our past, present, and future incarnations.

It's important to note that, according to the Book of Revelation, the Millennium is a *transitional* period in which linear time gradually dissolves, but does not completely disappear until the very end. Perhaps the Etheric Tide onsets gradually, meaning the transition to 4D takes place over several centuries.

During the Millennium, aspects of 3D existence would still be in effect, even if destabilizing. In quantum physics terms, this would equate to gradual delocalization and decoherence of the wave function defining our existence. For a period, linear timelines, parallel timelines, and alternate futures would still exist and timeline dynamics would still be active. Only at the end of the Millennium would the World Dream completely end and all this timeline business be put to rest. Thus the timewar could only exist until the end of time, and hence in the Book of Revelation, there is one final battle before we all go home.

Some clues about the final days of the Millennium can be found in Robert Monroe's books. In *Far Journeys* (pp. 206-227) Monroe chronicles his astral journey to a probable Earth located just beyond the year 3000 A.D. There he found the planet had been transformed into an Edenic state with a population of two million superhumans who had no clothes, buildings, roads, or other unnatural structures. They lived in complete harmony and mastery with Nature and mentally manifested all their needs. In *Ultimate Journey* (pp. 33-42) he encountered a very similar civilization and version of Earth but supposedly located one million years ago; this latter civilization was about to permanently phase out from physicality and linear time altogether. Perhaps these were both the same positive meta-civilization, projected into different parts of our linear timeline.

In *Far Journeys,* Monroe was also told about an unusual cosmic energy convergence that would irradiate Earth in our near future. This represented a rare and significant moment in our history. A great alien presence has gathered to observe this event and, I would add, influence the outcome. Monroe was told that the Edenic Earth was just one positive probable future, whereas the more negative ones could include extinction of the human race. Other timelines include genetic enslavement by some of these alien factions who have gathered here.

Monroe was shown that this irradiation event would be a cataclysmic period of chaos, crisis, and opportunity from which numerous probable futures split off. Thus it is *the* largest choice point on the timeline and the key focal point of the timewar, hence all the preparation spanning several thousands of years leading up to the events in our near future.

Competing Probable Futures

There remains the question of how precisely the timewar originated in the first place. An educated guess would go something like this:

There may have originally been a single positive timeline that produced a benevolent but naive human evolution; this timeline would have been a Golden Age of sorts. Earth could have been a completely different place in that timeline, an Edenic state without seasons, tilt of the axis, Moon, or other World Dream Symbols reflecting a fallen existence. This would have been a positive meta-civilization.

Then came a schism, an accident, or an intrusion of some kind. It could have been contact with a negative alien meta-civilization from elsewhere in the universe or from a parallel timeline where evolution had taken a negative direction. Or it could have been the genesis of negative factions within an otherwise positive meta-civilization, per the Lucifer Rebellion myth.

In either case, these negative forces would have hijacked the positive timeline and attempted to rewrite it in their favor. But the way timeline dynamics works, one cannot just rewrite the past with a snap of the finger since the past is held in place by the volitional momentum (freewill, consciousness) of the souls who are living in it. However, at the very least, their minds can be telepathically biased so that they make different choices than they originally did. Given enough time, such biasing can lead to a complete revision of culture toward one that helps engender the desired negative future.

The goal of negative timeline manipulators, therefore, would be to persuade the souls of the past to deviate into a different future. Hence all the finesse by the alien deception campaign in their use of disinformation to persuade us to choose them, instead of invading with full physical force.

What they are doing is much like an entrepreneur creating a new store and then persuading customers of a competitor store to shop at his place instead. If he can successfully win over these customers, the competitor store folds up and he becomes the only such business in town. But if he fails, then his investment in the new store would have been for nothing. This is an accurate metaphor for the quantum superposition state that exists between alternate futures. Negative timeline manipulators have initiated a new probable future where they reign supreme if only they could deviate past souls onto that future.

Before the timewar, the timeline may have been a single steady progression into the future, but after the timewar, the future is uncertain due to ongoing alterations, and therefore multiple probable futures exist, each one less than fully real because none has a monopoly over the past. The goal of each probable future would be to undercut the competition and consolidate the customer base entirely for themselves. This is how they could establish themselves as real and permanent.

What happens to a probable future that loses too many customers? It's difficult to say, but considering how our own lives get better when we receive positive feedback flow from the future but fall apart when we get on the wrong track and have lost such feedback, it would be reasonable to say that a probable future collapses in upon itself via negative synchronicities that manifest as mounting cataclysms. Hence, removal of the negative World Thoughtform that otherwise sustains the world as we know it, which is a product of negative timeline manipulation and largely the handiwork of the Corrupt Demiurge, would bring about cosmic destruction. The timeline must end before a positive timeline can take its place.

So the final implication is that via demiurgic technology, hijacking of the timeline originally took place in the "future" and reconfigured the past, initiating a war for balance by the positive forces. The hyperdimensional battle required going back in time, even incarnating into the past to continue the war on the terrestrial chessboard. The remaining positive factions of the meta-civilization would assist these ground forces. They would receive help in the form of synchronistic support, outright intervention in critical situations, subconscious training, and oracular avenues such as synchronicities, dreams, visions, inspirations, and direct messages if needed.

These soldiers of light must survive the conditions of the Matrix Control System by gaining mastery over their lower selves while nurturing and activating the full manifestation of spirit. The next part concerns their path.

The Heroic Avenging Fool

In the Finnish and Icelandic myths discussed in the previous chapter on polar mythology, a magical millstone was fought over until it sank in the ocean or else shattered upon the waves. The sinking millstone consequently churned a great whirlpool, symbolizing the genesis of our linear timeline. This act brought to a close the First Phase.

The story ends with the birth of a new hero, who would become the central character of the Second Phase. The previous protagonist, Väinämöinen, whose time has passed, builds a ship of copper and sails off toward the whirlpool, entering its eye and disappearing from our world. As he leaves, he promises to return one day when dire conditions necessitate his help. This is mirrored in the King Arthur myths about the magical sword Excalibur, which was bestowed and retrieved by the Lady of the Lake according to circumstance. All of this ties back to the idea of demiurgic technology as well as higher consciousness returning along with the Etheric Tide, and being removed as the Tide wanes.

At the beginning of the Second Phase, a new protagonist appears. His name in various myths includes Kullervo, Amleth, Amlodhi, Hamlet, Horus, Theseus, and Parzival. These are the avenging heroes, divine redeemers, and pure fools, who were born to right the wrongs that engendered the Second Phase. Within the World Dream, they carry out missions that originate from the Real World.

Horus, Parzival, and Amleth

One of the earliest avenging hero myths is that of Osiris, Isis, Seth, and Horus. Osiris and Isis were king and queen. The king's brother Seth became jealous and plotted to kill him. He did so by offering a contest where anyone who could fit into a coffin he had made would get to keep it. When Osiris laid down into the coffin, which had been custom built to his size, Seth sealed it shut and threw it in the Nile, where it floated north to Lebanon and got stuck in a tree. The tree had been harvested and, along with the coffin, became a pillar in a great temple in Lebanon.

Already, one can see how this cosmic archetype was mirrored in the historical episode of the Ark Stone being sealed in a box ('coffin') and taken north to Lebanon where the Phoenicians and Proto-Israelites used it to expand their empire. The pillar is an obvious reference to the World Pillar.

The myth continues with Isis finding the coffin and transporting it back to Egypt but leaving it in a marshland. This is mirrored in the Ark Stone being retrieved from Lebanon when Solomon's Temple was sacked by Thutmose III. The marshland reflects its subsequent location in the Great Pyramid, in Northern Egypt where reed marshes were prevalent.

In the marshland, Seth comes upon the coffin and subsequently dis-members Osiris into fourteen pieces. This is mirrored in the Semites occupying northern Egypt, where the Ark Stone and pyramids were located. Osarseph, the rebel priest of Akhenaten who became the historical basis for Moses, was one of them. The Semites of Egypt had always taken Seth as their patron deity; one could say they were alle-giant to the cosmic thoughtform represented by Seth, who was none other than Yahweh, the Corrupt Demiurge. In Egyptian paintings, Seth is depicted as a strange beast that has no analog to animals of nature; this is to indicate that Seth, or rather the Corrupt Demiurge, is an unnatural creation, and likewise, the timeline he engendered is corrupt, out of place, artificial.

Like the protagonists of the Finnish myth trying to find the shattered pieces of the Sampo, Isis was able to retrieve most of the pieces of Osiris, but not all. The fourteenth piece of Osiris, his phallus, had been swallowed by a fish. Likewise, in the Icelandic tale, the millstone had sunk irretrievably into the ocean. Consequently, Isis creates an artificial one of gold and resurrects Osiris who then impregnates her. Afterward, he is given proper burial ceremonies and withdraws from the world, like the Finnish protagonist entering the maelstrom.

Isis gave birth to Horus. He was the falcon-headed god, son of Osiris, and eternal enemy to his evil uncle Seth. Why the head of a falcon? The meaning of the falcon propagated through the ages, down to the old practice of heraldry. On family crests and coat of arms, the falcon continues to mean "a pursuer, one who will not rest until his objective is achieved." Horus was born because Seth killed his father, and he exists as a pursuer of Seth, as one who will not rest until the objectives of recrimination and restoration are accomplished.

In previous chapters, I have consistently referred to thoughtforms as entities that arise to fulfill a purpose and do not rest until their objectives are realized. The restorative mission of Horus, combined with his single-minded determination, shows him to be a thoughtform whose sole purpose is to right the primordial wrong that brought him into existence in the first place. Horus is none other than Christ, and his opposition to Seth is once more the Christ vs Yahweh conflict. So when conspiracy researchers point to parallels between Christ and Horus, the connection is quite a bit deeper than they might realize. Horus/Christ is an entitized correction mechanism sent by the Logos to counter the corruption of the timeline.

Now, Osiris was a god situated in a limbo state between the land of the living and the land of the dead. His original phallus was lost, but the gold one served in its place. Paralleling this, the Grail King Amfortas was gravely wounded in the groin, living in a half-dead state neither lying down nor standing up. The holy spear and Grail served to ameliorate his suffering and keep him alive long enough for Parzival, the redeeming, avenging, heroic fool, to restore him and become the new Grail King. Thus the Grail is to Parzival what the golden phallus is to Horus.

As explained, the Grail Stone is a physical mediator for the Christ thoughtform to illuminate, enliven, and instruct the Grail knights in their mission to carry out the divine will. Likewise, in Egypt, there existed a group known as the Followers of Horus, who were in charge of guarding and operating the Stone. They were the earliest record- ed example of the "Christian Progeny" spoken about in *Parzival,* to whom the neutral angels entrusted the Grail. Some researchers claim these Followers of Horus were not fully human, which would be in accord with what was explained in the sixth chapter of this book, that keepers of the Grail are likely human-Nordic hybrids.

A modern example of the avenging hero-fool archetype is Shake- speare's *Hamlet,* inspired by an old Scandinavian tale of an avenger named Amleth. Shakespeare transposed the "h" in Amleth to create the name of his character. Amleth was known as Amlodhi (or Amlóði) in Icelandic lore.

Hamlet had an evil uncle who murdered his father out of jeal- ousy, married and corrupted his mother, and usurped the throne. Under the oppressive reign of his evil stepfather, he carried out his revenge with great cleverness and patience. He pretended to be an insane idiot so that his enemies would not suspect his plans, thus he could exist among them while making preparations for his final move. When his enemies did have suspicions and put him through various tests to expose him, Ham- let's quick thinking preserved his cover, causing their plans to backfire.

In the end, Hamlet and Amleth succeed in their revenge, Amleth bringing the burning building down upon his drunken enemies, whom he had ensnared in a net, and then slaying his uncle. Hamlet's story ended with a sword fight in which he was victorious but soon after died from a poisoned blade wound.

The Meaning of the Fool

In the above stories, the father represents the divine Logos, evil uncle the Corrupt Demiurge, and mother the Matrix. The Corrupt Demiurge usurped the Logos and took control of the Matrix. The avenging hero represents the Christ intelligence, whose role is to destroy the Control System and bring the Matrix back into rightful harmonization with the Logos. The heroic fool, however, represents more the portion of this Christ intelligence that is working *within* the system to undermine it, the "ground team" so to speak. Jesus, more so than Christ.

The fool represents what *The Ra Material* calls "Wanderers," or what the book *Bringers of the Dawn* by Barbara Marciniak calls "Systems Busters." These are higher souls who have volunteered to incarnate into the Matrix Control System to help. Entering via the womb and being confined to a primitive human body means donning the shackles of mental and spiritual retardation. By default, they forget who they are and, like Tarzan, get "raised by the apes of the jungle."

Hence by entering this world, they become "idiots" relative to their original form. But underneath, they still maintain an innate sense of wisdom, freedom, and spiritual intelligence that puts them out of step with social norms. As much as they need to become human to survive here, they must also overcome or reject social programming that might interfere with their mission.

To society, they appear as fools for not buying into the Control System values. And should these souls awaken from their programming and begin the inner and outer search for truth and purpose, they would soon think, speak, feel, and act according to higher knowledge and standards that society simply cannot comprehend, thus they would once again be seen as fools for subscribing to "utter nonsense."

Everyone reading this knows firsthand how society too easily dismisses higher wisdom as lunatic ravings. I can say with certainty that if you have read this far, you are likely a Wanderer, and you have walked the Way of the Fool. Here I am simply revealing what this path signifies and why it exists.

Hamlet pretends to be an idiot to escape the suspicion of his enemies, so how does that apply to our situation? As explained, by becoming human we can exist here relatively undisturbed. We are still in the Second Phase, where the spiritual war is fought sub rosa. Amleth played a fool until the end. The time has not yet come for the open use of superhuman abilities, which is reserved for the Third Phase. Imagine being born with pyrokinetic, telekinetic, spacetime bending powers — how far would you have gotten before you were incapacitated and kept in some underground base for study and experimentation? We are born and live as fools, so that we may enter society as any other human might, and take up positions through which we can exert our subversive influences.

But just as the Christ intelligence has its alien and human representatives, so does the Corrupt Demiurge. We live under the watchful eyes of the evil uncle, under surveillance by higher dark forces. These are the demonic legions and negative alien factions that target, abduct, program, and manipulate us. They are the negative timeline manipulators that have been at this game for tens of thousands of years. Like our own efforts, their plans are currently carried out covertly. Abduction and programming happen in secret; demons move among us invisibly. The more we expose ourselves and threaten their agenda, the higher priority targets we become.

Like Amleth's enemies testing him to discover his true motives, these forces are very interested in discovering our true mission. They may sense we are threats and program us accordingly to lose faith and interest in our quest, but they may not know our specific missions because these remain locked away deep within our souls, unknown even to us, until the right time when they automatically unlock. This may explain the commonly reported practice in which an abductee is seated before a screen and shown random apocalyptic imagery; perhaps the locks are being picked. Not until the influx of the Etheric Tide and a convergence of other factors would the full cache of hidden knowledge and purpose be opened. Then, like Excalibur rising from the lake or the sword being drawn from the stone, it would signify the start of the Third Phase.

We also face everyday testing by the enemy in the form of provocations, temptations, and distractions that probe our weaknesses. These aim to extract "evidence of impurity" by which these beings acquire the metaphysical right to attack us further, which from our perspective seems like karmic punishment but to them appears as convenient openings in our defenses.

The Pure Fool

In the First Phase, pure beings were unwise and thus vulnerable, which brought about the Fall. In the Second Phase, purity was replaced by strength and cunning. Both conditions signify states of imbalance. In the Third Phase, purity, strength, and cleverness will combine into a balanced whole. These signify the perfection of spirit, body, mind, and soul.

The combination of virtues equates to having eaten from both trees in the Garden of Eden. These characteristics together form the base of spiritual chivalry, which will mature in the Third Phase but is already blossoming within the hero/fool during the Second Phase.

While the hero and fool act with purity and innocence, they also have cleverness and strength. They need strength to withstand the pressures of the Control System, and cleverness to navigate its obstacles. Their strength comes from not being divided within themselves, not saddled by self-doubt or social programming.

The Biblical character Samson was strong because his hair had never been cut; cutting of hair signifies a trimming of one's true nature to conform to the standards of the Control System. In the end, his remaining strength allowed him to push apart the columns of a building and crush all his enemies, much like Amleth casting a net over his enemies and bringing the burning building down atop them. Again, this pertains to the Christ intelligence destroying the World Dream, partly by removing/retrieving that which supports it – our collective ignorant participation in it.

It's easy to see how strength and cleverness are tactical advantages, but how might purity and innocence be likewise helpful? Because the hero and fool are aligned with their hearts, with spirit, with the divine will; they have synchronistic superiority over their spiritually inferior enemies who only have cunning and force on their side. Synchronistic superiority means things work out in unexpected ways when one stays true to one's higher, nobler Self. Ground troops receive "air support" as long as their positions are visible and distinct from enemy forces; if they lower themselves into darkness, they cannot be helped.

Dorothy was a pure fool who, out of concern for the Witch's broom being on fire, poured water to extinguish it but ended up inadvertently killing the Wicked Witch in the process. Amleth thrust his sword into a wall to test his strength and ended up killing an assassin who had been hiding there about to attack.* In our own lives, traps set by dark forces backfire when we maintain spiritual composure; their obstacles become our stepping stones. These examples illustrate how one can win a fight without fighting, just by acting naturally in a non-anticipatory manner and having the pieces fall into place.

Of course, as Wanderers or Systems Busters facing harsh odds, the best approach is to combine all our assets. While science and the stiffer esoteric schools advocate only strength and cleverness, and while certain religions and softer spiritual practices advocate only purity of soul, each has its shortcomings. There is no point reinforcing the front door when the rear door stays wide open. What we have, we must use.

---

* Compare with Logion 98 in *The Gospel of Thomas*:
  Jesus said, "What the kingdom of the father resembles is a man who wanted to assassinate a member of court. At home, he drew the dagger and stabbed it into the wall in order to know whether his hand would be firm. Next, he murdered the member of court."

Those who give up the intellect for the soul or vice versa are missing the point. Hence the dictum "be wise as serpents, gentle as doves," and why I emphasize combining a positive attitude with greater awareness.

The Unity of All Esoteric Training

The Way of the Fool is a spiritual school of hard knocks that employs life itself as the classroom. Its initiates operate in the wilderness like paratroopers launched into enemy territory. They learn their lessons through direct contact with the conditions of life in the World Dream. Hard experience, synchronicity, independent study, observation, dreams, and intuition are among the teaching tools.

Then there are occult teachers and formal esoteric schools that provide a more disciplined, protected, and accelerated environment for spiritual growth. Examples include Fourth Way, Inner Christianity, Sufism, Rosicrucianism, Toltec Shamanism, Anthroposophy, and Gnostic/Hermetic organizations.

Both formal and informal esoteric pathways share the same goal, to fortify spirit and enable its triumph over matter. This entails disengaging from lower/outer and engaging higher/inner, resulting in spirit influencing the World instead of vice versa. The opposite is true for people who are spiritually asleep; via genetics and environment, the world molds them into becoming mere instruments of the Matrix Control System. Esoteric training aims to reverse this.

To disengage from lower/outer means to observe and master (if useful) or reject (if harmful) everything the Control System has grafted onto us: all the bad habits, prejudices, mindless instincts, egotism, ignorance, chaotic thoughts and feelings, petty concerns, baseless fears, and illusory goals. It means to see through illusion and take back power from the World Dream.

To engage the higher means to get spirit back online in our lives, minds, bodies, and souls. Feelings are harmonized with spirit via devotion, humility, compassion, understanding, patience, forbearance, and love. Life is harmonized via higher thoughts and feelings initiating synchronistic support and wise action clearing the way of obstacles. And the lower mind is harmonized when it becomes aware of information streaming from spirit. The latter occurs in small flashes when, through contemplation, intuition leads to revelation, and revelation builds wisdom and discernment. But it doesn't become a constant light until the mind achieves continuity of consciousness between waking and dreaming states, so that even while awake one can access the dream state and thus receive communications from the subconscious, which is really a gateway to the higher mind. This bridge is enhanced by the development of psychic structures in the etheric body that mediate information between different aspects of one's being. This bridge allows under current conditions what would otherwise only be possible during an Etheric Tide.

Whether one examines the teachings of Rudolf Steiner, Jesus Christ, Buddha, Gurdjieff, Mouravieff, Baines, Mares, Castaneda, etc. they all basically boil down to disengaging from lower and engaging higher.

For Wanderers on a mission, it seems that life helps them achieve this up to the minimum threshold required for them to do what they are here to do, rather than spurring them on to superhuman perfection. Thus while we should strive to overcome the lower and activate the higher as much as possible, we should not get depressed if certain goals remain beyond reach, especially ones that are not mission critical.

Nonetheless, we would all do well to practice disengaging the lower, cultivating synchronistic support, and building up more conviction, courage, understanding, forbearance, and compassion. We have to be mindful of what originates from our lower nature versus higher nature and distinguish between them so that we can consistently choose the latter. This will "tide" us over until divine grace or some cosmic shift grants us etheric activation and spiritual transcendence that currently seem beyond practical reach.

If we want to reach that transcendental stage sooner, esoteric paths require the total death of the lower self for the Higher Self to take its place. In the Way of the Fool where life itself provides the catalysts, such a thing is quite painful; if such a thing becomes necessary for some of us, it's an unfortunate possibility that the appropriate catalysts will likely be provided by the aftermath of the traumatic global cataclysms on the horizon.

The Gnostic Teachings of Christ

How the foregoing discussion of fools, heroes, wanderers, and esoteric training fits into *Gnosis* is amplified and clarified by the wise and prophetic words of Jesus Christ. Or at least, what little remains of his original teachings.

Aside from the Beatitudes (the Buddhist-like lessons given via the Sermon on the Mount), the *Gospel of Thomas* is as close as it gets to the original teachings. As much as modern Christians might deny it, the four Biblical Gospels themselves were already part of the so-called "Great Apostasy," which is the turning away of Christianity from the original spirit of Christ's messages. They were propaganda pieces aimed at Jews, Greeks, Pagans, and Romans meant to hijack a burgeoning spiritual movement. Christianity became a weapon to bring diverse cultures under the control of a single political monster hiding behind the cross. Meanwhile, the original teachings of Christ propagated onward in secret until one version was set down in writing by the scribes of the Nag Hammadi, from which the *Gospel of Thomas* emerged into modern light.

At their core, the teachings of Christ are highly dualistic, apocalyptic, prophetic, and gnostic. Christ was not strictly concerned with getting us to live better lives here, or countering the karmic mind-traps that Yahweh installed in his people, but helping us get ourselves out of here. His primary mission was to end the World Dream and bring his spiritual kin home, to redeem the Fallen. So while modern scholars and theologians interpret the *Gospel of Thomas* from the viewpoint of generic spiritual wisdom we can apply in our everyday lives, make no mistake that Christ had more in mind than giving fortune cookie platitudes.

According to the teachings, humanity consists of the spiritually Living and the spiritually Dead. The Dead are products of this world, subject to its rules, obedient to its standards. They sacrifice spiritual priorities for personal and material pursuits. Meanwhile, the Living are in this world but not of it, they contain an inner quality that transcends worldly factors. We become more one or the other depending on where we place our priorities.

The Kingdom of Heaven is the original home of the Living, from which they fell and to which they will hopefully return. It is not a location within spacetime, but a higher realm surrounding and interpenetrating the physical world. It is all around us but invisible to the five senses. The Kingdom of Heaven has already come, but it has not yet been widely perceived. It is also within us but unrecognized by the everyday conscious mind. To transition into the Kingdom of Heaven externally, one must transition into the Kingdom of Heaven inwardly, for it's through an internal conscious and spiritual shift that we experience the corresponding external shift. The Kingdom is both a state of existence and a state of mind. In modern lingo, the Kingdom of Heaven is a higher density positive existence, both as a mode of being and realm of habitation.

Whereas the World operates on the principles of cunning, calculation, physical power, and determinism, the Kingdom of Heaven acts via synchronicity, nonlinearity, and nondeterminism. That is how the Kingdom of Heaven destabilizes the Control System and lends support to its own: not through sheer force, but through unfathomable elegance and subtlety. It employs the butterfly effect to leverage the smallest nudges into the greatest of outcomes, the ultimate form of spiritual jujitsu.

The World is an impermanent illusion, an ouroboros condemned to consume itself into nothingness. Therefore its epiphenomena, the Dead, likewise lack permanence in the greater framework of Eternity. The Living are immortal in that they continue existing even if the World ceases to exist, whereas the Dead would disappear along with it. Like with the dissolution of the physical body, one must possess spirit to consciously survive death. The Dead have no probable future extensions, no existence outside the World Dream; they are but hollow memories waiting to be forgotten.

The goal of spiritual discipline and training is to activate and build spirit within us. Spirit is not a product of the physical world, therefore it has permanence beyond the lifespan of the World. In building up everything associated with spirit, we translate ourselves into the Real World, the Kingdom of Heaven, and overcome death and dissolution.

The World as we know it will come to an end through a Great Revealing. A time will come when the Living have their spiritual eyes opened. This will occur when they succeed in being filled and activated by the same wisdom and intelligence that illuminated Jesus (and other avatars like Buddha). This is the so-called Second Coming of Christ. For the Living, it has already begun with a gradual opening of awareness and building of wisdom and intuitive perception. In the end, it will result in full etheric activation combined with harmonization with the Logos, whom Christ called the Father. Those who are activated will be able to see and recognize what was formerly hidden by worldly deceivers and the five senses. Secrets will be exposed, pretenses revealed, and illusions will fall away. They will finally see and enter the Kingdom of Heaven.

Presently we are controlled through our investment in illusions. We are attacked through gaps in our awareness. All our willpower and energy are useless if we lack the awareness of where and how to direct them. Thus awareness and vigilance are crucial. As long as we are here, we must be wise and discerning. The biggest illusions are those that employ false dichotomies; the World is spun from these. They can be as basic as the seeming separation between inner and outer. In reality, there is no separation, and in knowing this we can change the outer by changing the inner.

When you recognize an illusion for what it is, that illusion ceases to hold power over your choices. Thus to overcome the world, one must recognize the world for what it is and implement that higher understanding. In doing so, one steps away from the World and toward the Kingdom. The closer one approaches the Kingdom, the more one comes under its jurisdiction, and the more one lives by its principles, which override those of the World. As an example, the power of synchronicity easily trumps the forces of determinism. Worldly limitations and concerns that apply to the Dead may not always apply to the Living.

False opposites must be reconciled and transcended before a person can enter the Kingdom of Heaven. One cannot cling to illusion and leave the realm of illusion at the same time. To completely enter the Kingdom, one must therefore achieve non-dual consciousness in the sense of being permeated by an awareness that sees through false dualities and recognizes the higher truth beyond them. It is not just a superficial intellectual understanding, but a higher state of consciousness. In this state, one is not divided within oneself, rather there is total sincerity and complete unity with the heart, subconscious, higher mind, and other aspects of our being that are normally compartmentalized away during mundane waking consciousness. In this state, one acts with singular purpose and *knowing,* as Christ did. This state cannot be achieved by convincing yourself into seeming certainty, rather it must flow naturally from transcending the mortal mind and merging with your higher mind.

This non-dualism is not an endorsement of indiscriminate mindlessness, however. A higher kind of objective dualism is called for, one that discriminates between the World and the Kingdom and between the standards of the Living and those of the Dead. Thus the role of Christ is not to unify the World but to bring total division between the Living and the Dead, not to bring peace but to initiate *total war* between the World and the Kingdom. The role of false dichotomies is to distract us from this higher dualism, to keep us busy making false or irrelevant choices instead of the ones that truly count.

When the Great Revealing occurs and the Living fulfill their potential and increasingly see the Dead for who they are, there will be no alternative but polarization at every scale. In the same way we observe our own dark side and leave it behind, so will this happen on a collective scale. The role of Christ is to separate the weed from the crops, harvest the crops, and burn the weeds. Only at the time of the Great Revealing will it become absolutely clear what is weed and what is crop. Until then, each grows among the other unchecked.

Christ unifies the Living, but divides them from the Dead. The Living must recognize and love each other, for they are one in purpose, essence, and origins. They must cast off what does not belong to them: the fetters of social and biological programming, ego-based impulses, emotional addictions, material obsessions, illusory fears, and mortal personality. In the end, they will be stripped of these and will stand spiritually naked before the World, unassailable in their strength and purity, thousands of Christs holding torches to the framework of our sham existence.

END

FURTHER READING

Corruption of the Demiurge

- *The Way of Hermes: New Translations of the Corpus Hermeticum* (Hermes Trismegistus. Bristol Classical Press, 2013).

  Classic book from Hellenistic Greece on Nous. In the format of dialogues between Hermes Trismegistus and the Logos, and him and his son and disciple.

- *Gnosis: The Nature and History of Gnosticism* (Kurt Rudolf. Harper One, 1987).

  Excellent exploration of traditional Gnostic beliefs and their origins.

- *The Secret Doctrine of the Rosicrucians* (Magus Incognito. Red Wheel/Weiser, 2012).

  One of the few books that gets into Demiurge as the ender and initiator of World Ages or World Cycles, like a soul dissolving after death and reforming in a new body. This is highly relevant to the times we are now in.

- *Theosophy : An Introduction to the Spiritual Processes in Human Life and in the Cosmos* (Rudolf Steiner. Anthroposophic Press 1994).

  Good introduction to astral, etheric, mental, and other components of the human system. Steiner doesn't just describe, but fundamentally explains them logically from the inside out.

- *Initiation into Hermetics* (Franz Bardon. Merkur Publishing, Inc., 2001).

  Includes discussion on elementals, larvae, schemata, and phantasms — four types of thoughtforms, how they are created, and how they function.

The Philosopher's Stone

- *Mystery of the Cathedrals* (Fulcanelli. Brotherhood of Life, 1990).

  Modern English translation of Fulcanelli's first book from 1925, in which he explains the Alchemical meaning of the symbolic stonework found in Gothic cathedrals. Short, dense, and concise. Necessary companion and prequel to Fulcanelli's *Dwellings of the Philosophers*.

- *Dwellings of the Philosophers* (Fulcanelli. Archive Press, 1999).

  Fulcanelli's second book. This is a lengthy treatise by the most famous alchemist of the 20th century. Unfortunately he goes to great lengths to compartmentalize, rearrange, and obscure the secrets of Alchemy while simultaneously revealing them to the world in cryptic form. So this dense book takes some work to read and decipher and therefore won't be everyone's cup of tea. At the end of this book, Fulcanelli also strays into other topics like the mechanism behind the ending of World Ages.

- *Hermetic Recreations* (Anonymous. Rubedo Press, 2018).

  New English translation of an anonymous text on Alchemy from the 1800s. Likely used by Fulcanelli but without crediting it, because it was too open with the secrets of Alchemy. Probably the clearest, most concise, and straightforward explanation of making the Stone in print. If there's only one classic text on Alchemy to read, it would be this one.

- *The New Chemical Light* (Sendivogius. CreateSpace, 2011).

  A relatively clear text from the late 1500s. Entertaining explanation of creating the Stone, or at least the first stages. It's still done in riddle form, but he does a good job of explaining how alchemists believed metals are created. From that you can reverse engineer what they might have done to reproduce it in the lab, under their assumptions.

- *Hermes Trismegistus Old Natural Path* (I.C.H. Lulu Press, 2012).

  An obscure manuscript published in Leipzig, 1782, referenced by Cyliani. Key info on the technique for breaking down the raw starting material, and the proper order of the various phases.

- *Thirteen Secret Letters* (Adam Friedrich Böhme. Lulu Press, 2014).

  Compilation of thirteen letters received from alleged members of the 18th century Order of the Golden and Rosy Cross, which describe key aspects of making the Stone. Fulcanelli drew from this source, and up until now has never been printed in English. It reveals details not found in any other source.

- *A Rosicrucian Notebook* (Willy Schrödter. Weiser Books, 1992).

  Not a notebook by a Rosicrucian, but by a researcher into Rosicrucianism. It is an exoteric survey of anecdotes and quotations concerning the real Rosicrucian order. This is a compendium of occultism, mysticism, and weird science with tons of interesting tidbits concerning such topics as ever-burning lamps, remote healing, clairvoyance, the Stone, and other tools of Rosicrucian science. Everything is documented, so this book is a useful reference to find related sources on particular topics.

The Holy Grail

- *The Mystery of the Grail* (Julius Evola. Inner Traditions, 1997).

  Erudite work that spells out the meaning of the Holy Grail from an esoteric initiatory point of view. Evola provides numerous data points, which you can reinterpret from other perspectives.

- *Crusade Against the Grail* (Otto Rahn. Inner Traditions, 2006).

  History of the Cathars and their persecution by the Catholic Church, the Grail, and Gnostic philosophy. Written in 1920s by German researcher who was later employed by Nazis and ended his own life after growing disaffected. Rahn was not an academic on the outside, but one who immersed himself in Cathar and Gnostic outlook.

- *Lucifer's Court* (Otto Rahn. Inner Traditions, 2004).

  Travel journal by Rahn as he goes around Europe and Iceland in his hunt for the Grail. For each town he philosophizes and shares pertinent local legends. He rants quite a bit against the Catholic Church and sides with Lucifer as a light bringer. One antisemitic passage was thought to have been added by a Nazi editor of the book. Other than that, this book really captures a teutonic/pagan kind of spirit and is valuable in Grail research.

- *Parzival* (Wolfram von Eschenbach. Translated by Hatto. Penguin, 2004).

  The best medieval Grail story. Permeated with Gnostic/Cathar/pagan ideology despite an obligatory Catholic gloss. Story of a sheltered boy who becomes a knight and goes through many trials before becoming Grail King. Explains origins of the Grail as a stone brought to Earth by neutral angels.

- *The Ninth Century and the Holy Grail* (Walter Johannes Stein. Temple Lodge, 2001).

  Historical and Anthroposophical analysis of Parzival by one of Rudolf Steiner's disciples. Traces the historical events of Parzival to the ninth century A.D. Not a crucial book to read, but does provide historical context for the tale and explains the inner meaning of various passages.

Ark of the Covenant

- *Opening the Ark of the Covenant* (Frank Joseph and Laura Beaudoin. New Page Books, 2007).

  Traces the history of the Ark and Grail from ancient to modern times. I recommend this book for the broad spectrum of historical data it provides, but not for the lines of reasoning or conclusions that follow from that data.

- *The Sign and the Seal* (Graham Hancock. Simon & Schuster, 1992).

  Like the previous book, I value this one for the historical data more than the conclusions. Hancock believes the Ark resides in Ethiopia. But as reported on viewzone.com, a story inscribed on ruins dating from the 15th-16th century B.C. mentions a duplicate of the Ark being sent into Ethiopia as a decoy while the real one was hidden away. So a good portion of Hancock's research may have been tracing the history of this decoy. Still, Hancock does a good job of drawing upon obscure sources to paint a detailed picture of the alleged powers of the original Ark.

- *The Giza Power Plant : Technologies of Ancient Egypt* (Christopher Dunn. Bear & Company, 1998).

  Dunn examines evidence of advanced technology in the construction and design of the Great Pyramid. He concludes it was a power generator using plasma energy. I think plasma generation was only a means toward an even more sophisticated end.

Mosaic Abuse of Demiurgic Technology

- *The Stellar Man* (John Baines. The John Baines Institute, 2002).

  Synthesis of modern psychology and Hermeticism. Thorough explanation of the Hermetic Principles. Includes the occult history of Jewish origins and the intrusion of Yahweh into our world.

- *The Incarnation of Ahriman* (Rudolf Steiner. Steiner Press, 2006).

  Set of lectures discussing the interplay between Ahriman, Lucifer, and Christ — the three intelligences actively at work in our history, and the implications of that dynamic for our future.

- *Moses and Monotheism* (Sigmund Freud. Martino Fine Books, 2010).

  Freud's investigation into the origins of Moses and Judaism. He theorizes that Moses was not Jewish but part of the Egyptian priesthood and a follower of Akhenaten.

Nordic Aliens and the Grail Race

- *The Cryptoterrestrials* (Mac Tonnies. Anomalist Books, 2010).

  "A meditation on indigenous humanoids and the aliens among us." A meandering speculative essay on the hidden humanoid civilization.

- *Operation Trojan Horse* (John Keel. Anomalist Books, 2013).

  Comprehensive book on Fortean phenomena, especially the duplicitous, ambiguous, hidden nature of the alien presence. Cites anecdotes of human-like aliens as well. Good book to read on the subject of "cryptoterrestrials."

- *The Comte de Gabalis* (Abbé de Villars. HardPress Publishing, 2013).

  Series of discourses by a Rosicrucian, thought to be St. Germain or Francis Bacon. Published in 1670. Explains the practice among Rosicrucians of marrying themselves to non-human beings. Seems to put parasitic thought-forms and humanoid aliens under the same banner.

- *The Secret of the Saucers* (Orfeo Angelucci. Amherst Press, 1955).

  A 1950s contactee who had experiences with positive Nordics. What he says about them may be skewed or embellished, but nonetheless much of it correlates with alienology research coming decades later.

- *UFOs in the Gulf Breeze-Pensacola Area: Contact Since 1955* <geohanover.com/docs/contact1.htm>

  Anonymous contactee discusses his childhood visit to a Nordic alien base inside a mountain, their technology, and the nature of the Gray alien agenda.

- *My Experiences (Grey, Pleiadians and Oddities)*
  <montalk.net/fore.zip>

  ZIP archive of main forum threads by modern contactee Fore, where he details his life-long interaction with alien beings including a Nordic-like female who became his advisor.

- *Hair of the Alien: DNA and Other Forensic Evidence of Alien Abductions* (Bill Chalker. Gallery Books, 2005).

  Peter Khoury case of an odd sexual encounter with two humanoid females, where a strand of blond alien hair left behind revealed traces of Celtic, Basque, and rare Asian genetics.

- *The Morning of the Magicians: Secret Societies, Conspiracies, and Vanished Civilizations* (Pauwells & Bergier. Destiny Books, 2008).

  Discusses the occultic roots of Nazi Germany and the Aryan movement. Includes anecdote of Hitler being terrorized by superhuman beings.

- *Survivors of Atlantis: Their Impact on World Culture* (Frank Joseph. Bear & Company, 2004).

  An excellent compendium of historical and mythological information concerning the advanced post-Atlantean survivors and their cultural legacy. An important read if you are interested in where the earthbound descendants of the Nordic meta-civilization set up root, and what cultures and bloodlines were seeded by them.

- *Everything You Know Is Wrong, Book One: Human Origins* (Lloyd Pye. IUniverse, 2000).

  Book on human origins and anomalies in our genetic evolution pointing to alien tinkering. This book also implies a lot of genetic engineering was occurring around the time of the fall of Atlantis and afterwards, particularly with the domestication of grains and animals.

Polar Mythology

- *Hamlet's Mill* (De Santillana, Von Dechend. Godine, 1992).

  Classic book on comparative mythology. The authors propose a rather mundane hypothesis that mythology encodes knowledge concerning precession of the equinoxes. But beyond the astronomical layer there is a hyper dimensional one. Unhinging of the world axis is not just about equinoctial precession, but cataclysmic unhinging of our time axis that resulted in a fallen timeline we are now experiencing. Read it from that higher dimensional perspective.

- *The King of the World* (René Guénon. Sophia Perennis, 2004).

  Guénon explores esoteric traditions concerning the Grail, Shekhina, omphalos as center of the World, *Kali Yuga*, and other polar topics.

The End

- *The Exegesis* (Philip K. Dick. Houghton Mifflin Harcourt, 2011).

  Excerpts from PKD's personal writings wherein he attempts to unravel the meaning of his mystical gnostic experiences. PKD is an example of a true modern gnostic who had direct contact with a higher intelligence.

- *The Gospel of Thomas* (Jean-Yves Leloup. Inner Traditions, 2005).

  Translation and commentary on the gnostic Gospel of Thomas, a collection of the sayings of Jesus, of which most are straight out of the Bible but with some differences in how they are written.

- *The Hero with a Thousand Faces* (Joseph Campbell. New World Library, 2008).

  Comparative mythology that explores the unifying psychology of self-transcendence present in myths the world over. Some of these myths are polar in nature.

- *The Zelator: A Modern Initiate Explores the Ancient Mysteries* (Mark Hedsel. Weiser, 2001).

  An autobiographical account of Hedsel's initiatory pathway through various mystery schools. He goes into depth regarding the Way of the Fool.

Gnostic and Polar Entertainment

- *The Wizard of Oz* (1939)
- *Millennium* (1989)
- *Dark City* (1998)
- *The Truman Show* (1998)
- *The Thirteenth Floor* (1999)
- *Donnie Darko* (2001)
- *The Matrix Trilogy* (1999, 2003)
- *Noein* (2005-2006)
- *City of Ember* (2008)
- *The Frame* (2009)
- *Lost* (2005-2010)
- *The Adjustment Bureau* (2011)
- *Snowpiercer* (2013)
- *Dark* (2017-2020)
- *Westworld* (2016-2022)

INDEX

A

SPIRIT OVER MIND

MIND OVER MATTER

Printed in Great Britain
by Amazon